PRAISE FOR *ALL THE WOMEN FOLLOWED HER*

"I was totally captivated...it is a book to be read and savored."

-Marcia Cohn Spiegel
author of *Women Speak to God:*
The Poems and Prayers of Jewish Women

ALL THE WOMEN FOLLOWED HER "offers a stimulating variety of interpretations...These writers beckon us not just to dance with Miriam, but to study her and try to understand her – and ourselves."

-LILITH Magazine
Fall 2001

"...a wonderful entry into the field of feminist literature. (The pieces are) inspiring and thought-provoking. We need more books like this for our daughters to read and take pride in being Jewish women."

-*The Reporter*
Women's American ORT Fall 2001

All the Women Followed Her

A COLLECTION OF WRITINGS ON
MIRIAM THE PROPHET & THE WOMEN OF EXODUS

EDITED BY REBECCA SCHWARTZ

RIKUDEI MIRIAM PRESS

Published in 2001 by
Rikudei Miriam Press
2521 Valleywood Drive
San Bruno, CA 94066
[650] 568-7929
www.rikudei.com

Printed in the United States of America.

Cover art by Lydia Brose. All rights reserved.

ISBN 0-9668562-1-X
Library of Congress Card Catalog Number 00-192917

For information or additional titles, or to contact any of the authors in
this anthology, contact the publisher at
Rikudei Miriam Press
2521 Valleywood Drive
San Bruno, CA 94066
or visit www.rikudei.com.

❧

"And Miriam the Prophet . . . took a timbrel in her hand, and all the women followed her . . ."
Exodus 15:20

CONTENTS

ACKNOWLEDGMENTS

Any anthology is, by definition, a team effort. This book clearly would not exist without the beautiful words and timely effort of the more than thirty women whose writings make up this volume. Thank you to the women of Rikudei Miriam Press for their hard work and dedication to the voices of Jewish women. For my husband Roger, who watched and bathed and fed the baby while I typed, thank you for helping me create the time to give birth to a "second baby." And thank you Miriam, for your guidance, your spirit and your wisdom.

PREFACE

In the spring of 1994 nearly two hundred women came to a Passover seder entitled, "Dancing with Miriam." That title summarizes the essence of my relationship to Judaism. The image brought to mind is one of women in celebration: of their heritage, their freedom, and their voices. At the seder I sat mesmerized as woman after woman expressed her desire to explore Judaism through feminist eyes, and to delve deeper into the story of Miriam and the women of the Passover story. Women's voices are singing out like never before in Jewish history, giving birth to a very new and different Judaism. Passover, as the ultimate celebration of freedom from bondage, appeals to many women in their struggle, just as the feminist and civil rights movements have brought words like 'oppression' and 'liberation' into common parlance. These traditional Passover themes combined with images of Miriam and the Israelite women dancing at the shores of the sea, tambourines in hand, have led to an emerging tradition of women's seders, indeed women's celebrations of many Jewish holidays. Miriam in particular speaks to many of these women who are rewriting Jewish practice, as a leader, a teacher, a musician and a dancer.

Passover 2000 was the year of Miriam. Newspapers across the country from San Jose, CA to Allentown, PA to *USA Today* featured prominent articles about Passover highlighting the use of Miriam's Cups. Proclaiming this once radical, feminist ritual a new mainstream tradition, "Miriam's rise in Jewish culture has resulted in a flurry of Haggadot that set her at the center of the Passover Seder" (*San Jose Mercury News*, April 15, 2000). I even received a Miriam card as a Passover greeting from a friend bearing the lyrics from Debbie Friedman's "Miriam's Song" on the cover. The new Reconstructionist Haggadah, *A Night of Questions*, which received much praise at its long-anticipated arrival the same year, featured Miriam prominently. Invoking her name in the second paragraph of the seder's introduction, the reader is instructed to set out a Cup of Miriam beside Elijah's Cup. According to contributing author Dr. David Teutsch, "Miriam's Cup has become part of the seder ritual . . . Miriam reminds us of the redemption occurring daily in our lives"(p. 29). In the United States, mass marketing of consumer goods never lags far behind any trend in popular culture, and indeed often heralds its arrival. In Jewish merchandise catalogs one may now find: a $250 seder plate bearing a stylized tambourine in the center; a silver goblet embedded with semi-precious stones and an engraved dancing Miriam on one side; and a plastic goblet and tambourine sold as a "Miriam package" for children at the holiday season.

Miriam has never been so ubiquitous. The reasons for her popularity are numerous, and this volume will begin to explore them. From the simple desire to add women's voices to a text that has been silent about women's central role in the Passover story, to a recognition of a lost religious leader of great stature, women are turning to Miriam. This book offers those who yearn for more than the enticing remnants we are granted by the text a chance to hear the words of Miriam and the heroic women of Exodus. Many of the poems and midrashim included here speak in the first person, in Miriam's own voice. Women are seeking a new spiritual depth by climbing into Miriam's skin. Let us now pick up our own timbrels, and follow her.

Rebecca Schwartz
Summer, 2000

INTRODUCTION

Who is Miriam? She appears only eight times in the Bible, in seven of those by name, yet she captures the interest and imagination of Jewish women everywhere. Perhaps she lived, and played a pivotal role in the evolution of the Jewish people. Perhaps she represents a mythological composite of real women from the historical period, or even, as suggested by some, a humanized portrait of a desert water-goddess of ancient days. In viewing someone with so few lines of text assigned to her (she speaks fewer than thirty words in Hebrew), we might be surprised to hear her called "prophetess," or to see her challenging Moses for leadership of the people and for the right to speak for God. More than any other biblical character, Miriam appeals to the modern Jewish woman, and has emerged as a symbol of the Jewish feminist movement. She represents the struggle of Jewish women to find a voice in the tradition, demanding recognition and parity, and even symbolizes a messianic era of full equality.

The Passover story moves forward on the backs of women. We tend to think of the Exodus tale as Moses' story, despite the absence of his name from the Haggadah. But as we read the Torah we see that women surround and guide Moses like no other biblical hero. Two midwives facilitate his birth; his mother and sister hide him from Pharaoh's wrath; and that same Pharaoh's daughter pulls Moses from the reeds. Whereas the rest of these women disappear soon after their work is done, Miriam persists within the text, reappearing enigmatically as a leader of profound importance for the emerging Israelite nation.

Everywhere we see Miriam in the text, we find her near water. In Exodus 2, our introduction to Miriam, we learn that Moses' sister "stood from afar to see what would happen to him" as he floated along the Nile in a basket. We can envision her hiding along the water's edge, coming forward to approach the princess as Moses is lifted from the river. This scene is full of irony, since it parallels and reverses Pharaoh's decree that Hebrew boys should be thrown into the Nile. The water and the women who come to the water conspire to outwit Pharaoh and save the child who will save the Jewish people. Our next glimpse of Miriam, in Exodus 15:20, shows her leading the women of Israel in the Song of the Sea, following the parting and crossing of the Sea of Reeds and the escape from Egypt. Miriam, whose name (*mar yam*) means "bitter sea," stands at the shore of the sea filled with drowning Egyptians, and leads the people in singing God's praise. In the book of Numbers, the notation of Miriam's death comes with the mention that "there was no water for the community." All passages concerning Miriam are disappointingly brief.

One theory of biblical development, known as the documentary hypothesis, identifies different authors for different strands of biblical text. The "E" or Elohist author is connected with the story of the midwives, who are named Shiphrah and Puah, and with each passage of the text mentioning Miriam by name. While the "J" or Yahwist author is identified with most of the stories surrounding the women of Genesis, the Elohist takes on Miriam. Interestingly, "E" is associated with the northern kingdom of Israel, and with prophetic, rather than with royal, circles of influence. "J" supported David and the monarchy, whereas "E" was less concerned with earthly government, espousing rather the religious and ethical obligations of the community. Although the documentary hypothesis is not universally accepted, it is interesting to imagine Miriam having a supporter among the redactors of the Bible, especially one loyal to Israel's prophetic tradition.[1]

Still, if the Torah still considers Miriam a fairly minor character, the Talmud expands her role, especially her prophecy and merit. Her importance to the Jewish people as a legendary figure becomes obvious when we look at how the rabbis, despite their conviction that Miriam sinned by speaking against Moses, nevertheless depict her as a positive and righteous woman. Devora Steinmetz, in an article examining the rabbinic portrait of Miriam, notes their ambivalence toward this strong female character. The commentators chastise Miriam for speaking out of turn, yet applaud her for maintaining family ties and remaining loyal to God.[2] According to the rabbis, Miriam's special merit earned her the privilege of being one of only six people, and the only woman, to die by the kiss of God, without being taken by the Angel of Death.[3] The legend of Miriam's Well connects the magical source of water that followed Israel throughout its sojourn in the desert to the merits of this wondrous prophetess. The Talmud teaches that God built the Well at twilight on the sixth day of Creation and that it exists today, hidden in the Sea of Galilee. The rabbis told how the Well overflowed so that the women in the desert would visit each other in boats on great rivers. The waters springing forth from the Well contained healing properties, and lepers would come to the waters to bathe and be purified. All this Israel owed to the righteousness and wisdom of Miriam.[4]

As a woman, Miriam holds a unique position in biblical writing. First, the text shows her in relationship to other females. We see (briefly) a mother-daughter relationship, of which there are no others in the text. Mother-son or even father-daughter relationships are more common, but the only other mother-daughter interaction in the Bible is Leah's naming of Dinah. The Book of Ruth shows a close, active relationship between a mother and daughter-in-law, and represents one of the few exceptions to the biblical rule of women as rivals, not collaborators. Yet through Miriam the stage is set for a collaboration of six women to protect Moses and eventually bring about the liberation of the Jewish people. Miriam appeals to Pharaoh's daughter, even as a small child forming a connection with the Egyptian princess. This is but the first of many boundaries Miriam will cross, and together she and the princess represent an alliance of women that surpasses race, class, religion and every other form of personal status. Without all these women—Yocheved, Shiphrah and Puah, Bat Pharaoh, Miriam, and even Tzipporah—there would be no Moses, no Exodus, no receiving of the Law, and no Jewish people. The Bible moves from the book of Genesis, tracing the evolution of one family and their descent into Egypt, to Exodus, the emergence of a nation and their return to the land of Israel. These courageous, risk-taking women facilitate this transition, serving as a network of midwives to the infant Jewish nation.

In a book that values women primarily for their maternal roles, Miriam never married or had children. Instead, the Torah presents Miriam as a near-equal to her brother Moses, the unquestionable leader of the Israelites. Egypt historically preferred brother/sister ruling teams,[5] and such an alliance between Moses and Miriam, or between all three siblings, would have been recognized and accepted by the people of the time. Miriam, Aaron, and Moses are mentioned as equals in later writings (Mi 6:4), as co-leaders sent by God to save Israel. No other female receives such a high status on her own.

So where does Miriam's midrashic marriage to Caleb come in? The Talmud determines through a complicated juggling of names that Miriam was married to Caleb, and became the mother of Hur and the grandmother or great-grandmother of Bezalel, the famous architect of the Tabernacle.[6] The historian Josephus preserved a tradition that Miriam was actually married to Hur, and the mother of Bezalel.[7] These could be ancient oral traditions that never made the final edits of canonized text, or the rabbis' later attempts to place Miriam, a powerful and very independent female voice, safely into the nonthreatening role of wife and mother. An unmarried female presents difficulty in the *halacha*. A woman not under the jurisdiction of father or husband (or a widow whose position is common and understood) poses a threat to the social order. Could Miriam have remained celibate? Or taken lovers? The text offers no model for an unattached Hebrew woman who is not a harlot. On a more positive note, the Talmud gives Miriam the prominent position of becoming an ancestress of King David, probably the greatest reward the ancient rabbis could imagine for a woman. Since motherhood represented the ideal goal for a woman in their view, the establishment of a royal lineage for Miriam, as reward for her faithfulness to the unborn generations of Israel and her protection of the baby Moses, must have seemed to them the highest possible honor.

The most common depiction of Miriam throughout the centuries shows her dancing at the edge of the sea, tambourine raised, leading the women of Israel. The image of dancing holds connotations of joy and living spirituality, and the celebration of freedom. Miriam's actions compare to other textual images of women leading song and dance following a battle victory (Jgs 11:34; 1 Sam 18:6-7). But Miriam's cultic role as musician goes beyond the common biblical theme of women welcoming returning warriors with timbrels and dancing, for it is exactly this passage (Ex 15:20) that names her *nevi'ah*, prophetess. As the first woman in the Bible to receive this title, Miriam stands out as a member of a very small and exclusive club. Women's roles as cultic leaders in the Bible, and Miriam's in particular, survive only as fragments through centuries of editing. But this vision of Miriam, leading the women and speaking for God, resonated so deeply for the Jewish people that no patriarchal brush could fully erase it. Miriam remains a powerful figure for Jewish women, and her story speaks loudly to modern women in search of role models from our own tradition.

Many heroines of the Bible appear as victims, or as women known to us primarily for their famous sons. But Miriam held a position comparable to that of no other biblical woman except possibly Deborah, or the later queens. Miriam also differs significantly from other female leaders in that her position is *religious*, not military. The text preserves just enough evidence of female prophets and women in cultic roles to assure us these positions existed. Yet we have frustratingly little detail on how women served in the early Israelite cult, just how much leadership they did in fact hold, and how that leadership diminished. The women of Genesis characteristically use guile and deceit to bring about their desired outcome. Rebekah operates behind the scenes through her son Jacob, and Rachel conceals the truth from her father and husband. Miriam claims her power more openly. She stands boldly before Moses, Aaron, and God, and demands equality. Our image of Miriam dancing the *hora* with a tambourine does not do justice to her actions as one who confronts authority at every turn: familial, governmental, and religious. Miriam's challenge for the right to interpret divine word stands out as an attempt to transition from exclusion to inclusion. As women today try to imagine what Jewish life would have looked like with women's full participation from the beginning, they are echoing Miriam's call (Num 12:2), "Has God not spoken also through us?" At Sinai, at the receiving of the Law, Moses excluded women from hearing the word of God. "Be ready for the third day—do not approach a woman"(Ex 19:15). These are Moses' words, not God's. Not long after, Miriam calls Moses on his omission, and insists on restoration.

As a leader of women, Miriam took center stage, the Bible tells us, and "all the women followed her" (Ex 15:20). In recent years, growing numbers of modern Jewish women have been doing the same. As women take broader roles in Judaism and particularly in ritual, the figure of Miriam becomes central. She appeals to artists for her music and dance; to women in caretaking roles— mothers, healers, and teachers—for her guardianship of the baby Moses; and to professionals and community activists for her courage and leadership. Miriam in particular speaks to many of the women who are rewriting Jewish practice, and seeking new interpretations for the ancient texts that govern or guide our lives. Her story, and the interwoven stories of the women around her, form the basis of a resurgence within Judaism. The Cup of Miriam on the seder table, the proliferation of tambourines, and the growth of women-only seders as mainstream holiday observances, point to her eminence in the consciousness of the new Jewish woman.

One of the most widespread new rituals in modern religion has to be the observance of Rosh Hodesh, the new moon. In a tradition formed in the 1970s,[8] women have reclaimed the rabbinic midrash that God gave the new moon celebrations to women in honor of their loyalty during the construction of the golden calf.[9] We are taught that the women refused to give their gold toward the making of the idol, and remained faithful to God. We are not told whether women came individually to this decision, or whether a leader emerged from among them to turn them aside from the idolatrous practices of the men building the idol. But we can certainly imagine that someone stepped forward to speak on the women's behalf, and organized their resistance. In fact, Miriam and Aaron as priestly leaders of the Israelites have been contrasted in their roles during this incident. Aaron helped in the completion of the idol, while according to midrash,

Miriam's son Hur was killed trying to prevent its construction as Miriam led the women in a more appropriate ritual alternative.[10] We already know that the women of Israel had a leader in the desert, and she was unequivocally Miriam. We can envision Miriam as the symbolic mother of Rosh Hodesh.

Miriam's song and dance and the observance of the new moon, are all lost women's rituals, representing a revitalized "Miriam tradition." The women at the sea sang separately from the men, but next to them and in parallel. Here is a model for the modern Jewish women's movement: Create new rituals by adding women's voices, but without abandoning the tradition. Just as Miriam calls upon God and Moses, saying "Has God not also spoken through [me]," claiming the right of divine interpretation, modern women scholars of Bible and Talmud struggle for recognition of new perspectives on historical writings. Perhaps, as with the golden calf, women in some ways have stayed even more faithful to the spirit of the tradition—after all it was a man, not God, who excluded the women at Sinai. Miriam's rebellion serves as a model for modern Jewish feminists. Miriam may be seen as a "patron saint" for any woman rabbi or scholar who has had to fight for a place at the table.

Modern women have claimed Miriam like no other biblical heroine. Lilith may closely approach her in popularity, but there is no direct basis for Lilith in the text—she had to be invented. Miriam, in both text and midrash, gives us a more legitimate, traditionally sanctioned role model. For centuries, Rachel served as the closest thing Judaism offered to a real patron saint. Women facing infertility, or worried about an impending birth, would make the pilgrimage to her burial site near Bethlehem, wrapping a red thread around the tomb.[11] Rachel may have held some cultic status, as hinted at by the story of the *teraphim* (Gen 31:33), but she lives on in later texts as the weeping Mother Rachel. Since fertility and childbearing, and the fears and dangers associated with them, held foremost position in the thoughts and dreams of most Jewish women, Rachel's popularity as the object of women's prayers made sense. Where our foremothers looked to Rachel, feminists today look to Miriam. As a "career woman" rather than a wife and mother, she appeals to the concerns and passions of the women of the twenty-first century. We hold women's seders, which along with Rosh Hodesh celebrations and girls' baby-namings, mark the most popular innovations of Jewish women in the last two decades. This is not a passing fad. Our daughters will grow up never knowing that Miriam has not always been a part of the seder. We gather at Passover to read Miriam's story, to raise our tambourines, to sing together and even to dance. Drinking from the Cup of Miriam we are indeed "standing again at Sinai," with Miriam as our patron, leading the way.

∽

This book will explore four facets of Miriam's character as presented by the text and midrash— the leader and prophet, the musician, the bitter outcast, and the rebel. We will read about the other women, Shiphrah and Puah, Yocheved, and Tzipporah, who support and surround Miriam, as well as the unnamed women who stood at Sinai. In the final section we turn to Miriam as the mythic messenger of Eden yet-to-come, and as a symbol for modern women. Loosely following the order of Miriam's appearances in the text, we can trace the development of her spirit and reputation, and her growth as a prophet for biblical and modern times.

By playing on the origins of her name, this book will explore Miriam's connection to water, and to the bitterness of the Egyptian slavery into which she was born, and which often characterizes her life. We will also delve into the more subtle aspects of Miriam as an outspoken rebel and early advocate for women's rights. Miriam speaks for the women of our heritage—not the silent, nameless ones who lurk in the shadows of the text, but the women who pushed their way onto the pages of history. She stands for all those whose names were written down and passed along through generations of male editors who could not, dared not, wipe out the memory of these sacred and beloved figures.

NOTES

1. Norman Gottwald, *The Hebrew Bible* (Philadelphia: Fortress Press, 1989), pages 138, 183.

2. Devora Steinmetz, "A Portrait of Miriam in the Rabbinic Midrash," *Prooftexts*, 1998, p.54.

3. *Baba Batra* 17a.

4. Rashi; *Pesahim* 54a; *D'varim Rabbah* 6:11.

5. Savina Teubal, *Sarah the Priestess* (Ohio University Press, 1984), p. 6.

6. *Sotah* 12a; *Shemot Rabbah* 1:17.

7. Antiquities III, in Nahum Sarna, *Exploring Exodus* (New York: Schocken Books, 1986), p.122.

8. Arlene Agus, "This Month is For You" in Koltun, *The Jewish Woman* (New York: Schocken Books, 1976).

9. *Exodus Rabbah*; see also Louis Ginzberg, *Legends of the Jews* (Philadelphia: Jewish Publication Society, 1911).

10. J. Gerald Janzen, "Song of Moses, Song of Miriam, in *A Feminist Companion to Exodus-Deuteronomy*, ed. Athalya Brenner (Sheffield Academic Press, 1994), p.199.

11. Susan Starr Sered, "A Tale of Three Rachels," *Nashim*, Winter, 1998.

PROPHECY & LEADERSHIP

❧

iriam is the first woman in the Bible to receive
the title *nevi'ah*, "prophetess." This chapter
explores Miriam's religious role and her position
as a leader in the community. Here we read about the
crossing of the sea, and the ecstatic celebration of Miriam
and the women. In only two biblical passages in which
Miriam is mentioned by name does she actually speak. In
both of these, Exodus 15:20 and Numbers 12, Miriam
stands next to Moses, claiming leadership of the Israelites.
She leads the women at the Song of the Sea, and demands
the right to interpret divine word during the sojourn in the
wilderness. Miriam's position as a leader of the Israelite
women stands out through both text and midrash, and
characterizes every aspect of her life. The word *nevi*,
prophet, can be read as one who speaks for God, or one
who speaks for another person.[1] As a leader, Miriam
speaks for God and for the women of Israel. Her concern
for others—for family, and for the larger community,
overshadows her own needs at every point in the text. The
Bible takes note of Miriam's death and burial place, with
the comment that "there was no water for the people to
drink," connecting Miriam's life with the existence of the
magical Well of talmudic legend.

Works in this section include Ruth Sohn's
"Journeys" and Barbara Holender's "Red Sea," both
celebrating Miriam's spiritual leadership of Israel as she
leads the women in song and dance. Some writers delve
further into the character of Miriam, imagining her as a
midwife and teacher of the Hebrew women; seeing her as
a positive figure and role model for Jewish women. Erica

Brown's essay explores Talmudic views of Miriam's death, while Alicia Ostriker begins the chapter by painting Miriam's journey through the three biblical passages outlining her life, urging us all to 'follow her drum.'

NOTES

1. In Exodus chapter 7, God instructs Moses that Aaron will be Moses' *nevi* — spokesman with Pharaoh.

THE SONGS OF MIRIAM
Alicia Ostriker

> *And Miriam the prophetess took a timbrel in her hand;*
> *and all the women went out after her with*
> *timbrels and with dances.*
>
> Exodus 15:20

❧

I'm a young girl
My periods not started yet
Up to my waist in Nile water, I push
The baby basket through the bulrushes
Onto the beach
Come on, I say to myself, let's go
And they see it
And come running
My brother cries like a kitten
In the arms of that princess
Her painted face fills with the joy
Of disobedience, which is the life of joy
When she is hooked I walk
Out of the river
Bowing and bowing
I am Miriam, daughter
Of Israel

We gather the limbs, we gather the limbs
We gather the limbs of the child
We sing to the river, we bathe in the river
We save the life of the child.

If you listen to me once
You will have to go on listening to me
I am Miriam the prophetess
Miriam who makes the songs

I lead the women in a sacred circle
Shaking our breasts and hips
With timbrels and with dances
Singing how we got over
O God of hosts
The horse and his rider
Have you thrown into the sea—
That is my song, my music, my
Unended and unfinished prophecy—
The horse was captivity
And its rider fear—

O God of hosts
Never again bondage
Never again terror
O God of hosts.

Call me rebelliousness, call me the bitter sea
I peel the skin off myself in strips
I am going to die in the sand
Miriam the leprous, Miriam the hag
Miriam the cackling one
What did I have but a voice, to announce liberty
No magic tricks, no miracles, no history,
No stick
Or stone of law. You who believe that God
Speaks only through Moses, bury me in the desert
I curse you with drought
I curse you with spiritual dryness
But you who remember my music
You will feel me under your footsoles
Like cool ground water under porous stone—

Follow me, follow my drum
Follow my drum, follow my drum
Follow me, follow my drum
Follow my drum.

I who am maiden
woman and crone
I who am
Miriam.

IMMANENCE
Alana Suskin

Contractions tear the internal flesh
The container breaks at its mouth
And a world, the world,
slides with a rush out in a river of blood.
It was evening, it was morning, a full day.

All the broken pieces Miriam foresaw
Are woven together
Not perfect, a container patched
together with clay and tar,
Is put back into the river
Flowing away into time,
Bends around reeds,
Eddies behind rocks where she stands
in the water to free
The woven cradle from moments
Where it rocks trapped.
She stands there to catch the ark
At the end of the story,
which is the beginning of the new,
When she opens it.

Her hands are open
To catch or let go,
To push or pull or
do nothing,
To find our mother to nurse us
In the stranger's lap.

BIRTHS
Laurie Horn

> *I, YHVH , am your Healer.*
> Ex 15:26

∾

I am Miriam.

Sister of Aharon:

The one they called *ha-n'viah*—the prophetess.

All my life, I have searched for or run from water. When my mother pushed me out, her feet were damp with the mud of the Great River. I have walked in water, danced in it, sweated for it, swallowed it—even prayed silently in fear as my impatient brother, Moshe, beat stones for it. Hundreds of times, I have seen water and blood gush from between the legs of a woman with more force than it sprang from the rock at Meribah. The source of human life is between the legs, but the source of all life is YHVH.

Yocheved, daughter of Levi, was my mother. Amram ben Kohath was her nephew, my father. Kohath, my grandfather, was a son of Levi. Levi was the third son born to Yaakov *avinu* by Leah, our mother, may she be blessed. Both my mother and my father came down with Yaakov after Yosef into the Lower Kingdom of the Pharaohs. We called it *Mitzrayim*—the narrow land— because it was like a narrow serpent: a gray-green river in a sheath of black silt pulled long and straight in the burning desert. In *Mitzrayim*, we lived as though in a vise—oppressed by idolaters who worshipped the sun, fearful of what would happen if we left. There, the servants of Pharaoh first used our name—the name Yaakov *avinu* took at Peniel, after he wrestled with the angel. We called the servants of Pharaoh *Mitzrim*. The idolaters called us Israel.

I was born in *Mitzrayim* in the time of the great pharaoh Rameses the Builder in the new city given his name. In *Mitzrayim*, life was fixed on death. Because they believed that real life began in the tomb, the servants of Pharaoh enslaved us to build them monuments. They even made us build storage houses to hoard grain for their afterlife. Seeing them, did the Holy One laugh?

My mother was a midwife. Therefore I was a midwife. Both my brothers were born as I watched.

I was tiny when I began attending births. In Rameses, men and women of Israel toiled near each other in the fields, mashing straw, mud and sand into bricks. Nursing babies went to the fields on their mother's backs. Later, when we were weaned, we stayed, if we were lucky, in the huts with the elders.

But my grandmother died. My father was a stonecutter, an elder of Israel. In the evening, after we ate, he sat with a council of elders to settle disputes among the people. There was no one to stay with a baby in the huts— no one to nurse me when the messengers came, frantic, to call for my mother. Ima told the messengers to wait until the woman's water broke. Then, she simply wrapped me in her faded blue woolen veil and went.

Why are babies so often born at night? The messengers would knock and my mother would go quickly out the door, hiding me underneath the veil. Even after I could walk, we had to move too quickly for me to run. So I would wrap my legs around Ima's waist, breathing against the salty, moist warmth of her breasts. She would hurry, like a boat blown sideways, following a man with a torch through the marshy, twisted alleys of the Hebrew quarter.

Under the veil, it was dark and warm—almost like being inside Ima again. But when we got to the birthing rooms, the women would pull me away from her and push me into a corner. At first I was so small that I slept. Later, as I began to look and understand, I sat enthralled— fascinated by the intensity, the burning torches, the earthy smells of the birth room. Sometimes I would simply bawl for my mother as Ima shook the laboring women off their straw pallets and forced them to squat on the two *obnayim*—birthing stones. The stones were flat and massive, as high as I was tall, and they were placed just far enough apart that a mother could plant herself on them, pressing down away from the earth. Usually a sister or the grandmother pushed against the mother's back, so that my mother could position the baby properly and then kneel to receive the child.

"Lilith!" Ima would shout. "Demon Lilith! Keep your demon children away from this baby. This baby belongs to Adonai Elohim! This baby belongs to the Holy One of Israel! Protect this mother, Lilith, from your demon children!"

Sometimes, when I was in the desert, I would dream about *Mitzrayim* and my mother. In the dreams, I became at once both Ima and myself , and sometimes I even saw myself at different ages at the same time. At the start of the dreams, there would be nothing but the feeling of rushing, of desperation. Usually I was wrapped around Ima underneath the veil, merging into her body. "Baby," I would say as we wove, inseparable, through twisted, muddy paths separating the thatch of mud-and-reed huts near the river. "No, you're a big girl," my mother would respond, brushing her hand affectionately over my head. And I would bite her.

When women labored, my mother used to massage their bellies, standing behind them, bracing their backs. In the dreams, I would actually see myself leaving the womb, as though from over these women's shoulders. I would squiggle on my back towards the ground, first squeezing slowly and then dropping swiftly from between my mother's legs into the world. Sometimes, at the same time, I would even become the midwife with her hands between my mother's legs, ready to receive my own self being born. "Miriam, too, will deliver the children of Israel," the dream-women would say. And then they would laugh.

It became known in Israel that the children of Yocheved were most often born alive. New mothers rejoiced, and thanked her, and blessed her name. And in the house of Israel, her renown grew.

Eventually it became known even among the *Mitzriyot*—the women of *Mitzrayim*—that my mother was a midwife whose hands were blessed. "Tell them my name is Shifrah," my mother warned the mothers of Israel. "Don't let them know my husband is an elder. Tell them my daughter's name is Puah." But it did not take long before even the *Mitzriyot* began to call for her.

One time, my mother took me to a house in the court. The new mother must have been at least a minor princess—one of the hundred children of Rameses. Probably, she had been born of a concubine brought down the Great River from Cush, because she was as dark as the silt of the river.

I must have been about four. The house was made of stone. And the first thing that struck me was how strangely it smelled: of incense and burning ointments. The princes of the court thought we smelled bad. They were too dainty to allow field slaves into their houses. But we went, escorted by a sentinel, to a side gate, and the chief servant of the household, a *Mitzri*, pointed quickly to a corridor. Ima rushed down the corridor, toward the screams of a woman coming from a courtyard inside the house. But I looked behind, and when I did, I saw the *Mitzri* wrinkle his nose in disgust and bring his hand over his nose and mouth.

In the middle of the courtyard, there was a kind of sukkah—a booth covered with twisted vines and open to the sky. I didn't want to enter. I was terrified. But Ima would not leave me outside.

I walked into the booth, too scared to cry. Torches were burning brightly on all sides. To one side, the *Mitzriya* princess moaned on a couch—the kohl on her eyes running down her brown face in great black streaks. Women milled around her, chanting.

Why was I afraid? I, Miriam, daughter of a midwife, was not afraid of laboring women. After all, I had seen many. But in the middle of the booth was something I had never seen before. It was lit with torches, and it grabbed my attention like a claw reaching out to scratch my face.

There, set on a low table, a beast-idol loomed, reaching almost to the roof. The goddess was a hippopotamus with flaming eyes. Her teeth gaped and menaced in the flickering light. Her back was covered with the oily scales of the crocodile. Her breasts were long, like crocodile teeth. And she carried a knife pushed up into her jaw. "Who is she, mistress?" I said in their language to one of the attendants. "Holy Taweret," the woman replied. As their women walked past her, they kneeled and placed their heads on the ground.

Around the princess were at least four or five other women, fanning her, massaging her back. My mother went to the couch and felt the mother's belly. "The next time the contractions stop, stand up," my mother said in their language. The daughter of Rameses looked at her in shock. "Why does this Hebrew tell me what to do?" she demanded. "Isis! Look kindly on me! Hathor! Deliver me!"

"Stand up," my mother said again. Sweating, the princess bit her lip to catch the pain, and then she began to breathe very fast. In a moment, the contraction abated.

Desperate, my mother looked pleadingly at the attendants for help. They dragged the princess up, supporting her at each arm. She was completely naked, long-boned; her hips were narrow, her buttocks high.

"Take her to the birthing stones," my mother said. Slowly, the attendants walked the princess across the room. I could not imagine that a baby could squeeze between those narrow bones.

Standing on the stones, the princess struggled to open her thighs. "Great goddesses!" she called. "Deliver a child to *Mitzrayim*!" And four women stood around her, supporting her: one behind, one in front, and one on each side.

The contractions began again. Positioning the child inside the woman with one hand, my mother tried to slide her hand into the woman's vagina to ease the passage.

"Push," my mother insisted. The *Mitzriya* pushed, and at the same time she screamed. "I, who labor here, am the goddess Hathor! Isis stands in front of me! Nephythis behind me! Hekat massages my womb! Meshkenet greets me! Hathor, the great Mother, is here giving birth! Hathor the mighty pushes this baby out!"

I could see the tension in my mother's face. Something was not right. Looking straight at me, she said clearly in Hebrew in the most neutral voice she could muster: "Listen, Miriam, and do not forget: Only Elohim Adonai, our God, is God. This baby is dead, and if they kill me, you must try to go back to our own people, and you must remember." Once more, the princess pushed, and the baby suddenly slipped out fast. But the cord was wrapped around its neck. And it was lifeless.

Exhausted, the *Mitzriya* princess rolled off the stones onto the floor. Quietly, she began to sob. The women pulled her onto the stones again, waiting for the afterbirth. But the princess slumped to one side, whimpering.

At that moment, something moved me. I did not know how I began to move. It must have been an angel, an angel from the Holy One forming between the princess and me. The angel quickly grew very strong, and I found myself walking toward the princess—walking without my being aware. "Miriam, no!" my mother called, frantic. But the angel transfixed all of us—me, Ima, the princess' attendants—all except the princess herself, who was still collapsed to one side. The princess had begun to wail. I walked up to her and took her hand.

In her despair, the daughter of Pharaoh turned her face toward me and looked down to see what creature was holding her hand. Looking up, I saw dark, sad, frightened eyes—eyes that almost looked past me.

"Don't worry, mistress," I said to her. "The God of Israel, Adonai Elohim, will give you a son." The princess said nothing. But she changed her gaze. Her eyes narrowed, focusing on my face. From her attention, I knew she had heard me. Then, remembering that I was only a child, a slave, and a daughter of Yaakov, the princess turned away her eyes in despair and rested her chin on her chest. Ima, fearful, grabbed me and pulled me out of the booth. But, from the courtyard, the chamberlain of the house had watched. "Kind child," he said to me, "Go quickly with your mother before a messenger is sent to Pharaoh." Only the Holy One knew why they left us alive.

I do not know how many births I saw in those years in *Mitzrayim*. Probably hundreds—Hebrew and *Mitzriyot*. One of them was my brother, Aharon. At three, I was too young to attend my mother. But I was there, watching. Why did we toil there in such misery? For what purpose did YHVH keep us as slaves?

"I will bring you out," El Shaddai had promised. In *Mitzrayim*, the great monuments we built would last until the end of days. But each year, when the Great River spilled flat like a gray-green platter under the merciless sun, our huts were washed away once again. Would that be our life story—to evaporate like water? Would we crumble there in *Mitzrayim* like the dust and straw of our houses? The children of *Mitzrayim* walked in the sun in sheer linens and heavy wigs. Their heads were drenched in ointment, their eyes painted in kohl. In their narrow world, we were no better than *hayot*—beasts—wilder than the strange idols they worshipped, wild enough to be kept far away from their grazing cattle. Every year, our houses crumbled. But our houses, said the elders, would be built of generations.

"How long, Elohim?" I would hear my mother and father say. "How long?"

"I will bring you out." In *Mitzrayim*, we suckled our failing spirits on those words, feeding our hopes with them like infants at the breast. Faith was our only nourishment. We cleaved to the promise of Adonai as I to my mother Yocheved. The elders had promised us deliverance, Abba and Ima said. And the deliverance would come through the words and deeds of a child.

But then Rameses, son of the Sun, declared that Hebrew children would be killed. All newborn males would be taken from their mothers and killed by the sword or drowned in the River.

"There is no other solution," Abba insisted. Ima burst into tears.

"Yocheved," my father whispered in the darkness, "we cannot give over our sons to be killed by the *Mitzrim*. Pharaoh, may he be cursed, has made giving birth the path to murder." Behind the curtain separating our sleeping area from my parents' in the rest of the hut, I listened, frozen. Aharon slept beside me.

"No, Amram," said Ima, sobbing. "I can't lose you."

"There is no other way," Abba insisted.

"How will I live without you? Is this what El Shaddai wants from the daughters of Yaakov? Amram, you will let our people die? Is that what you want?"

"There is no other way," Abba said. "I will not bring sons into the world only to see them slaughtered like beasts by the *Mitzrim*."

And so he stopped sleeping inside the house. After cutting stone during the day, Abba would still come home to eat the evening meal. Then he would sit with the elders in the courtyard near our hut, and they debated late into the night.

But Abba began to treat my mother strangely. He always kissed me. But when he came to the house, he did not kiss my mother. My mother averted her eyes, angry and sad, and for the first time, when Abba was in the house, she covered her hair. She would not pour water from a jug into his cup. Abba would stand up himself to fetch the water. Sometimes the two of them would play, halfheartedly, with two-year-old Aharon and me, but I knew that after we children went to sleep, Abba would leave.

Hours after he had left, I would hear my mother crying on her pallet on the other side of the curtain.

To keep Abba in the house, I tried to stay up later and later. Mopi, a straw doll Abba had made me, helped me. Mopi would not go to bed, I said. I told Abba I had to stay up and care for her. As long as Mopi was awake, I said, I would not go to sleep. Sometimes Mopi would keep me up so late that I could not fall asleep even when I wanted to. Abba would put me on the pallet, and I would scream in anger as he walked toward the door. But then I discovered that if I pretended to sleep, sometimes he would stay awhile and talk to Ima. It was comforting to hear my parents talking, as they used to do. But the conversation was always the same.

"There must be another way," my mother would repeat.

"No Yocheved, they have twisted even birth into death. Better not to bring children into the world than offer them up for murder." And my mother would start to cry.

No matter what I did, Abba would not sleep in the house any more. Soon, just after I was five, he took Ima and me and Aharon to the public square. In front of ten elders and as many people as possible, he put a writ of papyrus into Ima's hands. She told me the paper meant he was no longer her husband.

"But is he still my Abba?" I asked.

"Yes, beautiful girl, Amram ben Kohath will always be your father. Do not forget." And she wiped her eyes with her veil.

Slowly, there were fewer and fewer babies born to Israel. At first, at night, I would trot beside my mother, fearful, and she would tell me that if the sentinels came, I should say nothing. I would not be harmed because I was a girl, she said.

That year was terrible. During that whole time, *Mitzriyot* midwives came to the house every day, trying to find out whose time was complete. Wordless, my mother would shut the door in their faces. At night, when the messengers came, we would go by indirect paths, and sometimes, to deceive the *Mitzriyot* midwives, my mother would trade veils with another woman of a different house so that the *Mitzriyot* would follow the wrong color and design on the cloth. It became the rule during those months for a woman of Israel never to give birth in her own house. Her family stayed behind, gaunt, worrying. The sons were hidden. A few survived.

Gradually, there were fewer and fewer births. And the less she was called out for her vocation, the more my mother became sad and silent. Bit by bit, she became gray, nervous. At night, I could hear her tossing on her pallet. In the mornings, she would stay motionless—ignoring Aharon and me until the foremen came. I, not she, prepared the morning grain for my brother. I, not she, washed him and cleaned him. I had just turned six. But I did a woman's work. Slowly, I began to see the way a woman sees. But I was a child.

In the fields, when I tired of bringing straw for my mother to mix, I played sometimes with Mopi. At first, over and over again, Mopi would emerge from my tunic, being born. I would pick the doll up by her straw legs, straightening them as my mother did the infants of Israel. I would pull a straw out of Mopi's belly and pretend to cut her birth cord. I would suckle her, singing softly the verse my mother had sung to me:

To Ima and to Abba.
This child comes from her Abba.
May Shaddai bring her *chuppah*,
Sons and grandsons and happiness.

Before, when I sang, Yocheved and the women would laugh. But during the bad time, Ima and the women around her would look at me sadly.

At first, my father came every day, but eventually, he started to visit us only about once a week. On evenings that he was scheduled to come, my mother began disappearing, taking Aharon.

"Be a good girl, Miriam," she would say. "He is your father." She would not tell me where she went. Then my father would arrive. But he didn't look like my father. His beard was dirty, his clothes unwashed. When I went to kiss him, he smelled funny. He brought me bread.

"Why do you wash only your hands for the blessing, Abba?" I asked, perplexed, as he splashed water from the jug over his hands before eating. "Why do you not go down to the River?"

"I wash for El Shaddai. For myself, no," he said. "I mourn for all the house of Israel."

I sat with Mopi, playing my game. I would put Mopi into the top of my tunic and hold her there under the dress. Then I would pull Mopi out and announce. "A boy! May you be like Ephraim and Manasseh!" or "A girl! May you be like Rachel and Leah!"

But one day, as my father watched, I pulled Mopi out from my tunic and I scowled. "See, Miriam, this child is dead," I said. "Only Adonai is God. If the *Mitzrim* kill me, you must remember."

"Stop that, Miriam," said my father curtly.

"No, Abba, I'm playing with Mopi," I said. I pushed Mopi through the top of my tunic again, looked at Abba defiantly, and pulled the doll out from between my legs.

"This child is dead!" I said again. "Mopi is dead!"

Swiftly, Abba got up from the table where he was sitting. He pulled Mopi out of my hands, and threw her straw body onto the cooking fire.

"No, Abba!" I screamed. Reaching into the fire, I nearly burned my arm. But Abba picked me up, restraining my arms, and I began to scream violently.

"No, Abba! No! Mopi is dead! We are all dead! And you are worse than Pharaoh! The *Mitzrim* kill only our boys. But you kill all of us. How are we to know that the next child Ima bears might not be the one to lead us out of *Mitzrayim*? You are worse than Pharaoh!"

Suddenly, Abba put me down. He brought his right hand to his face, spreading his fingers over his whole face the way he did when he prayed. He roared, and then the roar became a sob.

I had never seen my father cry. Frightened and guilty, I ran behind the curtain to my sleeping pallet. Abba followed me, still weeping.

He picked me up and held me close to his chest. "Forgive me, Miriam," he said. "Forgive me, child of bitterness. Forgive me, my daughter. Adonai Elohim has sent you to tell me. Adonai reproaches me. You do not. Forgive me, my Miriam, my prophetess."

The following week, as soon as my mother's time of uncleanness was over and she could immerse herself in the river, my father remarried my mother under a wedding canopy in the courtyard outside our hut. All the house of Levi was there, and seven blessings were said over their heads. Aharon and I danced around them, singing.

Seven and a half months later, Yocheved bat Levi bore a son.

He came quickly, unexpected. There was no one in the house but my parents. My mother's pains began sharply, just before dawn. Within minutes, the contractions were close together. As green and violet light began to rim the sky, my father grabbed Aharon and ran out to fetch the midwife of the house of Shimon, nearby. Meanwhile, I attended my mother.

There were no birthing stones in our house. We did not expect the child for another two months.

"Miriam, bring two stools," my mother said to me. "This baby is coming fast. May Elohim deliver him to us alive."

I brought the stools and my mother squatted. "Lilith, protect me!" she shouted. "Lilith, make yourself my ally in this birthing. This child belongs to the Holy One, be blessed!"

Almost immediately, Ima pushed. When she squatted, the child had already dropped. I did not need to massage her abdomen. This baby was only my mother's third child, but Ima's womb, bless YHVH, opened without pain. In less than a minute, the baby's head crowned.

"Kneel, Miriam, it is time," my mother said. I knelt underneath her to receive the child. As he came out into my hands, I could see immediately that even though he was early, his face was beautifully formed. His body was perfect, his color a bright pink. And even though he was small, he breathed immediately. I did not even need to slap him.

"I will not name him," said my mother. "He belongs to Elohim. May the Angel of Death never find him."

Just as my brother emerged, the sun pushed up over the eastern bank of the Great River, bathing the water and the mud and our huts in a brilliant light. The light was so bright that it surrounded the baby's face. Delicate but strong, the little face was so illuminated that we gasped. His eyes opened, and he stared out at Ima. "See, Miriam," my mother said as the baby began to make sucking motions with his lips. "The Holy One is with him."

But it was not Adonai Elohim—king, judge and ruler—who rested on Moshe when he still had no name. In that saving light, there was no judgment—only nurturance and innocence, only love. All the time that my brother grew to manhood in *Mitzrayim*, the love of the Holy One, be blessed, wrapped and hid him as my mother's veil had sheltered me. Every Shabbat, when we rested, we called the Holy One to us as a child calls its Mother, as a bridegroom waits under the canopy for the Bride. The Holy One suckled us. We rested easily between Her breasts. Other names for the Holy One we saved for other days—Adonai, El Shaddai, Elohim, El, Yah. But on Shabbat, YHVH was a tenderness among us, and we called her Shekhinah. She glowed within Moshe all the time that he grew in *Mitzrayim*—and we thanked and blessed Her.

By the time my Abba returned with the midwife, Yocheved's second son was nursing in his mother's arms.

JOURNEYS
Ruth H. Sohn

᭐

We stood at the sea, still astounded at our passage
through the waters. We stood, puddles forming at our
feet, our mouths open as the sea itself, as the waves came
crashing down over our enemies—horsemen and chariots
tumbling, like sand ploughed under by the surf. Legs and
wheels tumbling. We sang to Adonai. We sang of God's
awesome power and the incredible defeat of our enemies.
My brother Moshe led us in the singing (Ex 15).
   "*Ashira l'Adonai*—I will sing to Adonai, for Adonai
has triumphed gloriously. Horse and driver are hurled
into the sea." Our voices rang out strong and sure, so
different from our panicked footsteps just minutes before.
And then we stopped, the waters already subsiding. In the
silence, voices seemed to linger. I turned my head away
from the sea, away from my brothers and sisters. And I
saw . . . the desert stretched before us endless . . .
unyielding, sun-bleached white, burnt white and barren of
even one blade of green. Our path lay before us. But
where? There was no path—only sand punctuated by a
few scattered rocks and boulders. Where were we to go?
   Over the sound of the calming waters I thought I
could hear a new song. Someone calling: "*Mi zot olah min
hamidbar?* Who is this coming up from the wilderness?"
(Song of Songs 3:6). So we would some day rise up from
this wilderness, out of this burning desert. And someone
was calling us. We were being watched. If I had had any

doubts, I knew now for sure as the words came again, sung softly into the wind.

"*Mi zot olah min hamidbar?* Who is this coming up from the wilderness?" The voice was alluring, inviting, beckoning me forward. "*Rise up, come away, the time of song has come*" (Song of Songs 2:10-12). Suddenly, across the desert sands, I saw a well. A circle of deep, dark blue, surrounded by trees. Date trees and fig trees. Bright-colored flowers. Dark grapes hanging heavy on vines. The air was suddenly sweet with honey and light with birdsong. The others around me didn't seem to see. I blinked my eyes. Even in my wildest dreams I had never seen anything like it. But with all the heavily laden fruit trees and flowers and dazzling colors, it was the well that held my gaze. Waters deep-pulsing blue.

I wanted to sing. With the song I'd heard before still in my ears, I took a timbrel. "*Shiru l'Adonai*," I began. "*Shiru l'Adonai shir hadash*—sing unto Adonai a new song." A song of praise, a song of hope. A new song, a song of dreams redeemed. The women began moving toward me. I took a step and we were dancing. We sang with the timbrels, with the power of our hope, our bodies and hearts whirling. *Shir HaShirim*. The Song of Songs. We sang to God songs of praise, songs of love.

"Enclosed and hidden, you are a garden, a still pool, a fountain . . ." We danced in circles, our feet raising the dust, our voices lifting in song. "Living waters, you are a fountain, a well . . ." (Song of Songs 4:12-16). Could the others see this well we were singing of? Did they sense its importance? This well, I knew, would journey with us in the desert, in our midst. In a circle of deep blue, in clear waters that would soothe every thirst, the *Shechinah* would be among us, through all our journeys.

But first we had to endure several days of thirsty wandering. When they could bear the sun and their thirst no longer, the people cried out to Moshe.

"Is Adonai present among us or not?!" (Ex 17:7). This cry of despair was not their first. God showed compassion. Moshe struck the rock and water sprayed forth. And behind the rock appeared a well—*the* well. Its blue waters more welcome than any our eyes had ever seen. This was the well of my vision, the *Shechinah's* home among us, living waters in the midst of a burning desert. And because I had been blessed as the first to behold the well, it came to be known as "Miriam's Well."

This well, which some would later say had been formed by God already on the second day of Creation, would sustain us through our journey those many years (Seder Olam 5). The well would teach us we could turn to God thirsty, again and again, and have our thirst quenched. The well would sustain us with glimpses of the Garden with its sweet waters, and its songs of love, reminding us of the reasons for our journey.

Each night we would all circle the well and offer songs of praise to God. These were special times. Not only songs but long talks took place around the well. Talks of our journey, where we had traveled and where we were heading. Work that had to be done. And we told stories. Wonderful stories we spun those nights around the well. But mostly we sang. Songs of the *Shechinah*, songs of God, the Song of Songs.

When we were gathered all together around the well those evenings our journey made the most sense. These were the times we were most present to each other. The past and future came together. Renewed, reborn by the living waters, we would come away from the well each morning, ready to move forward in our journey.

So much happened over the months and years. I served the women as a teacher (Targum Micah 6:4), counselor, and spiritual advisor. Sometimes I would intercede with Moshe on behalf of a woman or a group of women. I frequently found myself in the role of mediator, seeking reconciliation between estranged people, much as I had done so many years before with my own parents.

The journey of our people continues from one wilderness into another, spanning centuries and continents, moving us forward into the unknown, ever closer to the Promised Land of dreams redeemed. If I could offer a prayer for my people today, it would be that each of you may find the courage and faith and patience to discover your own path to serve God, our people and humanity. And may God strengthen you, individually and collectively, on your journey.

MIRIAM AT THE RED SEA
Barbara Holender

Are you satisfied, Mama?
Am I free at last
of that one neglectful moment
your eyes accused me of?
All my young years I dared not ask
how long you thought you could hide
a baby in a basket in a river.

Even now, at water's edge
with the sand still wet between my toes,
I dread to hear a child cry out,
though it would not matter---
Pharaoh's men sleep on the far shore
with the sea in their throats.

And our lost child has brought us here---
my baby brother, this marvelous stranger
who makes us one and orders us about.
I'd like to ask him where he'd be
without his three brave mothers,
but he's been taunted enough
by these stubborn slaves grumbling
all the way to salvation. Look at them—
sleeping---at a time like this!

The sounds of these nights and days
rage in my ears:
the wings of the Death Angel whistling past,
the neighbors wailing for their sons,
the stifled cries of our babies

held so close; the sound of feet,
hundreds of feet, running, shuffling, limping,
slapping into the sea;
the swish of reeds and the gasp of fish,
the shouts and the horses' shrieks,
the waters crashing together,

and from our shore of the sea
that great Hosannah as of one voice.
The Lord lifted me, I felt His hands,
and my song poured out
and the timbrel shook in my fingers
and my feet never touched the ground.

MIRIAM'S WELL
Barbara Holender

*Due to the merits of Miriam, a mysterious well, created on the eve of
the first Sabbath, accompanied the Children of Israel in the desert.*

Midrash

ॐ

It followed her everywhere
like a lover, easing us to rest,
springing from hidden places
in our wanderings.

Always we were thirsty. Angered
by our wailing, she'd stamp her feet.
Even from the pools of her heelprints
we drank.

Once in anguish
she beat the rocks with her bare hands
again and again, weeping.
Water gushed, cleansing her blood,
soaking her hair, her robe.
She cupped her hands, rinsed her mouth,
spat; she splashed, she played.
Laughing, we filled our bellies.

She was the one we followed,
who knew each of us by name.
Healing rose from her touch as drink
from the deep, as song from her throat.

She was the well. In our hearts
we called her not Miriam, bitter sea,
but *Mayim*, water.

THE MIRRORS
Jill Hammer

"He made the laver out of copper, and its base out of copper, from the mirrors of the serving women (tzovot) *who served at the entrance of the tabernacle."*
Ex 38:8

"Miriam was a teacher of women."
Targum Micah 6:4

❧

When the Israelites received the Torah, they did not, at first, know what to do with it. Parts of it were law. Parts of it were story. Parts of it were poem. They began to read it and discovered that every time they read it, it had a new meaning. They also discovered that the new revelation seemed more clear if they studied it together. The people were occupied with the task of building the Tabernacle, and all its furnishings, as a dwelling place for God. Yet they also knew that it was an equally important task to study the words which they had been given at Sinai.

So at night when the work of building the Tabernacle had ceased for the day, the people began to gather in groups to learn the Torah together. Miriam, the prophetess, called to the women who had worked hard all day to spin blue, purple and scarlet thread for the Tabernacle's curtains. They wound their threads into skeins and came to sit in Miriam's tent. She taught them the Torah for hours, until their eyes drooped. The very beginning of the Torah fascinated them. They spent many days on the six days of creation, probing its mysteries, for they too were engaged in the work of creation. Finally, when they came to the creation of humankind, the women became confused, for they had read this verse: "God created the *adam* in his own image, in the image of God he created him, male and female he created them." They argued about the meaning of this verse. How could God create one creature that was also two? And how could God create a mortal creature, of any gender, in God's own image? They had seen on Sinai that the Eternal was a consuming fire. No mortal could approach that presence and live.

Miriam listened as the women argued. The debate grew more and more heated. Finally Miriam said to her disciples: "Go home and fetch your mirrors."

The women did not understand this strange request, but they hastened to follow Miriam's bidding. Each went to her tent to find the mirror into which she looked when she braided her hair or painted her eyes. Some opened carved chests of olive wood given to them by their mothers. Some unwrapped bundles of rags. Some begged from neighbor women or from grandmothers. Some brought two or three mirrors so that others could share. Soon all came back to Miriam's tent, carrying the precious bronze circles. The firelight reflected in the many mirrors made the tent blaze like a palace of light. Then Miriam told the women to look into their mirrors.

"What do you see?" she asked.

"I see myself," each woman answered. "I see my eyes, which reveal my soul. I see my mouth, which speaks and sings. I see that I am different from everyone else."

"Each of you is made in the image of God," Miriam explained. "Your soul and your speech are like God's, and your body is God's dwelling place. Each of you embodies the Divine presence in a different way. When you look into your mirror, you see a woman, but you also see the Divine image. If a man were to look into your mirror, he would see a man, but he would also see God. This is what the Torah means when it says: God created the *adam* in his own image, in the image of God he created him, male and female he created them. God is like the mirror: God remains the same, but reflects each of our images differently, men and women, young and old. This is why, when we study together, we can reveal different facets of the Torah to each other. Each of us is a different reflection of the One."

The women were silent, and for a long time they looked into their mirrors without speaking. Then one of the women said: "These mirrors are holy now, because each of them has held God's image. We can no longer use them for ourselves. They belong to everyone."

Some of the women were angry at this, for their mirrors were precious to them, but another woman said: "The people are all donating their most precious possessions for the building of the Tabernacle, and its instruments. Let us give our mirrors to become part of God's dwelling-place. Then their holiness will be honored by all the people."

Miriam smiled, for she was very pleased by what her students had said. Then Miriam said: "Let the mirrors be used to make the bronze laver which the priests will use to wash their faces and feet and hands. At each washing, they will look into the water, and they will see God's image. In this way, the mirrors will teach the priests what they have taught us."

Even the most grudging of the women consented to this plan, and each one gave her bronze mirror to be smelted for the priestly laver. And when the Tabernacle finally was finished, Moses arranged the Tabernacle, its curtains, its altar, its incense and its lamp. The Divine Presence settled upon the Tabernacle and shone radiantly throughout the camp. The women gathered and peered into the courtyard where the polished laver stood before the door of the Tent of Meeting. They made a covenant with one another to return again and again to the door of the Tent of Meeting, to pray, to study, and to see their faces in the basin made from their mirrors. And in that company Miriam was often heard to teach: On account of the one God's many images is the Eternal called *Adonai Tzev'aot*, Lord of Hosts; and some say, *Adonai Tzovot*, God of the women who serve the Divine dwelling-place.

THE WELL DRIED UP:
MIRIAM'S DEATH IN THE BIBLE & MIDRASH
Erica Brown

With the death of Miriam Israel lost a valiant heroine, and Jewish women, in particular, lost a role model of female leadership. Her loss was felt acutely enough to inspire the custom of pious women to fast to mark the day that Miriam died.[1] Despite the fact that her death was memorialized later in Jewish history, the Hebrew Bible contains little information about this tragic moment. The descriptions of her death in rabbinic literature however, do encapsulate some of the complexities of her character and shed light on her life and her leadership.

> "Then the children of Israel, the whole congregation, came to the desert of Zin in the first month and the people lived in Kadesh and Miriam died there and was buried there. And there was no water for the congregation and they gathered up against Moses and Aaron." (Num 20:1-2)

Miriam's death in the Hebrew Bible is an occasion of loud silence on the part of the text. Although her death is recorded, no communal mourning is mentioned. Her burial place is not marked nor are her brothers engaged in her burial; the text quickly moves on to the repeated complaint of lack of water. This is a sharp contrast to Aaron's death, which occurs in the very same chapter, and to which seven verses are dedicated and the presence of the grieving children of Israel is emphasized. Miriam protected the infant Moses (Ex 2), galvanized the women at the splitting of the sea (Ex 15) and expressed concern over Moses' relationship with his wife (Num 12); her death certainly warrants greater attention. A closer look at the text, its commentators and the midrash may fill in some of the narrative gaps.

In linguistic and thematic terms, Miriam's death parallels the attention her life was given in the Bible.[2] Miriam is one of the few women who occupy a frontal place in biblical lore and is not depicted as the supportive partner to a heroic male. In fact, no mention is made in the Bible of Miriam's spouse. She is a woman who appears assertive and alone, even from a tender age. Despite this portrait, we get very few glimpses into her character and her behavior. Those that we do have are usually brief -- one or two verses. In contrast to her two famous brothers, she is only mentioned a handful of times in the Torah and once in Chronicles (I Chrn 5:29). When we are introduced to her she is without a name and seems a distant figure in the early life of Moses: "And his sister stood afar off to know what would be done to him" (Ex 2:4). Her glorious moment of song at the Reed Sea only occupies two verses, and is diminished somewhat in uniqueness when we read in Judges 11:34 and Psalms 68:26 that it was a common custom for women to welcome men home from battlefield with timbrels and dancing. For example, "And it came to pass on their return, when David returned from slaying the Philistines, that the women came out of the cities of Israel, singing and dancing to meet King Saul with timbrels and with joyful song and with lutes" (I Sam 18:6-7). Perhaps Miriam's death is presented in a minimalistic fashion to convey that her life, like the verses that present it, shared this limited and ambiguous characterization. The narrative sparsity is enhanced in almost each instance that Miriam is mentioned in the Bible because her story is quickly eclipsed by the needs of the children of Israel. Immediately after Miriam's celebration at the Reed Sea the text states, "So Moses brought Israel; from the Reed Sea and they went out to the wilderness of Zur and they marched in the wilderness three days and found no water"

(Ex 15:20-21). As elsewhere, Miriam's moment is cut short by the travels of Israel in the wilderness and specifically by the persistent search for water.

The deaths of Moses, Aaron and Miriam also take on greater symbolic significance when viewed in light of their respective topographic locations, each suited to the characterization they respectively receive. Aaron died on a mountain in full view of the community in which he served as high priest, an elevated position. Moses died in Moav, in a valley out of view of the children of Israel, a lonely death at the end of a leadership of persistent contention summed up in the biblical words of Deuteronomy. "And he buried him in the valley in the land of Moav opposite *Baal Pe'or* but no man knows his grave to this very day" (34:6). Miriam died in the desert, the wide anonymous expanse of monochromatic land which signified the difficulties of the journey. It is a dry place, a place of constant human urgency and vulnerability and one where perhaps death itself is too commonplace to take sufficient notice.

The Midrash on Miriam's Death

The midrashim on Miriam's death tell a different story. Midrash is largely a product of the creative thinking of the same rabbis who composed the Talmud between the second and sixth centuries of the common era. The midrash embellished the biblical text on Miriam's death; for example, the Bible makes no mention of those who buried Miriam. In contrast, the Bible relates that Aaron was buried by Moses and Eleazar, his son, and Moses presumably merited divine burial: "Moses the servant of the Lord died there in the land of Moav, according to the word of the Lord. And *he* buried *him* in the valley..." (Deut 34:5-6). Yet in our verse, Numbers 20:1, we are only told ". . . the people dwelt in Kadesh and Miriam died and was buried there."[3] Who buried her and how was it done? One answer appears in the *Yalkut Shimoni*, a medieval collection of midrash from the thirteenth century. Moses is depicted as carrying Miriam's head and Aaron, her feet. The image is of a tripod that has lost one of its supports. Rather than the triumvirate standing in unison, two stand vertically and support the third who lies lifeless, horizontally. Elsewhere in the same collection of midrash, Moses and Aaron are described as being engaged in Miriam's burial and privately grieving over her death. At the same time, the children of Israel were searching for water and came upon Moses and Aaron in mourning. The congregation then went to the Tent of Meeting to call God. God appeared to Moses and Aaron and chastised the two of them for their private preoccupation with pain at a time when communal needs had to be addressed: "The Holy One, blessed be He, said to them, 'Servants of the community, leave here with speed. My children are dying of thirst and you are mourning over this elderly woman?'" Although this midrash does depict grieving, it also portrays a moral dilemma of leadership. Moses and Aaron are rebuked for ignoring communal needs at a time of personal difficulty. Particularly striking in this midrash is the way in which God dismisses the mourning over Miriam; her passing was not depicted as a loss for all of Israel; it was seen only as the loss of a sibling.

In one of the more well-known midrashim, Miriam's death is actually causally connected to the loss of water mentioned in Numbers 20:2. According to several rabbinic sources, the well that accompanied the children of Israel throughout the desert stopped providing water the day Miriam died. According to *The Ethics of the Fathers* (5:6), a miraculous well was created on the eve of the first Sabbath of creation to accompany the Israelites in their future journey in the desert. The Talmud states that this well was given as a gift to Israel in the merit of Miriam.[4]

Rabbi Yossi and Rabbi Judah said: Israel had three great leaders who were Moses, Aaron and Miriam and three significant gifts were given in their merit: the well, the cloud and the manna. The well was in the merit of Miriam . . . for when Miriam died the well dried up because it says, "Miriam died there," and right after that it states, "And there was no water for the congregation."

Many other collections of midrash and material from the second commonwealth period contain a similar attribution of the well to Miriam, this being a popular legend in the ancient Israelite world.[5] Although not stated outright in the midrash, the well may have been associated with Miriam because of the water imagery of her name and the good that she did through water.[6] She saved Moses through water and led the women in rejoicing when the sea was split. The cessation of the miraculous well when Miriam died prompted the rabbis to conclude that this is why the Israelites began once again to complain about water. The people felt her death palpably because without her the nurturing they received in her merit stopped. This midrash may have been the way that the talmudic Sages expressed the loss that was not expressed in the biblical text itself. The sixteenth century Polish commentator, R. Ephraim Lunshits, employed a different interpretative strategy to explain the causal connection between Miriam's death and the lack of water. He connected the two disparate verses, Numbers 20:1 and 2, by contending that the children of Israel suffered thirst *because* there was no recorded communal grieving over Miriam. In failing to appreciate their leader, the Israelites were denied the very gift given in her merit.

Another set of midrashim looks at the deaths of Miriam and her brothers as part of a larger theme of the death of the biblical hero generally. In these midrashim, the rabbis were clearly struggling with human death as an inevitable fact in contrast to the lasting legacy that the biblical hero leaves for the readers of later generations.

Our rabbis taught: There were seven over whom the angel of death had no dominion, namely, Abraham, Isaac and Jacob, Moses, Aaron and Miriam . . . Moses and Aaron because it is written in connection with them (that they died) "By the mouth of the Lord." But the words, "by the mouth of the Lord" are not used in connection with [the death] of Miriam? Rabbi Eleazar said: Miriam also died by a kiss, as we learn from the use of the word "there," in connection both with her death and with that of Moses. And why is it not said of her that (she died) "by the mouth of the Lord"? Because such an expression would be disrespectful.[7]

Through intricate word associations from verses in the Bible, the sages conjectured that there were a group of individuals who somehow fought death and won on two levels. On one level they were able to ward off the harshness of the actual moment of death because they died with God's kiss, a loving image of parting, instead of the image of death in a fearful guise. On another level, they were immune to the natural ravages of death symbolized by the worm imagery that make humanity seem existentially insignificant. Miriam is the only woman on this list and, for that reason, the sages explained that God did not kiss her as He did Moses; the male imagery used to describe God in this religious worldview vitiated the possibility that God would have kissed the heroine. Although the sages culled these lists of heroes based on word plays, they created an underlying theme of immortality for those who made significant contributions to the Jewish nation. These heroes may have died human deaths but they achieved immortality in the consciousness of their people.

The Text vs. the Midrash

In examining the biblical text and some of the midrashim on the death of Miriam, we find ourselves at a narrative barrier. On the one hand, the death of Miriam in Numbers is an ignominious and painful one for the reader. The sharp turn in focus from her passing to the needs of the community forces the reader into the same moral dilemma recorded in the midrash that faced Moses and Aaron. Miriam was first and foremost a communal servant and as such, we expect that the reader will understand the jarring move from her death to communal thirst. At times of urgency, the life of one—no matter how significant—is minimized in contrast to the lives of the many. In portraying Miriam's death so sparsely, the Bible succeeded in capturing the travails of life in the wilderness for the broader community. The children of Israel could not even mourn Miriam properly because, in many ways, they were mourning their own rapid demise. We know that thousands of Israelites were killed through plagues, skirmishes and thirst in the book of Numbers. Several medieval Bible commentators note in their explanation of the curious and seemingly repetitive expression, "the children of Israel, the *whole* congregation," (Num 20:1) that the numbers of the congregation were dwindling. For example, R. Hezekiah ben Manoah, a thirteenth century French exegete, makes the generational connection directly, "*And Miriam died there:* the death of Miriam and Aaron were placed here (in Numbers 20) because the generation was dying out." Miriam was just another one in the vast expanse of wilderness that consumed its inhabitants. Yet, unlike her brothers, Miriam's death is not a punishment. Hers is a natural death just as others of her generation pass on. Even though Miriam is often grouped with her brothers in the rabbinic consideration of her death, the biblical text forces us to separate the three. Death is clearly a punishment for Moses and Aaron. Numbers 20:24 and Numbers 27:14 offer a stinging condemnation of Moses and Aaron that brings about their deaths. They rebelled with the waters of Meribah and did not "sanctify the waters" as God had demanded of them. Miriam also suffered public punishment in her lifetime (Num 12) when struck with leprosy as a result of slandering Moses. However, her punishment was sickness and exclusion from the camp for seven days. When she died, she died without many words but also without any blame. In the deaths of both Moses and Aaron, the Bible uses the euphemistic expression, "to be gathered up unto one's people." However, Aaron died on a mountain high above his community, and Moses died alone. Ironically, it is Miriam who is truly gathered up to her people because it is she who dies the death of the community at large.

In Conclusion

The biblical text depicts Miriam's death in its full emotional rawness. Later rabbinic literature softens the picture, offering grief and personal loss as well as a grasp at immortality. The relationship between the text and the midrash mimics death itself. The actual moment of death is, for most, not a staged, beautiful closure. It is a jarring, abrupt cessation of life that leaves a wide gap for those left behind. But life and the biblical narrative continue despite the loss. This is the sentiment that is captured in the text. The midrash, however, offers death what the passage of time offers death - hindsight, reflection and a fuller, more gentle measurement of individual worth. The Sages rewarded Miriam with a beautiful death. Helen Keller once said, "Death is no more than passing from one room into another. But there's a difference for me, you know, because in that other room I shall be able to see."[8] When Miriam passed into "another room" those who read her story were able to see more, to offer the narrative more heft and weight. The two views of her death exist side by side in Jewish tradition. The minimalistic record in Numbers parallels the other narratives about Miriam both in length and style. There, she dies the death of her people and becomes part of the farewell to a turbulent generation of desert travelers. In the midrash, her death has communal consequences and is observed by the mourning of her brothers and the loss of the well. But the midrash also refuses to let her die and offers her heroic immortality. Both accounts of her death—the moment of death and its aftermath—capture the nature of death itself. Life does have a final moment but over time there is a refashioning of memory and characterization, and the final portrait comes out richer as a result.[9]

NOTES

1. This custom is mentioned in the *Makhzor Vitri*, 271 and in the *Siddur* of Rabbi Amram in his section on fast days. Eliyahu Kitov mentions this fast on the tenth of Nissan in *Sefer Toda'ah*, vol II (Jerusalem: Yad Eliyahu Kitov Publishing House, 1963), pp.31-32. For sources on the dating of Miriam's death see BT *Ta'anit* 9a, *Seder Olam Rabbah* (Milokovsky addition) 9, (D.H."*Va-yavo Benei Yisrael*") and Rashbam's comments on Numbers 20:1.

2. For more on the parallelism of life and death in the narratives of Miriam and her two brothers, see my, "In Death as in Life: What the Biblical Portraits of Moses, Aaron and Miriam Share," in *Bible Review* (June:1999).

3. Since the biblical text mentions the two verbs of death and burial together in relation to Miriam, an interesting Jewish law evolved with this verse as its basis. If both a man and a woman

died at the same time, the burial of the woman takes precedence. For a brief statement of this law, see the *Kitzur Shulkhan Arukh* 198:6.

4. BT *Ta'anit* 9a. Other versions of this appear in the *Mekhilta De-Rebbe Yishmael*, "*Be-shallah,*" 7 (D.H. "*Bnei Yisrael*") and the *Mekhilta De-Rebbe Shimon bar Yohai* 15:35 as well as the *Midrash Tanhuma, Bamidbar*, 2 (D.H. "*Vayidaber*").

5. For a brief citation of such material, see James Kugel, *The Bible as It Was* (Cambridge, MA: Belknap Press, 1997), pp.363-364.

6. It was customary for women to fast to mark the day that Miriam died. Ellen Frankel, in her creative conversations about women in the Bible, writes this about the association with Miriam with the well (in the voice of Miriam herself):

"Because of my merits - my powers of prophecy, my protection of my baby brother Moses, my skillful midwifery among the Hebrew slaves and my victory song at the Sea of Reeds - this well was restored to the Jewish people and was called by my name."

From *The Five Books of Miriam: A Woman's Commentary on the Bible* (New York: Grosset/Putnam Books, 1996), p.226. What Frankel does not do is provide a specific reason to connect Miriam's well to the water imagery associated with her. At the end of B.T. *Ta'anit*, there is a suggestion that Miriam died on the tenth of the Hebrew month of *Nissan*. A year later, on the anniversary of her death, according to the book of Joshua 4:19, the children of Israel crossed the Jordan River into the land of Israel. Thus, the water imagery associated with her life continued even after her death. For another water connection, see the commentary of Rashi on Psalms 110:7.

7. BT *Bava Batra* 17a.

8. As seen in Peter McWilliams, *The Life 101 Quote Book* (Los Angeles: Prelude Press, 1996), p.50.

MIRIAM THE MUSICIAN

⤖

Miriam's classic pose leading the women in dance and playing the timbrel represents the lost tradition of Jewish women's music. In *Miriam the Musician*, contributing authors and songwriters explore Miriam's role as cultic leader, singer, dancer and musician. In the new Reconstructionist Haggadah, *A Night of Questions*, Lori Lefkovitz comments that the timbrels the women played held the status of religious ceremonial objects. Observing the hurried packing of the Exodus, she notes, "Today we might remember to take candlesticks. Back then a good Jewish girl made sure she had her drum."[1] New scholarship has brought to light the hidden possibilities beneath the edited text as we have received it today. Scholar Phyllis Trible maintains that the Song of the Sea originally belonged to Miriam and the women, and was only later attributed to Moses.[2] The Dead Sea Scrolls offer evidence of missing words that were attributed to Miriam, highlighting the conquering of the strong by the weak, a reversal brought about by God's hand (a common theme in songs of praise by women).[3]

We begin with Rabbi Ruth Sohn's now classic poem, "I Shall Sing to the Lord." Scholar Cia Sautter traces the threads of a lost tradition through portraits of Miriam in four medieval Haggadot, and Susan Phillips' midrash imagines the life of Miriam the songwriter and psalmist. Several original songs about Miriam appear as well. Geela Rayzel Raphael's introduction to her songs, a commentary on *parashat shabbat shira*, highlights the importance of Miriam's role as songleader in her status as prophet, and its significance for women today.

NOTES

1. *A Night of Questions: A Passover Haggadah*, edited by Rabbi Joy Levitt and Rabbi Michael Strassfeld, The Reconstructionist Press (Elkins Park, Pennsylvania, 2000), p. 63

2. Phyllis Trible, "Bringing Miriam Out of the Shadows," in *A Feminist Companion to Exodus to Deuteronomy*, ed. Athalya Brenner (Sheffield Academic Press, 1994), page 172.

3. George J. Brooke, "A Long-Lost Song of Miriam," *Biblical Archeological Review*, May/June 1994, p. 63.

I SHALL SING TO THE LORD A NEW SONG
Ruth H. Sohn

I, Miriam, stand at the sea
and turn
to face the desert
stretching endless and
still.
My eyes are dazzled
The sky brilliant blue
Sunburnt sands unyielding white.
My hands turn to dove wings.
My arms
reach
for the sky
and I want to sing
the song rising inside me.
My mouth open
I stop.
Where are the words?
Where the melody?
In a moment of panic
My eyes go blind.
Can I take a step
Without knowing a
Destination?
Will I falter
Will I fall
Will the ground sink away from under me?

The song still unformed—
How can I sing?

To take the first step—
To sing a new song—
Is to close one's eyes

and dive
into unknown waters.
For a moment knowing nothing risking all—
But then to discover

The waters are friendly
The ground is firm.
And the song—
the song rises again.
Out of my mouth
come words lifting the wind.
And I hear
for the first
the song
that has been in my heart
silent
unknown
even to me.

THE DANCE OF MIRIAM
Cia Sautter

From a doctoral dissertation entitled*The Dance of Jewish Women as Torah**

᷽

*Miriam is considered a prophetess, and she sang a song of triumph
with the Israelite women after the crossing of the Red Sea (Ex 15:20).
A miraculous well accompanied the Israelites in the wilderness because
of her merits. When she died, Miriam's Well was transferred to the Sea
of Galilee, where its healing waters are still to be found. At the great
banquet, in the time of the Messiah, Miriam will dance before the
righteous. Mystics believed that the water of Miriam's Well helped
refine the body, and those who drank from it were thus able to
understand the teachings of the Kabbalah.[1]*

᷽

Who is Miriam, as a symbol of Jewish women in
celebration? With almost no written records describing
what Jewish women did when they met together, pictures
of Miriam from four medieval Haggadot (ceremonial
prayer books for the observation of Passover) may be the
best evidence of women's traditional practices in the
Mediterranean world. Analyzing the pictures from the
Haggadot reveals a history of women's leadership in the
music and dance of Jewish celebration, symbolized
through the figure of Miriam. At least, the Miriam pictures
inform us how medieval Spanish Jews understood the
meaning of Miriam, dancing at the shores of the sea, and
the significance of the dance of Jewish women for
Sephardic Judaism.

* My thanks to dancer and scholar Judith Brin Ingber, whose research
and assistance allowed me to explore the Miriam portrayed in the
Haggadot, and Sephardic women's dance traditions.

Visual evidence of dance must be read with a view of how performance was understood in a culture. Medieval Spain did have a significant amount of dance, so representation of this activity may have carried meanings lost through the years. Reading paintings in the Haggadot involves digging through written accounts of daily life of this time, as it relates to the images. While historical documentation concurrent with the Haggadot provides a major source of information on how to interpret visual depictions of the biblical character Miriam, continuing cultural traditions are also informative. There was a tradition of women's dance and drumming performance in Jewish communities around the Mediterranean. Evidence of this tradition exists in biblical texts, in supportive archeological material, and in the continuing dance practices of Sephardic women. Adding this evidence to the visual information in the Haggadot suggests that Miriam's symbolic meaning as a dancer who drummed was significant for Sephardic women.

I call this *Sephardiyot* practice the Miriam tradition, but cannot conclude Miriam was a conscious mythological archetype for the *Sephardiyot* (Jewish women of Spanish or North African ancestry). However, the image of Miriam dancing does appear to carry significant meaning in medieval Spain, occurring in Jewish visual and written sources. Since written texts indicate there was a continuous dance, drum, and song practice among Sephardic women, these documents may be compared with the images of Miriam in the medieval Haggadot.

The Sarajevo Haggadah

The motion of Miriam and the women in this painting involves a hand-holding line dance. Of the four women pictured, two have arms lifted and bent at the elbow. They are looking at each other. The young woman closest to the tambourine-playing Miriam is on the end of the line, and her free arm is bent. She and the young woman at the far end of the line look at Miriam. The women are dancing against a background of blue squares, reminiscent of tile work in Islamic Spain.

THE SARAJEVO HAGGADAH

Textual information from Spain during the thirteenth and fourteenth centuries suggests that the Sarejevo Haggadah might depict a northern version of the *zambra*, the Middle Eastern-influenced dance popularized in the Islamic courts of Andalusia.[2] Since the instrument played by Miriam is a hand drum, this might also suggest the so-called oriental influence. Most likely the dance is a blend of courtly influence and Middle Eastern or Persian styling, as is the music of the period. The painting is supposedly of a mythic Miriam and women, who in the Bible are escaped slaves. In this painting, the women are wearing fashionable clothes, and they are properly dressed, with Miriam shown as an older, married woman. Her head is covered in a white cloth, and she has a whitish-brown coat over her tunic. The dancing women all have long, flowing hair, and uncovered tunics, just as unmarried women of the day would have been clothed.

The tunics are in shades of blue and red. Presumably, they are also Jewish women.

When and why they are dancing is an interesting aspect of this depiction, as in all the Haggadot. At one level the answer is: because of the victory at the Red Sea. But the model for the dance is contemporary. The artist projects back in time, perhaps intending to portray the biblical version of Miriam and the women dancing. None of the paintings, however, include images of a seashore. The setting for Miriam in all the Haggadot suggests that artists portrayed contemporary scenes of Jewish women celebrating with drum and dance in medieval Northern Spain.

The Golden Haggadah

Determined to be the work of two artists by most critics, this Haggadah is from an earlier period than the Sarajevo Haggadah. The conventions employed in the settings and figures are in a French Gothic style, with some Italian features in the architecture included in the scenes of the biblical stories. It is called "golden" since the background for the scenes is golden foil with geometric figuring. In the scene with Miriam and the women, the geometric figures are also seen in the instruments the women carry.

The women's dance in this version of the Passover story is somewhat similar to that in the Sarajevo Haggadah, but there are noticeable differences. First, there are only two dancers proper, dancing in the right corner of the picture. They are looking at each other, and their back arms are raised, bent at the elbow. The forward arms are at approximately hip level. The hips seem to be swayed past the norm of a French Gothic style. Since the view of the dancers is from the side, the sway is more apparent in the figure of Miriam than the other women, who play musical instruments in the foreground. The body position of the women musicians does suggest a possible hip-shimmy movement.

All the women, including Miriam, are depicted as young and unmarried. Their heads and tunics are uncovered, their hair long and flowing. For the most part, they are musicians, with Miriam playing the box drum, the woman to the right of her hitting a round drum, one woman behind her playing cymbals, another percussive hand instrument, and one a lute. The elegance of their dress suggests that these are women of the courts.[3] Where and why the women are dancing again remains a question. In the scenes of this Haggadah, inside settings are specified through architectural features. There are none for the Miriam frame, but also no marks of an outdoor setting, such as trees, grass, flowers, water, or rocks. Why the women are dancing is unclear, other than to illustrate the biblical story of Miriam leading a victory dance. Why this image is the one chosen for Miriam and the women dancing in celebration also remains uncertain, given the lack of visual clues indicating the setting.

The Sister Haggadah

According to Bezalel Narkiss, The Sister Haggadah is similar to the Golden Haggadah, and thus derives its name.[4] In this depiction, there are eight young women, interlinking their arms, spaced in a pattern suggesting a circle. Off to the side, there is a Miriam figure playing a drum, and another woman with her, perhaps a singer. As to when and why these women are dancing, the Haggadah itself provides the script: "And Miriam the prophetess took a timbrel [*toph*] in her hand, and all the women went out after her with timbrels and with dances." The location and connection to the biblical account is made clear and direct with this inscription. Relating this original Passover celebration of Miriam and the women dancing with the dances of fourteenth-century Spanish Jewish women, again, was apparently not seen as unusual, given the images included in the Haggadot.

In all these paintings of women dancing, *men* never appear. They are not involved in the background or the musical accompaniment. The focus of the biblical account is on the women. Men were also part of the story, and men are depicted throughout various scenes of all the Haggadot. Traditional separation of men from women in the culture is evident. Unlike written texts of the period that lack mention of women, a question raised by the Haggadot is "Why only women?"

The Hispano-Morisque Haggadah

The Hispano-Morisque Haggadah picture of Miriam and the women dancing displays some significant differences with the other Haggadot. Stylistically, the paintings in the entire manuscript are of a different style than the other Haggadot. Rather than fine Gothic characteristics, the details here are more primitive. For the Miriam painting, this is especially noticeable in the ill-defined features of the dancers. Narkiss determines that the Haggadah is "archaistic, and may also depend on Italian origin."[5]

The dancers' hands in this painting show more clearly than in the other Haggadot the meaning of the dance. Of the two young, wreathed women dancing on each side of Miriam, one is holding percussive instruments in both hands. Her elbows are bent, with one arm raised and one arm lowered. The other young woman's hands display curled fingers, as if the hands were turning, or the fingers were going to snap. The dance depicted is decidedly more Moorish, judging from the hands and arms. The separateness of the women, and the strong curve in the hand-percussionist dancer also suggest Moorish influence.

Who the women might be is again determined by their dress. Miriam is the drummer, and her head is covered, as is proper for a married Spanish woman. Her drum displays the *fleur de lis*, a mark of courtly Castile. So the total image may be of upper-class women playing in the court. The architectural columns framing the dancers in the painting suggest the court setting, as does the dress of the dancers. Who then was Miriam, in symbol and reality, for medieval Spanish Jews? Given the dance and drum tradition among the *Sephardiyot*, what did the symbolic image of Miriam mean for Jewish women of medieval Spain?

Symbols of Miriam: The Drum-Dance-Song Ensemble History

Mention of Miriam and the dancing women in Jewish texts of medieval Spain begins to unravel at least some of the mystery of their depiction in the Haggadot. At the very least, the written text offers some perspective on what the figure of Miriam meant to medieval Jews. Comparison of recorded history from Spain from around the fourteenth century may offer clues about the cultural context of the Miriam images.

Records conveying details of dance practices in medieval Spain indicate that it was a popular activity. Therefore, the use of dance for religious celebrations by women might be interpreted as normative. However, because of the strength of the Haggadot images of Miriam, the symbolic function of the figure of Miriam remains in question. Judging by Amnon Shiloah's description of the dance and drum tradition among Jewish women in the Mediterranean, the association between Miriam and Jewish women's performance ensembles has a long history, stemming from biblical times.[6] So one possible, simple interpretation of the Haggadot paintings might read Miriam as a symbol of the dance and drum practice. However, Miriam is associated with much more than dance in biblical tradition, and her representation in the paintings might signify far more than the existence of a dance tradition among Sephardic women.

Ilana Pardes explores the meaning of the biblical Miriam, in *Countertraditions in the Bible*. In her examination, she considers the rank of Miriam as "prophetess," the strands of biblical material mentioning her, and her relationship to goddess traditions in the Near East. Through her investigation, Pardes finds a mythology of Miriam, partially continued by the rabbis in the legend of Miriam's Well.[7]

Carol Meyers, on the other hand, considers biblical stories about women leading victory dances, including the Exodus passage about Miriam (15:20). Meyers considers archeological findings, and interprets the evidence through feminist ethnomusicological perspectives. She describes a women's drum-dance-song ensemble tradition, with women serving as dance and music leaders in Israel. Meyers derives her information from the evidence of terracotta figurines found mainly in Cyprus. Many appear to be women holding a round, flat object, such as a hand drum. Although there is a noticeable lack of these figures in Israel itself, she suggests that the figures are relevant, since they match textual information about women drummers and dancers in the Bible. Meyers examines biblical evidence, looking at the text for details about women's performance ensembles. Citing biblical passages naming types of instruments and times of performance from Isaiah, Psalms, and from history books, she states:

> It is clear from artistic depictions of musicians recovered in archaeological

excavations in the near East that women as well as men played all the instruments in these Canaanite or Phoenician ensembles...In these texts, the women playing drums are associated with dances (*m'holot*) and also with song . . . Perhaps the best example is the so-called Song of Miriam.[8]

Meyers concludes that biblical texts referring to women drummers and dancers indicate the existence of a women's performance tradition in ancient Israel, and that the fact of their public performance constituted a leadership role in the society. Meyers also notes that there was an ongoing tradition of women's performance leadership in Israel, including during the Second Temple period. Women were lament leaders, temple singers (Ezr 2:41; Neh 7:44; 1 Chr 25:5) and also "daughters of song" (Eccl 12:4).[9]

Adding this information to Pardes' claim that there are fragments of a Miriam tradition present in the Bible, the total picture suggests women's music and dance leadership may have existed within formative Judaism, and remained active through the ongoing music and dance of Jewish women. However, talmudic writings suggest that Jewish women's leadership eventually went underground; that is, women's ritual leadership was tangential to sanctioned rabbinic ritual, and practiced primarily among women, for women.

What we view in the Haggadot may depict a drum and dance ensemble as performed in Spain in the thirteenth and fourteenth centuries. The paintings of Miriam and the women may simply indicate a continuing existence of women's performance ensembles in medieval Spain. If so, the figure of Miriam was important to a culture that valued dance. The symbolic use of Miriam, however, may also indicate the worth of a continuing women's dance and drum ensemble in Judaism. While Jewish women did not provide dance and music leadership for the medieval synagogue, their performance did have meaning, depicted through the image of Miriam in the Haggadot.

Biblical and Talmudic Accounts

According to Susan Grossman's analysis of the drum-dance-song ensemble in the book of Judges, "women sang and danced at festivals. . . . However, it is not clear whether the dances were part of the official cultic ceremony or just part of a general popular celebration of those who attended." Passages she mentions include the daughters of Shiloh dancing for a festival (Jgs 21:19), victory ceremonies that were also religious celebrations (I Sam 18:6-7), the Song of Deborah (Jgs 5:1-31), and Jephtah's daughter's song and dance (Jgs 11:34).[10]

Of the Second Temple period, Grossman notes that "male and female singers are mentioned in Ezra and Nehemiah as part of the community returning from exile (Ezr 2:65; Neh 7:67). She concludes that "in both books, it is difficult to determine whether these women singers were part of the Temple retinue, or just entertainers. Only male singers are mentioned when ceremonies or services are described." Heiman's three daughters are mentioned in Chronicles as trained for service in the Temple. Grossman supports her assertion with a reference to Psalms 68:26, which describes "maidens playing timbrels among the musicians as part of the procession bringing the ark to its place, probably in Solomon's Temple."[11]

Meyer's research, and studies by ethnomusicologist Alfred Sendrey, strongly support the claim for music and dance leadership by women in the Bible. They report that the text in no way denotes these women as merely entertainment. In *Music in Ancient Israel*, Alfred Sendrey attributes the entertainment evaluation of the women singers to the medieval talmudic commentator Rashi. He counters the claim by arguing that if the women were merely entertainers, they would not have prepared for return to the Jerusalem Temple by practicing singing in Babylonian captivity. Sendrey states that "it is indeed highly probable that the 'male singers and female singers' mentioned by Ezra and Nehemiah must have been in part non-Levitical Temple singers, whose functions have not terminated with the repatriation. . ." Finally, Sendrey notes that women were dance and song leaders at religious festivals that occurred outside the Temple. He describes the rituals as times of "entertainment," but not in a derogatory manner:

> "Besides their participation in the Temple choir, women have had in the sanctuary another important function, which is not mentioned in the Bible . . . but which constitutes an indispensable requirement for certain ritual ceremonies. . . After the daytime's religious devotions in the Temple, the festivity was brought to a climax by a popular entertainment, in which dances were the main feature. These dances were performed, according to ancient custom, by the sexes separately, or by women alone."[12]

Grossman and Sendrey both report women's continuing participation in Temple practices for sacrifices and offerings in the Herodian period, and also in the water-drawing ceremony, *Simchat Beit ha-Sho'evah*. The celebration involved dance and rejoicing.[13] In *The Hebrew Goddess*, Raphael Patai suggests *Simchat Beit ha-Sho'evah* was a time that men and women danced ecstatically together, as a rite of fertility, based on "descriptions contained in the Mishnah and in talmudic source."[14] Whether women participated or were separated in worship and celebration is at issue in these reports. Women's dance and music participation for the holiday might indicate their religious status, and help determine the significance of women's dance and music in Judaism at this time. In any case, the biblical and talmudic texts strongly suggest a long history of a women's drum and dance ensemble in Judaism. Comparing this historical information with the images of the Haggadot, the representation of the tradition cleanly matches written records. Yet, research on the development of synagogue worship suggests that the value of the women's drum-dance ensemble changed, as dance and music of women became separated from official, sanctioned worship.

Jewish Women and Medieval Spain

The Jewish community in Spain lived under Islamic domination for centuries. A religion noted for extreme separation between men and women, Islam did seem to influence some rabbis of the time, including the medieval Spanish Jewish scholar Maimonides. Similar to the comments in the Talmud, his remarks on music and women's voices reveal strong opposition to men listening to female performers.[15] From the information we have on the *zambra* parties in medieval Andalusia, both Islamic and Jewish communities had liberal interpretations of the prohibitions on music and women. Maimonides' restrictions seemed to be aimed at music for secular occasions, such as these parties, where women played instruments and danced.

Given Maimonides' comments and the information available about the *zambra* parties, it is fairly safe to assume that medieval Jewish women were singing and dancing before men and, on occasion, with men. Rabbinic condemnation of mixed couples dancing verifies this assumption.[16] However, the remarks objecting to women dancing in front of and with men provides little information on what women were doing when they met separately, and whether they used music and dance for their own ritual celebration. The Miriam paintings of the Haggadot offer insight. The iconography from these Haggadot is curious, given the prohibitions against men hearing a woman's voice during prayer. But if Jewish women maintained separate music or prayer groups, historical data from medieval Spain suggests that the Miriam imagery may be derived from women's rituals occurring outside the synagogue.

The imagery in the Haggadot may derive from women's gatherings for ritual, and the paintings might reflect women's separate ritual performance. Following Jewish custom and law, the women depicted in the Haggadot were celebrating a religiously significant event, rather than performing a secular dance. Religion and culture are never separated completely in a society. In medieval Spain, women dancing before and with men would be on the more cultural end of the spectrum. Religious values of Jews of medieval Spain allowed for some members of Jewish society to accept the behavior. Since rabbis controlled the religious end of the spectrum for Jews, and they did not approve of women dancing in front of men, it appears women's ritual performance was removed from sanctioned rabbinic Jewish worship. However, despite the prohibition against men hearing a woman's voice during prayer, the image of Miriam's ritual leadership retained enough meaning to be depicted in the visual rendition of the Passover story. Artists for the Haggadot were then perhaps painting what they knew of the Miriam tradition in their lifetime, with this tradition living through the dance and music of Jewish women of the period.

The Kabbalistic Texts

Questioning the meaning of Miriam and the dancing women in Jewish history raises issues of symbolic and lived reality. The illuminated Haggadot do not present us with images of the actual life of medieval Jews in Spain. Rather, we have an interpretation of biblical history, with parts of the Exodus story portrayed through chosen contemporary medieval images. Kabbalistic material of approximately the same time period may offer clues to the significance of the Miriam imagery.

From a passage in the Zohar (3167b) commenting on Miriam's victory dance, it appears that the Haggadot pictures were an idealistic but living image for medieval Jews. Impressively, the Zohar describes Miriam dancing in the royal courts of heaven. Despite reports of negative opinions of women's dance attributed to Spanish mystics, the description contains extremely positive commentary on Exodus 15:20. Shiloah's report of this passage emphasizes the singing of women in the heavenly courts, where female performers constitute a third and upper "band" of heavenly choirs, which includes Miriam. She leads singing and dancing of the women's choir. Additionally, Miriam's mother Yocheved sings with the women. They join with Yocheved for "the Song of the Sea three times a day." Miriam is mentioned in the song, which refers to her taking up her drum. After Miriam has her drum, the Zohar states that "Yocheved sings alone."[17]

This is an amazing report in that, in a medieval Jewish text, women are of a superior rank as singers, although their voices have been condemned by rabbinic texts. The women sing in separate chambers from men, but nevertheless have an important role to play. Moreover, while in the biblical account Miriam is a leader of song and dance, and some believe the composer of the Song of the Sea, her mother Yocheved is not even mentioned in

Exodus 15:20. We can wonder why Yocheved takes over for Miriam in the Zohar's description of the women's court. Possibly the medieval commentator assumed that a drumming woman also danced.

Rivka Haut gives her version of this passage from the Zohar to stress that women had separate prayer groups, and that the story is a reflection of the tradition. Haut's English translation of the Zohar passage notes that "Yocheved" (meaning God's glory) and the "thousands and ten thousands with her . . . praise(s) the Lord of the Universe"; then she sings the Song of the Sea . . . and "all the *tzadikim* in Gan Eden listen to her sweet voice." Miriam, the dancer, is replaced by Yocheved, in an apparent symbolic shorthand. It is as if Miriam's drumming and dance brings in the *Shechinah*.[18]

Presumably this passage depicts an idealized women's drum and dance group. To what degree it portrays the reality of life for Sephardic women remains in question. Recalling that the Spanish kabbalists used Neoplatonic ideas, for them, what happened on the earthly plane affected the heavenly realm, and this world was an imperfect version of the celestial realm. Considering the possible symbolic meaning of the figure Miriam, and the continuing use of drum-dance-song ensembles by the *Sephardiyot*, the Zohar passage on Miriam in the heavenly courts may be based on knowledge of women's song and dance practices of medieval Spain. The match with the Miriam pictures of the Haggadot is not exact, but comparison and contrast between the images in the visual and written texts reveal striking similarities.

Conclusion

The Haggadot pictures offer snapshots of women's existence in medieval Spain, which perhaps included separate women's music and dance groups; a type of continuing Miriam tradition. Along with kabbalistic writing and Sephardic cultural history, these paintings render much more than biblical illustrations for a Passover seder. The imagery may be revealing of life circumstances for women of the period.

The textual information of the Zohar, and the visual imagery it provides, imply that the kabbalists of Spain were placing their own interpretation on the meaning of a women's drum and dance ensemble, signified through the figure of Miriam. Because there are visual texts of the women's ensemble available through the Haggadot, the kabbalistic interpretation appears to be based on actual practices of Jewish women of the period. The kabbalists weren't inventing a heavenly reality; they were looking at Spanish Jewish culture and rendering it in terms of their own theology. Again, this is a possible interpretation based on cultural influences in Spain during the thirteenth and fourteenth centuries, and on the background of that culture in Islamic Spain. The Haggadot were products of artists commissioned by wealthy families, but the artists' vision may have been influenced by kabbalistic ideas circulating in the culture. Comparison of visual and written texts suggest this possibility, although the match is not exact.

In a way, traditions of dance and music among the Sephardic women support the idea that the women's performance ensembles were prayer groups. *Tanyaderas* were the leaders of these Spanish groups, and as leaders, might be considered teachers of prayer in the tradition of Miriam. They were not instructing women in traditional Jewish prayers, or even in Hebrew songs. Instead, they created times for rituals of dance and songs within the Jewish life cycle.

Music and dance may be considered Jewish prayer, if it is defined through meaning rather than through the spoken word. Like Miriam, the *tanyaderas* also led women in prayers of praise and celebration, through the medium of dance. If their tradition is taken seriously, it must be in terms of the type of nontextual, movement-centered prayer encompassed in the extra-ordinary activity of dance.

The Bible teaches that when Miriam went out with timbrels and with dances, "all the women followed her." At the shores of the sea, in medieval Spain, and here today, we still do.

NOTES

1. Alan Unterman. *Dictionary of Jewish Legend and Lore* (London: Thames and Hudson, 1991), p.136.

2. Anna Ivanova, *The Dance in Spain* (New York: Praeger Publishers, 1970), p.44.

3. Therese Metzger, *Jewish Life in the Middle Ages* (New York: Alpine Fine Arts Collection, 1982). Metzger discusses the luxurious dress of the Jews in these paintings, saying that this was typical, and giving reasons why this was a common depiction, pp.146-147.

4. Bezalel Narkiss, *Hebrew Illuminated Manuscripts in the British Isles: Spanish and Portuguese Manuscripts* (Jerusalem and London: The Israel Academy of Sciences and Humanities and the British Academy, 1982), vol. I, p. 77.

5. Narkiss, vol. I, p.45.

6. Amnon Shiloah, *Jewish Musical Traditions* (Detroit, Michigan: Wayne State University Press, 1992).

7. Ilana Pardes, *Countertraditions in the Bible: A Feminist Approach* (Cambridge, MA: Harvard University Press, 1992).

8. Carol Meyers, "The Drum-Dance-Song Ensemble: Women's Performance in Biblical Israel," in *Rediscovering the Muses: Women's Musical Traditions*, Kimberly Marshall, Editor (Boston: Northeastern University Press, 1993), pp.60-61.

9. Meyers, pp.64-66.

10. Susan Grossman, "Women in the Jerusalem Temple" in *Daughters of the King: Women and the Synagogue* (Philadelphia: Jewish Publication Society, 1992), p.18. In this description and elsewhere in this article, Grossman suggests that the women

song and dance leaders were either a part of the official cult, or "just entertainment." I find this evaluation misleading, as there are many other possible interpretations. Women might have lead rituals that were meaningful to their community, but conducted outside the Temple or synagogue.

11. Grossman , p.18.

12. Alfred Sendrey, *Music in Ancient Israel* (New York: Philosophical Society, 1969), pp.520-21.

13. Grossman, pp.20-24; Sendrey, pp.520-21.

14. Raphael Patai, The Hebrew Goddess, [3rd enlarged ed.] (Detroit: Wayne State University Press, 1967, 1978, 1990) p.85. Patai lists his source as M. *Sukkah* 5:1.

15. Shiloah, p. 85.

16. Shiloah, pp.212-213, refers to some of the comments the rabbis made concerning men and women dancing together in medieval Spain.

17. Shiloah, p. 145. In the Bible, the Song of the Sea is attributed to Miriam.

18. Rivkah Haut and Susan Grossman, eds, *Daughters of the King: Women and the Synagogue* (Philadelphia: Jewish Publication Society), p.144; note 40, p. 156.

THE PROPHET AND SINGER
Susan Phillips

They were living in terrible times, in a land where just being born put them in jeopardy. The children of Israel were slaves to Pharaoh of Egypt. Every day brought new fears, new terrors. Every night she fell asleep listening to the moans and cries of the people around her. Nonetheless, Miriam had faith in the future. Over and over, as she worked in the fields, as she cooked meager soups, as she lay at night trying to blot out the sounds around her, she told herself stories. Over and over, she repeated the stories her mother Yocheved had taught her years before.

Sometimes, to make the tales easier to remember, she turned them into songs. As she worked, she hummed the tunes and repeated the lyrics silently—stories of the matriarchs Sarah, Rebekah, Rachel, and Leah. Stories of Jacob and his children: of lost Dinah, and of Joseph who was sold into slavery and then rose to high rank in Egypt.

At her most melancholy, she sang that *A new king arose over Egypt who did not know Joseph* (Ex 1:8). Or *Your offspring shall be strangers in a land not theirs, and they shall be enslaved and oppressed for four hundred years* (Gen 15:13).

At times old lyrics gave her joy. *In the end they shall go free with great wealth* (Gen 15:14). "Go free with great wealth, great wealth," she sang again and again. "Free, free, all with great wealth."

One day a new song came into her mind while she was thinking of something else. This was a story she had never heard from her mother.
Sing to the Lord, for He has triumphed gloriously;
Horse and driver He has hurled into the sea. (Ex 15:21)
As she sang the new song over and over, she added verses.

The Lord is my strength and might;
He is become my deliverance.
This is my God, and I will glorify him;
The God of my father, and I will exalt Him. (15:2)

She hummed the new tune until she perfected it. Sometimes, without realizing it, Miriam sang the song aloud. Often, at the end of the song, she heard—echoing over and over—other women's voices singing also.

Sing to the Lord, for He has triumphed gloriously;
Horse and driver He has hurled into the sea. (15:21)

When she lay down at night, when words and tunes tumbled through her mind, she wondered what the song meant.

In Your love You lead the people You redeemed;
In Your strength You guide them to Your holy abode.
(15:13)

Where is that place? she wondered. When will it happen? Miriam never doubted that her life of slavery in Egypt would end. She closed her eyes and felt desert sand beneath her feet. She tasted milk and honey and fresh spring water. She saw beautiful hills and valleys. But in the morning, she did not know how to turn the dreams into reality.

One day Elisheva, her brother Aaron's wife, came running to tell her great news. "Moses is back," she exclaimed. "Moses is back!" And she burst into tears even as she began laughing and dancing in joy. Now Miriam saw everything clearly.

You will bring them and plant them in Your own mountain,
The place you made to dwell in, O Lord. (15:17)

Miriam listened with eagerness to all the news—of the rod that turned into a snake and later turned the Nile to blood, of the frogs and insects and locusts that ran and flew everywhere, of the great darkness that descended over the Egyptians.

As the night of the great Exodus approached, she readied herself and her household, as did all the Hebrews. Many women ran here and there, begging and borrowing gold, silver, clothing from the Egyptian women they knew. *God had disposed the Egyptians favorably toward the people, and they let them have their request* (12:36).

Miriam realized that she lacked one thing. One night she crept out and went to the hut of an old Egyptian musician she knew. "Ah, Miriam," the old woman said. "So you have come, like all your Hebrew sisters, to take my gold and silver."

"No, Mother," Miriam replied, "but there is one thing I beg you to give me. Please, Mother," she said, "may I take your tambourine?"

The old woman laughed and tossed the instrument to Miriam. "Take it," she said. "I have no more use for it. I am too tired to dance. My voice has become rusty, and I cannot remember the songs I used to sing. You shall have my gifts now."

Miriam returned to her hut with her treasure. That very night she found materials and began to fashion tambourines for other women. They, in turn, made more instruments for still other women. And when, at midnight, the Hebrews left Egypt, the women carried their tambourines with them.

When the people stopped to rest and camp, Miriam, Aaron, and their families joined Moses. Because he stuttered badly, Moses needed Aaron nearby. When Moses spoke to the people, Aaron repeated the words loudly and clearly so that everyone would understand. As they sat together at night, Moses realized that he also needed Miriam. He listened to her clear, sweet voice:

Who is like You, O Lord, among the mighty;
Who is like You, majestic in holiness,
Awesome in splendor, working wonders! (Ex 15:11)

Over and over, she sang her song for Moses until he learned every verse.

As the Israelites were departing defiantly, boldly, the Egyptians gave chase to them, and all the chariot horses of Pharaoh, his horsemen, and his warriors overtook them (14:8-9). Moses could not hurry the people along fast enough. *As Pharaoh drew near, the Israelites caught sight of the Egyptians advancing upon them. Greatly frightened, the Israelites cried out to God* (14:10). Most were ready to return to Egypt, to return to the life of slavery that they knew. But Moses listened to God. *Moses held out his arm over the sea, and God drove back the sea with a strong east wind all that night and turned the sea into dry ground* (14:21).

When she saw how the *floods stood straight like a wall and the deeps froze in the heart of the sea* (15:8), Miriam could hardly contain her joy. Eagerly she followed the first people who half-ran, half-swam into the water. *The waters were split, and the Israelites went into the sea on dry ground, the waters forming a wall for them on their right and on their left* (14:21-22). As soon as the last of the Hebrews had crossed, *Pharaoh, with his chariots and horsemen, went into the sea; and God turned back on them the waters of the sea* (15:19).

When she realized what had happened, *Miriam the prophetess, Aaron's sister, took a timbrel in her hand, and all the women went out after her in dance with timbrels. And Miriam chanted for them:*

Sing to the Lord, for He has triumphed gloriously;
Horse and driver He has hurled into the sea. (15:20-21)

≪↶

Strong and proud, she had definite ideas about what should and should not be done. Her husband, Caleb ben Jephuneh, thought Miriam the loveliest woman he had ever seen. He spent their entire marriage dazzled by her, boasting of her beautiful music and prophetic insights. In turn Miriam was proud that of the twelve spies sent out to report on the Land of Israel, only Caleb and Joshua ben Nun had defended the beauty of the land.

The freedom from Egypt Miriam had dreamed of so long meant years of wandering through the desert. For the rest of her life, Miriam did her best to keep the people's spirits up. She led the women in song and dance and taught them to turn to music when life was difficult. Miriam listened to women's troubles and offered sound advice. Every woman she met assumed that her place in Miriam's heart was a special one. Her faith ran deep, and she assumed everyone felt as she did. But that was not always true.

As the time for revelation from God drew near, Moses instructed the men how to prepare for the great day. He *warned the people to stay pure, and they washed their clothes* (Ex 19:14). He took the men aside and said, *"Be ready for the third day; do not go near a woman"* (19:15).

In another part of the camp, Miriam taught the women new songs and dances to celebrate the upcoming event. On her advice, the two groups separated for days. Away from their husbands, the women listened intently as Miriam explained that they would soon receive the laws and rituals to follow in the Land. She promised to advise them whenever they felt confused or needed her help.

And then Moses left the Israelites to speak with God on Mount Sinai. They waited the forty days he had said he would be gone. But their restlessness grew and, on the forty-first day, the people demanded that Aaron make them a god, a golden calf, to worship.

Miriam was scornful. "Does anyone believe that a calf of gold is God?" she asked Caleb. He shrugged. "Perhaps we should join them," he said, "to be sure that nothing goes wrong." Miriam hesitated. She respected her husband's opinions, but she felt uneasy. Reluctantly, she agreed.

The next day she stood with a group of women, squinting against the sun to see what would happen. The people argued; her beloved brother Aaron argued back. Feeling both worried and proud, she watched her son Hur defend his uncle. Hur gestured toward the crowd, then pointed to the mountain where Moses had ascended. He shook his head, he shook his fist at the men closest to him. Suddenly, a group of men grabbed Hur's arms and legs. Before her horrified eyes, before she could do or say anything, the gang attacked and killed her son. She was still, as still as stone. The women surrounding her stopped talking. The quiet grew by degrees until the entire crowd was silent.

Aaron looked up and saw his sister. "Take her away from here," he ordered. Immediately, his wife, Elisheva, and Moses's wife, Tzipporah, led Miriam back to her tent. Aaron looked down at his favorite nephew's body. Who would be next in his family to die? *When Aaron saw this, he built an altar before it; and Aaron announced: "Tomorrow shall be a festival of God"* (Ex 32:5).

A festival of mourning, I hope, thought Miriam, as she allowed her two sisters-in-law to lead her away. In the morning she sniffed the air and was repulsed by the smell. *Early the next day, the people offered up burnt offerings and brought sacrifices of well-being.* It was quiet, too quiet, for hours after that. *They sat down to eat and drink.* In the distance she heard music. And again she knew anger. She heard familiar music, the voices of men and women singing the songs she had taught them. She heard the sound of many feet dancing, and she felt betrayed that anyone could use her gifts to debase God. *And then [they] rose to dance* (Ex 32:6).

For a long time after the incident, Miriam refused to sing and dance with the congregation. Aaron can forgive them, she thought, but not I. Moses will forgive them and even God, but not I. Nothing will bring back my son.

Her sorrow intruded on the great joys that followed. Eventually, she forgave the people. Aaron helped her, of course. He visited all the tribes and spoke to the leaders. "Miriam suffers so," he said. "She wants to forgive you for the death of her son, but her pride prevents her."

And then he spoke with Miriam. "If you only knew how the people long for your forgiveness," he told her. "They need you to lead them in song and dance." He hesitated. "No one dares approach you," he continued, "no matter how much they miss you."

After Aaron left, Miriam wondered if her anger and isolation had gone on long enough. Staying by herself, refusing to speak to her friends, only added to her own sorrow. As she suspected, Moses and Aaron had forgiven the people. The worst sinners had already been punished. If she continued to stay apart from the congregation, someone might be tempted again to use her songs and music to worship strange gods.

And there was another reason to rejoin the congregation. Without her, they might die of thirst! For Miriam controlled the water supply. As she trudged through the desert, Miriam's well, shaped like a beehive, rolled along behind her. "It was created on the eve of the first Shabbat at twilight," she told the young children who asked about it. At night she called softly, *"Rise up, O well"* (Num 11:17), and the waters rose. The well grew so large at some places that it became a river. Women who wanted to visit their friends used small boats to travel. They gathered herbs and made themselves sweet-smelling perfumes. From the well's waters grew herbs, vegetables, and even trees.

Sometimes toward evening as they drew the sweet water, or made their beds from its fragrant grasses, the women would hear, softly:

Sing to the Lord for He has triumphed gloriously
Horse and driver He has hurled into the Sea.
In Your love You lead the people You redeemed;
In Your strength You guide them to Your holy abode.

And they knew that Miriam still dwelt among them.

STILL DANCING WITH MIRIAM
Geela Rayzel Raphael

In *parashat Shabbat Shira* we look for clues in the text to contemporary women's leadership. We have seen enormous changes in the Jewish community regarding women's participation in the past twenty-five years. I would like to examine one sentence in this portion— "Miriam took her timbrel out and all the women danced"— to find out what the text actually says and what our historical medieval commentators, the *miforshim*, have said about this verse. As we look for female role models and mine the biblical text for clues as to women's roles and voices, this verse is loaded; it gives us clues to women's participation and we are struck by Miriam as a figure of importance.

What does the text say or not say about her? We are curious as to what the rabbinic commentators say about her because we want to try to understand their world to see if they can shed any light on ours. I am particularly intrigued with her standing as a prophetess—and we may want to go beyond their interpretation—for this contemporary age demands a fuller view of women.

To set the scene: The Israelites have crossed the Red Sea; Moses has sung the *shira* song, and then it says, *'v'tikach Miriam, ha-nivea achot Aharon et ha tof b'yada, vtaytzena kol ha nashim aharecha, b'toofim u-v'mcholot'* (Ex 15:20); which translates as, "and Miriam the prophetess, sister of Aaron, took timbrel in her hand and led the women in dance." Immediately several questions jump to mind:

Where did they get the instruments?
Why does Miriam dance separately with the women?
Why does it mention she is the sister of Aaron?

Why does the text call her a prophet?
Is there a connection between her leading the dancing and being a prophet?

For the sake of brevity I will focus on the image of Miriam as a prophetess—a powerful figure in our tradition—and how she is seen by our tradition. There are two historical interpretations of this passage. Rashi, the eleventh-century French commentator who comments on just about everything, asks why she is called a prophetess. He says it's "because she is Aaron's sister," that this defines her status. He also mentions that Miriam predicts that a son will be born, after Aaron; hence she *foretells*, and that could be what defines her prophetic status. Rashi also goes on to say that she is defined by Aaron because he was ready to give his life for her when she was stricken with leprosy. Aaron was devoted to her with his whole soul, like Shimon and Levi, brothers of Dina.

Rashi, not content with just this explanation, however, goes further, bringing in the story from *mekhilta shira perek yod*: Miriam had said to her father, "You are destined to beget a son who will arise and save Israel from he hands of the Egyptians." Immediately, there went a man from the house of Levi and took a wife . . . and the woman conceived and bore a son. . . . Then her father reproached her, "What of your prediction—we have to hide our son because of the decree of Pharaoh!" But she still held onto her prophecy, for it is said "and his sister stood far off to know what would be done to him." Why did they have the timbrels when they were fleeing? Because the righteous women of Israel knew they would be rescued. They had faith.

Ramban, a philosopher of the thirteenth-century Spanish community, asked "Why is Miriam singing again?" He says we find Miriam singing again because she repeated the *shira*; she leads a call and response for the women. He believes the text says that she is the sister of Aaron because it has already mentioned Moses and Miriam, and does not want us to forget that Aaron is part of the story. Ibn Ezra, a rabbinic commentator of the Golden Era of Spain, asked, "Why is she called prophetess? Perhaps she is called this in *Mitzrayim* (Egypt), to distinguish between her and some other Miriam, like a last name." Rashbam says the text mentions Aaron's name to give *kavod* (honor) to the eldest of the siblings, but she is called prophet because this is a term for *ba'al d'varai shevach*, a master of praises.

Why are we concerned with why the commentators are concerned as to why this woman is called a prophetess? Because this allows us to see the evolution of Jewish tradition. It bears relevance to our concerns—by noting that she is distinguished in her day, and in their day, as well as in ours. In the biblical era Miriam is one of the trio leading us to liberation, but unlike Moses, whose legal legacy lives on, and Aaron, whose priestly lineage is established, Miriam is not marked by a major impact on Jewish tradition. In fact, her traditions of prophetic call and dancing women are actually limited through the ages by restrictions on women singing and the cessation of prophecy. The rabbis restore some of her prophetic license, calling her *ba'al shevach*, but as we have seen, they are mostly concerned with Aaron's status. By calling her *nive'ah* they are giving her the credit she deserves—that of one of the founding figures of this religion. But only today is she being restored fully to her proper place.

On closer examination of the text, I believe if I were adding a commentary today about what makes Miriam a prophetess, I would say it is the word *kol*, all. All the women went out after her. For the new image of women is not one voice but the collective voice. All the women were drawn to follow her, for I imagine she knew her descendants—both men and women—would be dancing in joy for centuries to come.

∽

During the past twenty-five years we have seen an explosion of Jewish feminist creativity. The tension between feminism and Judaism catalyzed this artistic outburst of ritual, poetry, midrash (interpretation), crafts, and song. Fueled by the feminist movement, contemporary Judaism has stretched its boundaries to include women's voices in public song and prayer. Feminism has given cause for a reexamination of Jewish tradition and the creation of new women's rituals. Jewish women of all ages are trying to reclaim women's oral legacy. Feminist historians are researching famous Jewish women and musicians are setting their stories to music. The biblical text calls to us for reinterpretation. Women gather monthly in the light of the new moon to sacralize their lives and the cycles of the seasons. These Rosh Hodesh meetings have become sacred time—the laboratories for a new and holy dimension, enriching the celebration of Jewish women. It is as if Miriam the prophetess herself has come dancing and singing into our lives—fanning our passion for spiritual expression.

Miriam, the charismatic leader of the Israelites, stands out for us as a paradigm of women's power. For she is not one of the forgotten, unnamed, tragic figures reflected in the *Tanach*, but rather an inspiration and role model for Jewish women through the centuries. Miriam, one of the righteous women upon whose merit the Israelites were redeemed from Egypt, is very much with us in spirit today. We cling to the shreds of Miriam's story, in order that our own lives will not fragment. We add new and stronger fibers—our own stories—and reweave them to make the text relevant to us today. She is the inspiration for new songs and dances. She validates our artistic forms as the blessings they are.

Miriam is not only a guide for music, dance, and drumming, but she is also our archetype for prophecy, giving sanction to women to use their own oracular power. Modeled on her divine healing from leprosy, we are experimenting with healing ourselves and our wounded world. Chanting circles of women, courageously sharing their pain, break the silence and soothe their injuries—all graced by Miriam. Miriam's Well, that magic source of water which nourished the Israelites in the desert, following them from camp to camp, has become the symbol of our own internal fountain of wisdom. Miriam charges us to draw from our "collective unconscious" in order to blossom into full participants of Jewish life.

Today Miriam takes her place beside Elijah as the great female prophet. She ushers in the golden age of Jewish feminist literature, without which the Messiah will not come. The following songs can be attributed directly to Miriam's inspiration, signifying that her chimerical spirit roams freely, sparking our imaginations wherever we are.

MIRIAM / BY THE SHORES
Geela Rayzel Raphael

By the shores, by the shores,
Of the Red, Red Sea,
By the shores of the Red, Red Sea;
The light of day lit up the night
The children, they were free.

CHORUS
And Miriam took her timbrel out and all the women
danced. (2X)
*Va- te-kach Miriam ha-nivea et ha tof b'ya-da, va'taytzeh-na kol
ha-nashim ah-cha-re-ha.*

They danced, they danced
Oh, how they danced
They danced the night away
Clapped their hands and stamped their feet
With voices loud they praised.

They danced with joy
They danced with grace
They danced on nimble feet
Kicked up their heels, threw back their heads
Hypnotic with the beat.

CHORUS

They danced so hard, they danced so fast;
They danced with movement strong
Laughed and cried, brought out alive
They danced until the dawn.

Some carrying child, some baking bread
Weeping as they prayed

But when they heard the music start
They put their pain away.

CHORUS

Enticed to sing, drawn to move
Mesmerized by such emotion
The men saw us reach out our hands
Stretching across the ocean.

As they watched, and they clapped, they began to sway
Drawn to ride the wave
and all our brothers began to dance
They dance with us today!

They danced, we dance
Shechinah dance
They danced the night away
And all the people began to sing
We're singing 'til this day!!

FINAL CHORUS
And Miriam took her timbrel out and all the people
danced. (2X)
*Va- te-kach Miriam ha-nivea et ha tof b'ya-da, v'a'taytzeh-na col
anashim ah-cha-re-ha.*

coda: And the children were rockin' just as far as you could
see, by the shores, by the shores, my God, my God we
were free.

BATYA
Geela Rayzel Raphael

Long ago in Pharaoh's time a princess felt alone
Longing and praying for a child to call her own
One day by the riverside - while washing her hair
Looking down she saw - a basket floating there.

CHORUS
She drew him from the water, water, water
She drew him from the Nile
Today she sits in Paradise
underneath God's smile

Mother and sister watched as the princess held him near
Breathing sighs of relief, fighting back their tears
Batya now knew her task, she must stand up to the hate
Confront her own father, and she must not hesitate.

CHORUS

As the princess looked across the banks at the women
        standing by
Knowing of their sacrifice, the child she held might die
Woman to woman they gazed, eyes locked in embrace
Not a word was spoken, yet a covenant was made.

The silent bond of sisterhood is stronger than the chains
For arms linked through the ages, soothe the knots of pain
To nurse each others' children,
        and listen with a willing ear
Creates a legacy of love, defiant in the face of fear.

Miriam
Elaine Moise

Miriam was the daughter of Yocheved and Amram
When she was five came Pharaoh's harsh decree.
When Amram then divorced his wife and others did the
      same,
Said Miriam to them, "This must not be!
If future generations are denied their chance to grow,
There'll be no one remaining when they let our people go!"
And Amram heard her wisdom; he could see that
      it was so:
Miriam knew they would someday be free.

Chorus: For Miriam was a prophet from the time
                that she was small
                She saw what the future could be.
                And she knew the day would come when
                they would dance and pray and sing
                Filled with joy, by the shore of the sea.

Yocheved was with child, and Miriam prophesied again,
She said "My brother will our leader be;
For he will grow in wisdom, and will learn to speak with
      God
And he will bring us out of slavery."
The boy was born, they wrapped him up;
      he floated down the Nile,
And Miriam, waiting hidden there to see what would
      befall
Saw Pharaoh's daughter take him up and bring him to her
      hall.
And she knew they would someday be free.

Chorus

So many long years later, Pharaoh let the people go,
They all went forth from Egypt joyfully.
But when they reached the Reed Sea's shore they once
again knew fear:
How could they cross away from slavery?
God raised a strong east wind that caused the waters to
        divide,
And women, men, and children quickly gained the other
        side.
And Miriam stood among them, and she raised her timbrel
        high,
"Let us sing, for we're now to be free!"

Final chorus: For Miriam was a prophet from the time
                that she was small
                She saw what the future could be.
                And she knew the day would come when
                they would dance and pray and sing
                Filled with joy, by the shore of the sea.

                Yes she had been a prophet from the time
                that she was small,
                She'd seen what the future would be.
                And the day had finally come when they
                could dance and pray and sing
                Filled with joy, by the shore of the sea.

"...and all the women went out after her..."

THE WOMEN OF EXODUS

❦

The text assures us that Miriam did not dance alone, and therefore we must also look to the women whose stories intertwine with hers. Shiprah and Puah, Pharaoh's daughter, Yocheved and Tzipporah—all these women connect fundamentally with Miriam's story. In Sara Adler's midrash "On the Birthstones," Shiphrah and Puah are not Hebrews but Egyptians, colleagues of Miriam, and they struggle between following Pharaoh's decree and doing God's will. Naomi Graetz's midrash "Yocheved" tells the story from her point of view, as Yocheved muses like a stereotypical Jewish mother over her daughters Miriam, Zipporah, and Elisheva. The pieces on Zipporah look to Exodus 4:24 as she saved Moses and their son, and also describe her bitterness, much like Miriam's, at the unacknowledged religious role she plays. Finally we read of an often overlooked woman of Exodus, Aaron's wife Elisheva, and her relationship to the members of this unique family, particularly to her sister-in-law Miriam.

These women, the first to "follow" Miriam, paved the way for the women of the modern era who follow their inspiration.

ON THE BIRTHSTONES
Sara O'Donnell Adler

One

The year my daughter was born it seemed like everyone was giving birth. Alone I was on the birthstones, but for *Khnum* standing over me, fashioning the child that emerged from between my legs. Because so many women were giving birth that year, I had no one to attend to me in my own labor. So I took the screaming child in my arms, wiped away her blood and mucus, cut the cord that joined her to me and drew her to my breast. Because my daughter cried tears, I called her *Puah*. Because of her tears and my own straining and struggle to bear her, she is Puah, for I knew then that she would in turn strain and struggle to give birth to others. Like me.

I am a midwife, and I live near the fields where Pharaoh's slaves cut straw and bind them into bricks. All my life I have delivered the babies out here in the villages that border the fields, as well as the places that are near the *Ya'or*. But the year that Puah was born, I began to deliver babies for the Hebrew women, because there were so many children being born to them. It happened slowly at first, and then there were stories of women giving birth to three or four children at a time. There could never be enough hands to help all these women and all these newborns, so I added myself to the number of hands that pulled forth the life from their wombs. There was always a need for a midwife for the Hebrew women, especially because of the pain involved in their birthing more than one child at once. So, when the time came for Puah to come forth out of me, there was no one there to help, but *Khnum* and the god of protection.

Two

Since I was five I've gone with my mother to births. I hold the woman's hand and whisper in her ear that *Khnum* is taking care of the baby. *Khnum* sits at a stone like she sits on stones, only *Khnum* forms in his hands the life that will come out of her. *Khnum* is a potter and from his stone comes a new child, fully fashioned by his hands. I lay grain at the woman's feet so that *Khnum* will be happy and help us with the birth. I tie blue stones around her neck because no trouble comes through the color blue and my mother makes sure all the doors are open and unties any knots on her clothing because they make the birth easier. The woman sits on stones and when she screams I hold her hand tighter. Her knees tremble and her legs are rigid and hard like the stones she rests upon. This is how I can tell that the baby will come any moment, when her legs are like *Khnum*'s stone. I wipe her face and neck with a damp cloth to calm her. When the baby comes down, my mother catches it. Then she wipes it clean, cuts the cord and smears dung on the wound, which stops the bleeding and keeps away the sickness.

Sometimes the mother of the newborn doesn't stop bleeding and sometimes her arms go limp and the other women in the room become frightened. But my mother knows to put the baby on her breast. That stops the bleeding. And then she brushes the woman's hair and sings soothing songs and wipes mother and baby clean. This is why they call my mother *Shifrah*. Because her touch soothes the pain and because her hands make all who are caressed by them know that she is beautiful.

Three

When we go to midwife to the Hebrew women, there are children everywhere. Their eyes are a wide and deep shade of brown and their hands are busy exploring all that is around them. When there are young children and their mother is giving birth, I go to them and blow bubbles in wine to make them giggle and coo. Or I dangle my bracelets from my ears and nose and make funny faces. This way, there is laughter when a brother or sister emerges, screaming into the world.

When we go to midwife to the Hebrew women, my mother tells me not to whisper *Khnum* in the birthing woman's ear. Why not say *Khnum*, I ask and she tells me it must not be said to them. When Hebrew women are in trouble, they point their eyes upward and look to a place I do not know.

Four

Mother is talking with a woman by the *Ya'or*. She bends over and breaks off the long narrow leaves of the plant that eases pain. Mother shows how you crush the leaves with a round stone and mix it with water and mud. The woman has a daughter called Miriam and she and I wade into the *Ya'or* among reeds that are taller than us. I pull out long blades of the thick grass on the bank and Miriam and I braid them and I show her how I know how to make a bowl that will dry in the sun. Miriam's mother is learning from my mother how to be a midwife because of all the Hebrew babies being born. I'm glad because this means Miriam and I will be able to see each other almost every day.

Miriam tells me that her mother is going to have a baby boy. I ask, how do you know that? And she says, I just know. But how do you know? She says, I just know things.

Five

Mother and I are standing in Pharaoh's court and there are guards all around us and Mother's face looks tight, like the way it does when a baby comes out of a woman backwards. I've never seen Pharaoh up close before. He is wearing gold and purple and blue and a deep, deep red, and when I look at him I want to squint because it feels like there is sunlight in my eyes, with all those bright colors. The next thing I know he is telling my mother that we need to instruct all the other midwives to kill all Hebrew male babies when they are born. Pharaoh tells us to look at the birthstones and if it is a boy we should cup our hand over its mouth and nose so it will die. He is saying that we should tell the other midwives to do it quietly and to make sure the Hebrew women don't catch us doing it or else no one will allow us near enough to the babies to do it and then where will we be? I am holding Mother's hand and her grip is tight on mine and I can feel my heart pounding and my face is hot and my eyes begin to burn with the threat of tears and I don't understand why he is telling us to do such an awful thing.

I turn my face towards Pharaoh and tell him we can't do that because that would be wrong and he stands up from his chair and he is very tall and his face is powerful like the sun and how dare I speak to him in such a way and I should be punished for my behavior. And tears stream down my face and I think of Miriam and her brother and how she knows that she will have another brother and I can't imagine what it would be like to kill Miriam's brother and what are we going to do? Mother tells Pharaoh to please understand that I am only a child and that I am too young to know what I am saying and that he should not worry, that we will do what Pharaoh bids us. And now I'm really confused because surely I'm not too young to know what I'm saying and how can she say such things and what about Miriam's brother and all those Hebrew children with the wide deep brown eyes?

Six

I am walking through the fields where the Hebrews are making bricks and when they see me they turn their backs to me and walk away. Even when I go to the areas where all the Hebrews homes are gathered together, the walkways clear when I come through them. I see Miriam and her little brother and her father and her mother with her large belly and none of them speak to me when I smile and wave. They look through me as though I were water and I don't know why all of the Hebrews are keeping away from me until all of a sudden I remember the mother and the baby that came out on the birthstone facing down towards the earth, which meant it was a boy and so I covered its mouth and nose with my hand and felt it sneezing and moving under my fingers until the small body shuddered and was no more. And I remembered the blood on my hands and the mother screaming at me and all the Hebrews are now turning their backs on me because I am a murderer and obeyed Pharaoh and broke *Khnum*'s potter's stone and *what have I done, what have I done, what have I done?*

Seven

It is late at night and the crescent moon dips its reflection into the *Ya'or*. I hid myself in the darkness to bring food and medicine to a couple of Hebrew women who are still weak from giving birth. I go at night when it's hard to see the bundles of bread and clusters of fruit I carry on my shoulder. Walking home, I hear crying down by the river, and here in the middle of the night is my Puah, my daughter, with her face as white as the sinking moon. I turn her towards me and feel her trembling, saying, what have I done? She says she could feel the baby boy

sneezing under her hand and says, Mother, I am so afraid. I kneel beside her and wipe the hair from her eyes and the tears from her cheeks and tell her it was a dream, that it really did not happen, that she shouldn't be afraid. She says, but she *is* afraid. She tells me that there is fear like she has never felt before. She says that she fears something that is oh so much greater, so much more terrifying than Pharaoh would ever be.
Me, too.

Eight
It is hard to reach back into memory and conjure up the who-what-wheres of the years. Yet I can recall the events of how the child was pulled forth from the river by Pharaoh's daughter, like I can recall the rays of a perfectly angled setting sun. My mother and I stood on the bank of the *Ya'or*, watching Miriam, as she watched her brother wobbling over the waves of water in the basket we all made.

That was sixty years ago and now it is my people and the land we live on that gasps for air. My mother is old but she joins me and my daughters and my daughters' daughters as we travel from home to home, applying salves that we make from the bark of trees, and pitch, and crushed leaves. Since Moses came to face Pharaoh, we have not been in the habit of greeting women on birthstones. Instead we run to heal open sores caused from lice bites that ooze red and yellow and brown. We apply warm towels to the painful knobs that sprout out of foreheads, arms and backs. And all the time when the land is dark and thirsty and full of the smell of the rotting flesh of cattle, our family's houses are quiet, and safe. I come home one evening and there are frogs all over the land, grunting in the mud and clicking in the trees. But at our door the frogs are not. Inside our houses there is no darkness, no disease, no lice that hang on clothes or on our bodies, sucking our blood , causing us to gouge ourselves with our nails. No locusts, no frogs.

My mother says it is because of Miriam and her family, for none of the Hebrews have sickness in their homes, either.

Nine
One afternoon as the sun goes down and the sky becomes brilliant Miriam is at my door. Her gray hair reflects the orange pinks and blues of sunset, and in her arms is a sheep. She puts the animal down beside me and tells me that I must listen, that I must do as she says, as awful as it may seem. She tells me that I should slaughter the sheep whose head is like *Khnum*'s at this time tomorrow and place its blood on our doors. She pleads me to do this or I will lose all that I love, for tomorrow's will be a night more terrible than anything we have ever seen. Miriam touches my cheek and tells me that when the sun comes up on the next day they will be gone. Come with me, my friend. You know that I cannot. Please, she says. *Please.* But you know I cannot. There are tears in our eyes and I can see her now standing with me by the river, cutting down reeds and laughing and braiding baskets in the sun. You know I cannot go. And so we say good-bye.

Ten
There is blood on my hands and on our doors the next day. My family huddles with me in the night and when the winds begin to blow, screams rise out of the darkness, up into the feeble silver rays of the moon. Death comes in waves of wind and the screams are terrible, loud, and distant—far greater than those of childbirth, but at the same time I know that it is birth that is taking place.

Our house protects us like a great hand cupped over a flickering flame. I hold my children to me and cry that I'll never again see my dear friend Miriam and run to midwife to the Hebrew women on the birthstones. My mother wipes away the tears and explains that so it is with us. Birth is letting go, she says. We pull people through the narrow space between life and the other world, and then we must let them go.

Come with us, she said. Really, I cannot. This is where we need to be. *Please.* You know we cannot.

IN PRAISE OF BATYA*
Davi Walders

You could have turned from cry, from reed, good daughter,
stayed on the bank, in bounds, ignored the need, good daughter.

You stopped, descended, refused to leave. You would not make a
sister plead. Gladly you took him in, good daughter.

You brought him, held and taught him inside palace walls,
let Yocheved cradle, feed him, good daughter.

You blended two worlds, bent his fire into strength
to honor, serve and lead, good daughter.

Knowing all the while he'd leave, it must have hurt
to see him flee, freed by rage and blood, good daughter.

And then the return, arguing with your father, this son
growing distant as each new plague was decreed, good daughter.

His second leaving worse, the loss of servants, slaves,
the child you raised, guarded, paying you no heed, good
daughter.

So few women's stories, but there in the beginning,
we read of Miriam, Shiphrah, Puah, and you, all lively daughters.

You live on in praise, in word and wonder,
each deed remembered by another, good daughter.

*Source of Pharaoh's daughter's name, Leviticus *Rabbah* 1:3,
'daughter of God.'

YOCHEVED'S DAUGHTERS
Naomi Graetz

*"A certain man of the house of Levi went and married
a Levite woman."*
Exodus 2:1

❧

Yocheved sits in her succah, a booth with some
palm leaves over it to protect her from the intense sun of
the desert. It is a hot day and she has put in a long day's
work. This is her time, and she is sipping a drink of
brackish well water, carefully boiled, rationed, and
disguised with dried and preserved *nanna* leaves from
their garden in Goshen, Egypt. Besides her daily chores,
she is expected to keep an eye on Moses and Tzipporah's
two sons Gershom and Eliezer, who are fairly easy—
passive in fact, and neglected terribly by their father and
their bewildered mother.

*Later this day, there will be a meeting in the Tent and
I'll be expected to look after Aaron and Elisheva's four unruly
sons: Elazar, Itamar, Dotan and Avihu. All these boys! Where
did they come from—I at least was blessed with Miriam. But my
daughter does not seem to want to marry anyone—she enjoys
being a leader too much.*

*At least Elisheva is expecting a girl, which Zipporah,
with her mysterious powers, has predicted by running her hands
over her belly and Miriam, with her own gift of prophecy, has
confirmed. What a family! How is it that each of my immediate
family has been chosen to lead the people of Israel through the
desert? What a long trip this is. If I can only survive it and make
it into the Promised Land!*

Yocheved is a woman with a long white mane of
hair, flowing in all directions. Her eyesight is still pretty
sharp for a woman of her indeterminable age, which is

why her daughters-in-law trust her so much as a caretaker—but they also trust her as a marriage counselor and confidante. "Could I tell some tales," she often says, "if I were so inclined." She chuckles, "That would certainly change Moses' and Aaron's claims to the authority of the books they are constantly scribbling, insisting they are Yahweh's inspired words." Too bad she does not know how to write, though she might use one of Elisheva's scribes to jot down her reminiscences—so that HER story doesn't get lost, drowned out by Moses' and Aaron's version of truth.

Which of her daughters would she write about? Would it be her favorite, the impetuous Miriam who could have been the leader of the people, had she not been a woman? As it was, the people came to her and looked up to her and all her time was taken up listening to their complaints, serving as advisor and problem solver to her brothers. The three of them were engaged in a power struggle. Some days Miriam and Aaron allied themselves against Moses—some days, it was Moses and Miriam against Aaron—and sometimes Miriam stood alone—against both of them. She worried about Miriam; she was too outspoken. Moses was clearly the reluctant leader of people, chosen by Yahweh and preferred over Miriam—she was resentful of her "little brother's" chosenness. After all, it was she who'd saved him, watched over him in the bulrushes before Batya, Pharaoh's daughter, found him. She was the one who'd kept in touch over all those long years and brought Yocheved in, openly, at great risk to herself (Ex 2:6ff), to nurse her son, who was an illegal alien and doomed to die by Pharaoh's decrees.

Miriam keeps on going to Moses and telling him that he'd better find some time for Zipporah, that things cannot keep on the way they are—she hints that she knows something and is threatening to go to the Meeting Tent and confront him in the face of God and get him to change his ways.

Miriam was playing with fire—she had let her power get to her head and had no real sense of a woman's place. She'd actually saved the people, and was given credit for it. She went to Amram and challenged him to procreate when all the other men were afraid to have intercourse with their wives, after Pharaoh's decrees to throw all the little baby boys into the Nile to annihilate the Hebrews. Amram bragged about that while laying bricks and the other men emulated him. *That act of boldness, magnified and retold as one of the legends which saved us from dying out and which also provided us with our Moses, prince of Egypt, made her reputation.*

She had her women's groups around her; she had her phenomenal insight into finding water, when they were thirsty—was it instinct, or was it Yahweh's gift of power to her, to compensate her for not choosing her to lead the people to the promised land? *Actually, I never understood why it was Moses who was chosen, not Aaron, or Miriam. The first time he was away from anyone's restraining influence—actually from the influence of women, now that I think about it, he went and lost his temper and killed an Egyptian—in typical Levite fashion. And the rest we know; it is history. He went and got married—to you know who . . . no real good judgment—just because of that Levite quick temper, which he loses so easy—hitting the rocks to get water, instead of speaking soothingly and listening to the water flowing beneath the stones, like Miriam.*

They thought her daughter had magical powers. To this day they sang this song whenever they looked for water. She composed it, just as she composed the song of praise to God for successfully crossing the Sea of Reeds. She loved to sing and she taught all her songs to the women—and the men learned these songs from their wives and mothers.

Spring up, O well—sing to it—
The well which the chieftains dug,

Which the nobles of the people started
With maces, with their own staffs.

Miriam was a special child—she was born after Aaron, but she always acted the big sister and collected the other children around her the way a stone does moss—and then they always stayed faithful to her. She had this charm, this power, this talent—she never wanted to be married, like the other children—she wanted to do things—worse than that—she wanted to run the world, or if not that, to tell others how to run the world—that was the source of her conflict with Moses—her willfulness. If only they could cooperate—if only she could stop seeing herself as the big sister—she even bossed us around and told us what to do. I remember so well (Lev Rabbah 17:3).

And that's why they called her a prophet—although no one usually acknowledged that about her—except God, when it suited Him (Ex 15:20). There was too much built-in discrimination against women in our laws—Miriam was so frustrated about that—first, because of how it affects her and second, in how unfair it is. She railed against injustice; she hadn't learnt to moderate her tone. She will be punished for this—cast out. My husband, Amram, gave up on her a long time ago. He said, "what harm can her willfulness do—she'll outgrow it—let her enjoy herself while she can." So he encouraged her. I think he doesn't perceive how serious a problem it is. Aaron does—but he doesn't know what to do—and when he can he uses her, uses her disdain for injustice, so that both are temporarily allied against Moses, and then when HIS schemes don't work, Miriam gets the blame.

It was rumored that God's presence would be revealed to one of Yocheved's three children, but no one knew which of the three it would be. No one thought that it would be Moses, since he was being raised as an Egyptian—but it was Miriam's job to see to it that he would be nourished on the Israelite traditions just in case! Miriam, of course, hoped it would be her and strutted around the community as if she were the chosen—bossing Aaron around, who didn't strike anyone as a leader in those days

Everyone knew that Aaron wouldn't be chosen—but could Miriam, a girl, be God's choice?

Elisheva came over to the succah. She saw Yocheved lying down in a reverie. She was alarmed. "Yocheved, are you all right?" she asked. "I was just coming over to ask you if you can watch the boys, since I want to go to the meeting at the Tent—but if you don't feel up to it, I don't have to go. Can I bring you anything?" Elisheva had never seen Yocheved so contemplative before.

Yocheved's white mane was strewn all over the place—she was still in a prone position, having fallen asleep while in thought. She looked at Elisheva like a stranger—her eyes so intensely focused on her. What do I look like to her? Elisheva wondered.

Elisheva was actually quite startling-looking—her face was relatively pale for an Israelite and her long brown hair was light colored, streaked from exposure to the sun. She had been teased for this and also for being taller than most women in her tribe—the women of Judah were known neither for their height nor for their light looks. Hints had been made about her paternity—thus she was known only as Elisheva *bat* (the daughter of) Aminadab and her mother's name was not usually referred to (not that too many daughters' names were known, nor, in fact, their mothers' names). She was closer to Yocheved than to her birth mother. To see her standing next to Zipporah was quite a contrast. With her stomach protruding (she was about eight months into her pregnancy), slightly stooped with the burden, her face flushed, she looked like some of the ancient goddesses their ancestresses must have worshipped—Ashtoret or Asherah, or Rachel's famous *teraphim*, the house gods of Laban.

Yocheved wanted so much to record the inside story of women in the Menstrual Compound. This was Tzipporah's contribution: She had organized it. She deserved the credit for it. As an outsider she had questioned the loneliness that the Israelite women felt every month and thought that if they could all be together, like she and her six sisters were, the women would look forward to this time period rather than be outcasts. Thus had begun the tradition of Rosh Hodesh—the celebration of the new moon by women—who all seemed to menstruate around the same time. It had become a holiday, an expression of womanliness, rather than a punishment.

"I want to attack the Levites' view of the menstruating woman as unclean. How dare they take our tradition away from us?" Yocheved thought indignantly. Another story that must be told was their friendship with the Egyptian women who sent them on their way with presents so that they would not go away empty-handed. *Each woman gave us from her house a gift to remember her by; usually a goddess made of silver and gold, or a simple piece of jewelry or clothing for our sons and daughters that their children had outgrown, since they knew we would need it for the long trip.* For some reason, rather than see it as an act of generosity and compassion by their friends, it was recorded by the scribes as an act of trickery—it was said that the women "borrowed" these items, implying that they stole them in lieu of the back pay owed them.

The men never realized that we had good friends and allies among the Egyptian women, a relationship that goes back in time all the way to Sarah's friendship with Hagar (before that went sour). And what of our contribution to the Exodus itself? Who was it who stayed up all night preparing and baking unleavened cakes of the dough we took out of Egypt? True, we were "driven out of Egypt and could not delay," but not by the women. Our Egyptian friends were there helping us to bake, crying tearfully with us about how much they would miss us— even Batya came over, sneaking away from her entourage to say a special good-bye to Moses. She knew we had no time to prepare any provisions for ourselves, so she brought us some special goodies.

This would be Yocheved's contribution, her way of making history. Miriam, too, was part of history, though not always mentioned by name. I will preserve the other side, the softer side. And then I will no longer be considered JUST a mother, a daughter. This will set the record straight. Now I can get a good night's sleep. In the morning there will be more to think about.

TZIPPORAH: EXODUS 4:22-26
Alana Suskin

I licked the salt from your skin
Like a deer.
You said to me, I will not touch you
In your impurity
Meaning my blood.
Did you think that Egyptian daintiness
Made you well-bred?
Did their niceties protect you
on the road as you traveled back
to their disdainful cities?

Bridegroom of blood, you are to me,
The blood of your son is my blood
Smeared across your penis.
How embarrassing to be saved by the flooding Nile,
The rising tide
Which should have drowned you.
My impurity which frightens away angels.
My fertility which caused you life.
How delicate your court language:
Feet for genitals -
Turning my anger into sex,
Into my bowing myself to the ground:
Sex into slavery

How Egyptian of you,
When it was I who rode you
As you shifted slowly beneath me
Like dunes over a season of winds.
The sands think themselves an ocean
Covering everything that rests upon them,
Sliding into crevices,

Then gently brushing themselves over:
A father's hand on his sleeping son's hair
Smoothing the covers
To gentle rounded hills.
But when the sands reach the sea,
the windy, roaring, salty sea
That rushes back and forth,
Like us, along the roads to Egypt,
like blood in your veins,
They rear back, fold under,
as the sea covers them up:
Scissors, paper, rock; a child's game.
The sands, too, are swallowed up.

My father called me Tzipporah,
He knew that I would fly away.
Don't call me "little bird,"
Only an eagle rends flesh in flight.
The splash of blood on your doorstep
Is mine. Does it defile you
or protect you from the shadow
of death that steals
across Egypt's roads and pauses
at the thresholds?
Is it the sea that splits for you
to walk across: safe,
To a fertile land?

DRAWING BACK: A MIDRASH ON EXODUS 4:24-26
Virginia (Beruriah Avniel) Spatz

Moses and I have long agreed that our journey left us in very different places. Only recently, though, have I come to wonder if we even shared a starting point . . .

In the beginning, I remember, both boys[1] were almost trampled to death when the elder tried to push his new brother off my breast. Plus, the little one wasn't nursing well and screamed himself to sleep without drinking enough for that day's heat. When I couldn't rouse him at first, I began to panic. So, of course, my milk wouldn't let down when I was finally able to awaken him. It was just eight days after the birth of our not-yet-named son, and I was losing blood again. I was exhausted, missing my sisters, and wondering again if this trip was truly necessary. But my husband seemed so sure—about some things anyway.

First, he'd gone to Father, telling him—with an urgency I had not seen since that long-ago day at the well[2]—that he must see how his brethren were faring.[3] With Father's blessing, he rushed through the preparations and we made our good-byes. Then, when he was all but on the road, he returned in another rush, telling me that the boys and I should accompany him: that we would all live in Egypt. Finally, as the donkeys were already proceeding, Moses rushed back once more for the staff he used in shepherding.

In fits and starts through the day's journey, I had heard more words from that man than he ordinarily spoke from one new moon to the next. He'd told me again about the bush[4] and the staff, the promise of redemption and his need to be among his people. Mostly, though, he'd repeated the same fears: "Why would Pharaoh receive a man of the slave people, a man who'd actually fled court to become a shepherd? Would any Israelite trust a man raised in Pharaoh's palace? Would they recognize him as a fellow?"[5]

Moses wasn't hearing my responses, and I knew those were not his only fears, so I let the silences grow. Then just before nightfall, Moses began to speak again, this time of a land of milk and honey and a river of blood; the need to bring the people into God's presence and the terrors that faced everyone before the redemption could take place. That was when he began to shiver.

The night was quite warm, so at first I assumed the shivering was exhaustion. Still, I remember hesitating to halt our journey, thinking Moses might tell me more if we kept our pace. Eventually, though, I felt the need to lie down and suggested we stop.

Moses barely spoke as we settled in for the night. The boys were already sleeping, and I was beginning to drift off, when he suddenly sat up and shouted, "Not my firstborn!"[6] Moses shook in his cloak, mumbling something about that river of blood and where it would lead. He was sinking deeper into the grip of the fever.[7] He began struggling for breath, and each gasp seemed to be emptying the little room of its air. For a time I feared Moses' struggle with the fever might engulf the boys and me as well.

I remember thinking how easily men seem to link blood with death and how constantly they must be reminded that blood is also the source of life. Still bleeding myself from bringing forth the exquisite new life sharing my wrap, I suddenly pictured Moses shortly after Gershom's birth, demanding that he be circumcised according to Israelite custom. How I'd railed at Moses then![8] And, as Moses continued to shiver, I found myself repeating aloud what I'd shouted at him over Gershom's birth: "Why should your fathers' God want the blood of this perfectly formed babe? Haven't I shed enough?"[9]

But that night, kneeling between new life and near death . . . that's when I experienced a clarity as sharp and all-encompassing as a birth pain . . . and as impossible to recall after it has passed.

I can tell you that my fingers refused to uncurl afterward, so hard had I clutched the flint.[10] I can relate how I touched Moses with the blood, telling him, "You are a blood bridegroom," and how, soon after that, I saw Moses' fever depart. But none of that explains how the wound I inflicted allowed our family to breathe again that night, or how its scar eventually became a lifeline drawing Moses back to us.

I can tell you how, when Moses finally sat up, I recognized his expression. I'd seen it many times before, on the faces of men at festival rites with my father—only there was no joy in Moses' face, just awe and determination.[11] I can repeat what I told Moses then, "You are a blood bridegroom to me." I can describe Moses' response, his solemn nod, the way he carefully placed my hand on his shoulder before pulling our wide-eyed Gershom to his side and picking up our bandaged infant. And I can tell you that it wasn't to me or to the children that Moses looked when naming our youngest. But does that explain how, even as I felt his shoulder under my hand, I knew that I could no longer hold Moses? Does it give you any clue to the terror I felt as he leaned forward and away from me, intoning "Eliezer—God is my help"?[12]

There is so little of that night's experience that translates into everyday language. If I tell you that Moses and I lived the rest of our marriage from opposite shores of that river of blood, am I speaking your language? Perhaps I should simply tell you how glad I was to let Aaron and Moses continue on alone after that night.[13]

Over the years I've come to be grateful that I was not destined for prophecy or priesthood. I do still regret that I never succeeded in making anyone else understand what was so clear to me that night . . .

I was never quite sure what Aaron knew in the beginning, and after the tragedy[14] we couldn't speak of such things at all. Miriam, who received and responded to prophecy as naturally as most people breathe, simply could not—or would not—understand how different things were for her brother—or for me.[15]

Even Father—who was able to help Moses share the burden of his prophecy, to get through to him when no one else could[16]—couldn't unburden me.[17]

NOTES

1. Gershom, Moses' and Tzipporah's first child, is introduced and named in Exodus 2:22 and again in Exodus 18:3. In Exodus 18:3-4, two sons are named. I am following a line of commentary that assumes both boys had been born at the time of this trip, although the second had not yet been named (or circumcised; see, e.g., *Shemot Rabbah* 5:8). Other commentary has the second child born during this trip, and so outside Midian. Still others assume that only one child was born before this incident, leaving the second to be born back in Midian, while Moses and Aaron are in Egypt.

2. Exodus 2:16-21.

3. Exodus 4:18.

4. Exodus 3:1 – 4:17

5. Exodus 2:1-15.

6. Sarna's note on Exodus 4:23 (*The JPS Torah Commentary*) links this verse, which closes with "Behold, I shall kill your firstborn son," words Moses is told to speak to Pharaoh, with the incident at the lodging place that directly follows.

7. In *The Depths of Simplicity: Incisive Essay on the Torah* (New York: Feldheim, 1994), R. Zvi Dov Kanotopsky suggests that it is the potential leader's tension between obligation and fear that causes Moses' illness, and that Tzipporah's cure is a reminder of the covenant and his role in its unfolding. I have blended this midrash with the picture of Tzipporah that emerges from the myriad other commentaries and midrashim on this odd passage.

8. The brevity of the "night lodging" passage and its use of pronouns and verbs without clear referent leads to much confusion, and has become food for comment, ancient and modern. Who does the threatening—an angel? God? Who is

threatened—the elder child, the younger child, or Moses? Who is circumcised here—Moses or one of his children? And who does Tzipporah touch with the blood? Who is the "bridegroom of blood"? Are there two separate referents in the two uses of this term? In addition, commentators disagree about why the attack took place: Was it punishment for a failure to circumcise? A pre-leadership test of Moses? Nor is there agreement about why Tzipporah took the action she did. As a magical rite of Midian origin? As a sign of the Israelite covenant, which she understood from her husband's teaching? An action that seemed necessary to her, based on the situation alone?

9. Some traditional commentary on Exodus 4:24-26 suggests that Jethro forbade circumcising his grandsons; Tzipporah's opinion is not recorded.

10. Exodus 4:25.

11. Jethro is known as "the priest of Midian" (Ex 3:1, 18:1).

12. Exodus 18:4.

13. Tzipporah is not mentioned in the text between Exodus 4:26 and 18:2, when Jethro comes to Moses in the desert with "Tzipporah, Moses' wife, after she had been sent home." Rashi's commentary has Aaron suggesting that Tzipporah and the children, not being Israelites, not be forced to suffer, and Moses agreeing to "send them home."

14. Aaron's sons Nadab and Abihu die "offering alien fire" before to the Lord (Lev 10:1ff).

15. See Numbers 12:6-8, where God tells Miriam and Aaron that they do not understand the difference between Moses' prophecy and those who receive visions and dreams.

16. See the account of Jethro's visit to Moses in the desert in Exodus 18:1-27, especially Jethro's telling Moses, "The thing that you do is not good. You will surely become worn out—you as well as this people that is with you—for this matter is too hard for you, you will not be able to do it alone. Now heed my voice . . ." (Ex 18:17-19).

17. Tzipporah is a footnote lover's dream. She appears only three or four times in the Torah; she is called by name only in Exodus 2:21, 4:25, and 18:2 and is possibly the "Cushite" woman who is the focus of Numbers chapter 12. Yet it is this marginal character who stares down God (or a messenger thereof) in order to save her family—and, as a result, the Israelites. In three short

verses, a woman who lives largely in the footnotes, or in the white space between the Torah's letters, makes possible the redemption of the Israelites and the birth of the Jews.

TZIPPORAH'S FLINT
Davi Walders

Raise
the flint
alone

sharpen
cut
the foreskin
now

our
child this
son

Gershom
this skin
his skin

blood
our blood
his blood
by my

hand
holding
a cry

binding
mother
and
son in

covenant.

ELISHEVA BAT AMMINADAB: THE SILENT WIFE SPEAKS
Susan Phillips

Elisheva bat Amminadab, sister of Nahshon, wife of Aaron, mother of Nadab, Abihu, Eleazar and Ithamar, grandmother of Pinchas, is mentioned only twice in the Bible. She says nothing, does nothing, has no story. Midrash surrounding her is almost as scanty. One day she had five crowns—her brother-in-law Moses was a king, her brother Nahshon a prince, her two sons High Priests, her grandson Pinchas a priest anointed for war (Exodus 6:23). Then Nadab and Abihu take strange fire into the Holy of Holies, and she is left with nothing.

But surely she, too, has a story somewhere. Was Elisheva a patient, loving wife and mother? Was she close to her sister-in law Miriam? How did she deal with her heartbreak?

๛

Once I thought life could run smoothly. Once I thought after this or after that is settled, all will go well. I no longer believe that. I'm old and sick and tired. I long to join my husband and my two oldest sons. I want no more troubles, no more unhappiness, no more glory.

In those early days, when we first left Egypt, I often found myself nearly bursting with joy and pride. What woman, what creature, had ever experienced the happiness I felt! My brother-in-law Moses was considered a king among the Hebrews, mightier than Pharaoh. With God's help, he had rescued us from Egypt. My brother Nahshon was a prince among men. Had he not shown his faith in God even more strongly than our father Amminadab? When all the people cried out at the Red Sea, fearful to cross, Nahshon jumped in and began to swim. Cries turned to laughter as we realized that the water became not deeper, but shallower, the further out he swam. Nahshon stood up, covered with mud. As others followed him into the water, he and Moses led us all across.

And I was proud to be Miriam's sister-in-law. After all the women had crossed the Red Sea and arrived on the other side, Miriam *took a timbrel in her hand, and all the women went out after her in dance with timbrels.* As we danced together joyously, we joined Miriam in song. *And Miriam chanted for them:*

Sing to the Lord, for He has triumphed gloriously;
Horse and rider He has hurled into the sea.

(Ex 15:20-21)

When we had finished, she approached me. "I saw your face, Elisheva," she said. "You looked so proud of me and our entire family. I hope you always feel that way. I hope none of us ever causes you shame." She was silent a moment. "Let us share all our moments of joy and all our moments of despair with each other," she added.

And so it was. In times of trouble or fear, we backed each other up. We trusted Moses and followed his lead, though sometimes Miriam was uneasy about Moses' leadership. "For a patient man," she would grumble, "he doesn't always know how to wait."

Miriam was always by my side. She was there at my times of high joy—when my grandson Pinchas, Eleazar's son, was born. "I see great things for him, Elisheva," she said. "I know he will be a great man, a prophet himself, a prophet anointed for war."

And she was there when Aaron was anointed High Priest and when he taught our sons Nadab and Abihu all the intricacies of God's work. How proud I was then! I felt like a queen—crown after crown set upon my head.

There were also hard times in the desert—all the wanderings, the fears. Sometimes I felt I was always tired and dusty. Except on Shabbat. Every week, a few hours before the sun set, Miriam came to our tent. She would look in and beckon with her finger. I would stop what I was doing and follow her. Every week, no matter where we were, Miriam found a cool spring to bathe in. The two of us washed, then floated in the water and talked. When we left, we noticed others walking to our secret spot. But we were always there first, when the water was cleanest.

"It's as if you drag a well around behind you," I teased her.

She smiled. "Who knows?"

The bright spots got me through the hard times. When Aaron separated from me to ready himself for God's presence, I imagined him inside the Tent, at the altar, performing sacrifices. I thrilled with pride and joy each time he left the Tent of Meeting. His face glowed; he looked young again. As soon as I saw him, my uneasiness and loneliness disappeared.

We went on, trudging through the desert, month after month, year after year. Aaron and I were no longer young. We were all getting old. Sometimes I'd come across the boys talking together. Boys, I say, but they were all grown men: Nadab and Abihu, Ithamar and Eleazar, and Moses' sons, Gershom and Eliezer.

"There's no place for us." That was Gershom, always the stranger, never finding his own way. He wanted to follow in his father's footsteps, but Moses preferred Joshua ben Nun's independent spirit and courage. "Don't worry. Some day our time will come. There is enough work for everyone." That was Ithamar, even more patient than his uncle Moses.

"Now is when I want to be in charge. I'm ready now." My heart sank. Nadab—wanting everything today, not tomorrow. Wishing perhaps that Aaron were dead and that he could take over as High Priest. I should have stepped in then. Instead I listened as Abihu agreed with his brother.

I walked away, shaken. The two of them were always conspiring. I hoped their brothers and cousins would calm them down.

That night we were awakened by a huge burst of lightning, running toward the Tent of Meeting. I was frightened. For days it had been dry, and the sky had been completely clear at sunset. Suddenly I heard shouts and cries, the sounds of people running. And then, just as suddenly, complete silence.

Miriam entered our tent. "Elisheva," she said. "I have something dreadful to tell you. Please, don't interrupt. It's Nadab and Abihu." She broke off, began to cry, stopped herself. "I must not cry," she murmured. She paused again. "I'm not sure what happened," she said finally. "And we may never know. Moses says that Nadab and Abihu *each took his fire pan, put fire in it, and laid incense on it, and they offered before the Lord alien fire, which He had not enjoined upon them. And fire came forth from the Lord and consumed them; thus they died at the instance of the Lord.* That is what Moses says," she told me (Lev 10:1-2).

I was silent. My sons, two jewels in my crown of pride and glory. And then I couldn't help myself. I started to cry, loudly, hoarsely, until I felt weak and sick. I lay down and cried and cried until I cried myself to sleep. When I awoke, Miriam was looking down at me, holding my hand.

After that I felt no more joy. At first I was ashamed, ashamed of my sons and of myself. Rumors spread quickly. Nadab and Abihu had been drinking for hours. They were drunk when they entered the Tent of Meeting. So Aaron and our two remaining sons refused all drink for days before they were to offer sacrifices.

Instead of the pride I used to feel, I was fearful each time they went into the Tent. I paced and paced, unable to work, until each emerged safely. Although I pretended to feel as joyful as I used to be, I felt used up, as if my heart and soul had burned up along with my sons.

There was no one to console me when Miriam died. It was just before Shabbat, a dry and dusty day. As we were preparing to leave and find a cool spring, she collapsed in my arms. "There's a spring not far from here," she whispered. Before she could tell me its location, she died. That evening the people realized there was no spring, nowhere to clean up and cool off before Shabbat, no water to drink. They quarreled, they cried out against Moses and Aaron. Moses found us water to drink that night, and every night after. But never again did I find another place to cleanse myself before the Shabbat. Never again did I look for one.

And when Aaron died, I only found out afterwards. He and Moses and Eleazar went up to Mount Hor. I saw them descend days later—two men, walking slowly, one dressed in the vestments of the High Priest. Where is Eleazar? I thought. Where is my third precious son? I have lost two already. Am I to lose a third also?

As I watched them approach, I realized it was Eleazar, not Aaron, dressed in the High Priest's robes. Eleazar walked toward me, but I ran off to my tent, so lonely and empty now. I cried and cried. Again I cried myself to sleep. When I woke, it was night, dark and cloudy. There was no one to hold my hand and console me, as there had been after the death of my two sons.

STANDING AT SINAI

⤜

The ultimate moment in Jewish history, the creation of a people, indeed a nation, came at the foot of Mount Sinai. When the Hebrews received and accepted the divine commandments and agreed to live by a set of theologically disposed rules, they became Israel. But Moses' oft-quoted warning to the people, "Go not near a woman," has led to centuries of marginalization for Jewish women. As the people prepared for the ultimate moment, the giving of the Law at Mount Sinai, Moses replaced God's words with his own, and created a rift wider than the parted Sea. By speaking for God, and speaking only to men, Moses caused generations of women thousands of years later to still feel the bitterness of Miriam.

Each of the writers in this section looks through the eyes of a woman of Israel, at the moment of covenant. Through Miriam and the unnamed women standing with her at Sinai, these poems give voice to feelings of exclusion now three thousand years old. Beginning with Merle Feld's classic, "We All Stood Together," let us explore the meaning of standing together in covenant as the poets dialog with each other, with Miriam, and with the nation of Israel.

WE ALL STOOD TOGETHER
Merle Feld

For Rachel Adler

～

My brother and I were at Sinai
He kept a journal
of what he saw
of what he heard
of what it all meant to him

I wish I had such a record
of what happened to me there

It seems like every time I want to write
I can't
I'm always holding a baby
one of my own
or one for a friend
always holding a baby
so my hands are never free
to write things down

And then
as time passes
the particulars
the hard data
the who what when where why
slip away from me
and all I'm left with is
the feeling

But feelings are just sounds
the vowel barking of a mute

My brother is so sure of what he heard
after all he's got a record of it
consonant after consonant after consonant

If we remembered it together
we could recreate holy time
sparks flying

SINAI
Merle Feld

The men rushed ahead
They always do
in battle, to defend us
in eagerness, to get the best view
to be there with each other
as a community

We followed later
some of us waited
till we were done nursing
others waited to go together
with those who were still nursing
most of us were herding several children
carrying a heavy two year old
On one hip
(it's hard to move forward quickly
with a heavy two year old on one hip)
last came the very pregnant ones
when you're that far along
it's your instinct to be afraid of crowds
afraid of being jostled
you hang back
you feel safer being last

Anyway, I was one of the ones
with a heavy two year old on one hip
such a sweet body he had
warm soft delicious flesh
he was afraid of the noise
he clung to me so tightly
his fingers in my neck
his face buried in my neck

I showered him with little kisses
not so much to comfort him
as out of habit
and my pleasure

The earth shook, it vibrated
And so did I
My chest, my legs
All vibrating
I sank to my knees
All the while with this little boy attached to me
Trying to merge himself back into me

I closed my eyes to be there more intensely
It all washed over me
Wave upon wave upon wave...

And afterwards, the stillness
of a nation, a people
who had been flattened
forever imprinted
slowly raising themselves
rising again from the earth

How to hold onto that moment
washed clean
reborn
holy silence

STANDING AT SINAI
Chava Weissler

For Merle on her birthday
Simchat Torah, 5745

᠀

The missionary asked me
"Do you believe the Bible is the word of God?"
I answered him by beginning to chant
"*Ba-hodesh ha-shelishi*—On the third new moon
After the Israelites had left the land of Egypt
On that very day, they entered the wilderness of Sinai."

Ten years ago,
When I first learned to chant from the Scroll,
That was what I learned—"On the third new moon."
And every time I chant it from the Scroll
I remember again how it was.

Do I believe? I was *there*!
I remember what it looked like,
A bare mountain, not very tall,
With some scrubby bushes growing on the lower slopes.
They put up a fence around it
To keep the sheep from grazing in the scrub,
And warned us we'd be stoned if we went up there.
They didn't need to frighten us—
That mountain was scary enough all by itself.

Three days before the Big Event
They told us to get ready.
"Wash your clothes," they said,
And told the men
"Keep away from women"—

Not that it made much difference in *my* life.

On the Big Day
There were voices—
Thunder and lightning and a long blast of the shofar;
The mountain was covered with clouds and smoke.
On that day
We *saw* the voices.

When you see voices
You never forget it as long as you live.

Breathing hard, eager, filled with terror,
We all pressed forward towards the mountain
Where God hid and beckoned.
I started to walk with my friend Merle
But like most of the women
She had her kids with her—
She had to carry the two-year-old—
And I just couldn't walk that slowly.
All *I* had to carry was my briefcase,
So I pushed right up there with the men.
I stood next to Miriam.
Now *there* was a hard-bitten career woman if I've ever seen
one,
Tall, gaunt and bony
With a shock of frizzy black hair
A hawk nose
And haunted eyes.

The gossip about her in the camp was nasty
"Haggard old maid, no wonder she thinks she sees God."
"I hear she has quite a thing for Caleb ben Jephuneh,
But he won't give her a second look."
"You'd think, with all her brother's influence,

He could prevail on him to take her."
She looked just the person to dicker with Pharaoh's daughter
About a nursemaid's hire
But I couldn't believe
She had ever taught Aaron to dance.
I never saw her smile.

We stood and waited, men and women.
The mountain smoked and steamed
It trembled and we trembled
The sound of the shofar got louder and louder
Moses spoke and God answered—

Ten years ago,
When I first learned to chant from the Scroll,
That was as far as I got.
And every time I chant it again
I stop before God speaks.

WOMAN FREE FROM FEAR
Abbe Don

This drash was written in response to "Yitro" which is Exodus 19,
in particular Exodus 19:15 in which Moses says,
"Be ready for the third day: do not go near a woman."
This passage has raised the question among many feminist scholars,
most notably Judith Plaskow in Standing Again at Sinai:
"Where were the women when Moses received the Torah at Sinai?"

This drash offers one imaginative answer to the question:
"What was your experience at Sinai?"

❧

Alone, behind a rock, I slowly undressed, trembling.
I washed days of dust and years of pain from my sun-
wrinkled skin.
The sweet taste of freedom followed by the bitter aftertaste
of fear.
Mount Sinai silhouetted against the night sky.
The desert stretched out in all directions.
Endless waterless desert.
Torture and brutality,
Dark armies of men chasing away foreigners, pillaging
what little we carried on our backs.

The cold crisp, not-yet-dawn air, overpowered my fear.
The dew clung to the otherwise dry brush as desert
aromas began to stir.
I stood naked facing the mountain.
The dark black fear nightsky slowly, almost imperceptibly,
transformed to
warm dawn early-light blue.

I began to pray like I had never prayed before.
An unknown sense of strength pulsed through my body.
My feet burned pleasurably with energy that ran up my
legs and swirled around my thighs.
My belly felt full yet I had not eaten in two days.
My heart pounded evenly and loudly as if announcing my
presence to the desert.

"I am here." I called out to no one in particular.
A woman's voice answered, "And I am here."
And another's affirmed soothingly, "We are here."

I slowly rocked back and forth to the beat of my heart.
The energy flowed through my arms. I was dancing.
The whisper of women's voices gathering at the foot of the
mountain broke the silence.
I knew the others would be looking for me.
I reluctantly put my clothes on.
I ran to join Miriam and the other women as they walked
towards the foot of Mount Sinai.

Moses had already gone up to the mountain.
The women were silent.
I could still feel the energy pulsing through my body.
I wanted to dance and sing.
But instead, I stood quietly with the others.
The fear began to rise again just as intensely as the as the
energy pulsing through my body.
My heart began to beat rapidly and irregularly.
My breath was short and I gasped for air as the sound of
the *shofar* pierced my ears.
Loud, rumbling thunder shook the ground and the
mountain erupted in flame.

The wind was so strong that it blew right through me and blew away the rest of the world.

I was completely alone, facing the mountain.

Though I could not see the others, I was aware of their presence.

A voice called out to each of us simultaneously with our own message, a chorus of
individual meanings...

"You are woman, woman who loves women, woman free from fear."

ON EXODUS 19:15
Susan Gross

Dreary rain.
We sleep in soggy tents
and trudge through the daily desert mud.

We watch Moses descend.
He startles at lightning zigzags.
No one else moves as
he picks his way through the wet boulders.

I sense tragedy.
He speaks, and my premonition is confirmed.
He has erased us.

My friends fling bewildered looks at me
as when I stepped into the sea.
Back then, though, the world was ours.
They followed me bounding
into the waves, splashing,
watching the waters part.
This time, there is no way out.

> remember the other covenant
> the penis business
> it's Abraham all over again
> I tell you

We are chilled. Some of us cry.
I gather a damp shawl
around my shoulders.

"...and their lives were embittered..."

MIRIAM THE BITTER

⋘

Miriam's name, which translates literally as "bitter sea," contains multiple plays on the words that surround her life. The word *mar*, bitter, is repeated in the text following references to Miriam, both after the Song of the Sea, and after Miriam's death (the *mei meribah*, waters of strife, in Numbers 20:13). The themes of bitterness (*marah*) and water (*mayim*) or sea (*yam*) intermingle in Miriam's name and in her story. The waters of the Nile, into which Hebrew babies were thrown, is bitter water indeed. Midrash has often painted Miriam as a bitter woman, complaining and lonely, as she sat in the desert in Numbers 12. The bitterness of Miriam runs through many of the contributions to this book, as felt by women reading her story: bitterness at being silenced; bitterness at being excluded from a more central place in the tradition.

The title quote for this chapter comes from early Exodus, and refers to the enslavement of the entire people of Israel. Here, the authors imagine the anger, pain, and disappointment of Miriam and the other women of the Exodus as they are denied full participation in the creation of their people's history. Marjorie Agosin's poem "Miriam" contrasts the roles of Moses and Miriam and speaks to the bitterness of exclusion. Davi Walders offers a modern look back, in an angry letter to God titled, "Re: Sister Miriam." In Naomi Graetz's essay, "Did Miriam Talk Too Much?" she explores the punishment of Miriam for the sins of gossip and slander. Graetz's poem connects Miriam's name to *maror*, the bitter herbs eaten at the seder.

MIRIAM
Marjorie Agosín

Translation by
Monica Bruno Galmozzi

Mi hermano y yo
fuimos los testigos de Dios
en el desierto.
El anotaba la vida
sobre las piedras y
yo imaginaba el agua
sobre la arena áspera y
oscura.

My brother and I
were God's witnesses
in the desert.
He wrote life down
on the stones and
I imagined water
on the rough, dark sands.

Mi hermano fue el eleguido.
Recibió el don de todas las
palabras.
A Dios le gustaban sus
pasos
y su aliento.

My brother was the chosen
one.
He had the gift of words.
God was pleased with his
steps
and his breath.

Dios se enfadó ante mi
deseo
de ser peregrina, como mi
pueblo.
Me llenó la piel
de escamas y de peces
muertos.

God was angered by my
desire
to wander, like my
people.
He covered my skin
with scales and dead fish.

En la oscurísima oscuridad
me quedé en un calabozo,
en la luz de este jardín del
desierto.
Las mujeres me esperaban.
Cantaban mi nombre.

In the darkest darkness,
I was trapped in a cell,
in the light of this desert's
garden.
The women waited for me.
They sang my name.

De pronto,
me di cuenta
que tan sólo mi hermano
escribía entre las piedras
los dictados de Dios,
ese Dios que me había
dejado muda
y tan sola
en aquella vasta soledad.

Permanecí
con mis mujeres,
sin nombre,
sin historia,
sin Dios.
Me llamo Miriam,
guardiana de la fe.

Suddenly,
I realized
that only my brother
wrote God's words
on the rocks,
that God who had left me
mute
and alone
in the vast loneliness.

I remained
with my women,
without a name,
without history,
without a God.
My name is Miriam,
guardian of faith.

MIRIAM'S BLUES
Carol Anshien

I am Miriam
(in menopause)
filled with memories
some magnificent
some mournful

I remember watching
my baby brother
wrapped in a soft blue blanket
afloat in the blue Nile
praying for his protection

I remember working with him
organizing the logistics
for each family's
going out of Egypt.

I remember leading the women
in joyous dance and song
at the other side of the sea

When my brother Aaron's sons, my nephews
were burned alive in God's brutal flames
I mourned for them
while he could not
I loved them as if they were my own
the ones I never had
time to have

I have had to be tough
All my life
I have had to support

everyone else

And now, I am challenging
Moses' leadership

I don't know why
I am angry
                my moods keep changing

DID MIRIAM TALK TOO MUCH?[1]
Naomi Graetz

At the beginning of Numbers 12 we read: "Miriam and Aaron spoke against Moses because of the Cushite woman he had married . . ."(Num 12:1). The rabbis wonder why the Hebrew word used for "spoke," *wattedabber*, is in the singular form, rather than *wayyedabberu*, in the plural form, since the text says that Miriam *and* Aaron spoke. They also ask why Miriam, a woman, precedes Aaron, since "ladies first" was not a principle in ancient times. The chapter is problematic, and many questions can be raised upon studying it. First let us consider it:

1. When they were in Hazeroth, Miriam and Aaron spoke against Moses because of the Cushite woman he had married: "He married a Cushite woman!"
2. They said, "Has the Lord spoken only through Moses? Has He not spoken through us as well?" The Lord heard it.
3. Now Moses was a very humble man, more so than any other man on earth.
4. Suddenly the Lord called to Moses, Aaron, and Miriam, "Come out, you three, to the Tent of Meeting." So the three of them went out.
5. The Lord came down in a pillar of cloud, stopped at the entrance of the Tent, and called out, "Aaron and Miriam!" The two of them came forward;
6. And he said, "Hear these My words: When a prophet of the Lord arises among you, I make Myself known to him in a vision, I speak with him in a dream.
7. Not so with my servant Moses; he is trusted throughout My household.
8. With him I speak mouth to mouth, plainly and not in riddles, and he beholds the likeness of the Lord.

How then did you not shrink from speaking against My servant Moses!"
9. Still incensed with them, the Lord departed.
10. As the cloud withdrew from the Tent, there was Miriam stricken with snow-white scales! When Aaron turned toward Miriam, he saw that she was stricken with scales [leprosy].
11. And Aaron said to Moses, "O my lord, account not to us the sin which we committed in our folly.
12. Let her [Miriam] not be as one dead, who emerges from his mother's womb with half his flesh eaten away."
13. So Moses cried out to the Lord, saying, "O God, pray heal her!"
14. But the Lord said to Moses, "If her father spat in her face, would she not bear her shame for seven days? Let her be shut out of camp for seven days, and then let her be readmitted."
15. So Miriam was shut out of camp seven days; and the people did not march on until Miriam was readmitted.
16. After that the people set out from Hazeroth and encamped in the wilderness of Paran.[2]

Some of the questions that arise about this text are the following:

1. Who was this Cushite woman to whom Miriam and Aaron referred?
2. Why was Moses silent when accused by Miriam and Aaron?
3. Why did God have to defend Moses' honor in such a drastic way?
4. Why was only Miriam punished and not Aaron?
5. Why leprosy?
6. Does the Bible downplay Miriam's importance to keep the focus on her brother, Moses?
7. Finally, did Miriam and Aaron pose a real threat to Moses?

I suggest that Miriam was punished with leprosy because women in the biblical world were not supposed to be leaders of men, and that women with initiative were reproved when they asserted themselves with the only weapon they had, their power of language—a power which could be used viciously and was, therefore, called *lashon ha-ra*, literally, the evil tongue.

Miriam is recalled in Deuteronomy where it is stated: "Remember what the Lord your God did to Miriam on the way as you came forth out of Egypt" (24:9). She is "a marked woman, a warning for generations to come," a woman so important "that detractors tabooed her to death, seeking to bury her forever in disgrace."[3] Yet she is also a woman whom the rabbis chose to see as a positive role model, an advocate of the biblical command to humanity to "be fruitful and multiply." Specifically, she criticized Moses for not having sexual relations with his wife, and encouraged the Israelite males to marry while in Egypt despite Pharaoh's decrees against Jewish male babies.

Examples of Praise

First, let us look at the many examples of the Miriam whom the rabbis admire. One instance is their explication of Numbers 12:14f., where it is written clearly that it was *the people* who did not journey until Miriam was returned to them. The rabbis, however, say it was the Lord who waited for her. Not only that, but the "Holy One, blessed be He, said: 'I am a priest, I shut her up and I shall declare her clean'" (Deut *Rabbah* 6:9). If God, portrayed as a concerned doctor, intervenes in Miriam's case and personally treats her illness, surely it follows that Miriam was someone to be reckoned with.

There are many midrashim which have to do with Miriam's "well," which is said to have been one of the ten things created during the twilight before the first Sabbath of the creation (B.T. *Pesahim* 54a). One of the few songs of the Bible, an obscure fragment of an ancient poem, is read by many rabbis as referring to this well:

Spring up, O well—sing to it
The well which the chieftains dug,
Which the nobles of the people started
With maces, with their own staffs.
(Num 21:17-19)

Since the verse which comes after Miriam's reported death (Num 20:1) is followed by a statement that there was no water for the congregation (20:2), the rabbis write that Miriam's gift to us after her death was *her* song, which could cause the waters of her well to flow. The proviso was that the right person had to know how to address the well to get it to give water. Moses, who knew only how to hit the rock, was not that person; clearly a woman's touch was needed. The rabbis actually located her well in Tiberias, opposite the middle gate of an ancient synagogue lepers go to in order to be cured (Deut *Rabbah* 6:11).

Miriam is called a prophet in Exodus 15. Though the Bible does not relate any examples of her prophecies, the rabbis interpret the passage "And his sister stood afar off" (Ex 2:4), to mean that she stood afar "to know what would be the outcome of her prophecy," because she had told her parents that her "mother was destined to give birth to a son who will save Israel." That prophecy, they say, is "the meaning of: 'And Miriam the prophetess, the sister of Aaron, took a timbrel'" (Ex 15:20).[4]

A fifth midrash concerns the virtuous midwives who saved the Israelite babies from the wicked Pharaoh. The rabbis decided that the Hebrew midwives, Shifrah and Puah, were none other than Yocheved and the very capable five-year-old Miriam. In this guise she performed pleasing (*safrah*) acts to God and lifted (*hopi'ah* from *pu'ah*) her face against Pharaoh, whereupon Pharaoh became so angry that he sought to slay her. In this same midrash her father, Amram, is shown as a coward who stopped having intercourse with his wife, and even divorced her because of Pharaoh's decree to kill the baby boys who were born to the Israelites. In this story, Miriam pointed out to him that "your decree is more severe than that of Pharaoh; for Pharaoh decreed only concerning the male children, and you decree upon males and females alike." As a result, Amram took his wife back, and his example was followed by all the Israelites (Lev *Rabbah* 17:3). In this midrash, Miriam is praised for outsmarting her father, and for encouraging the people to be fruitful and multiply so that they will survive.

To the rabbis, Miriam is a perfect role model, except for one thing: She is not married and does not have any children. So, to fix that, the midrash explains that the meaning of the passage, "And it came to pass, because the midwives feared God, that He built them houses" (Ex 1:21), is that "they were founders of a royal family." They show that Miriam founded a royal family, with David descending from her. The genealogy is a bit complex but, essentially, Miriam marries Caleb, who begets Hur, who has Uri, who begets Bezalel, leading ultimately to King David (B.T. *Sotah* 12a and Ex *Rabbah* 1:17).

Many problems are solved by this marriage: Amram's line is continued; Caleb, the faithful spy, is rewarded; and Moses' children (sons of a black woman) are written out of Jewish history. But most importantly, Miriam is not an anomalous, unmarried spinster anymore; rather, she is a happily married mother and wife whose offspring bring fame and glory to her. Were it not for the incident when Miriam asserts herself and attacks Moses (God's choice), Miriam would be one of the few women in the Bible about whom the rabbis have nothing bad to say

(B.T. *Ber.* 19a). That this is not the case we see in the examples of castigation concerning her punishment by leprosy.

Examples of Castigation

In Numbers 12, it is not clear who is the Cushite woman, and whether Miriam's case against Moses was just or not. Both she and Aaron claim that God speaks through them as well as through Moses. They both speak up against God's chosen leader. Yet, the popular interpretation is that Miriam was behind it. God, the father figure, reprimands them both, but punishes only Miriam with a skin disease. The fact that Miriam is punished and Aaron is untouched is a discriminatory decision against her, and has the effect of ending Miriam's "legitimate public aspirations."[5]

To see this we must look at the story's textual context, which deals with the people's discontent and their questions concerning authority. We see this in the texts both before and after chapter 12. Chapter 11 depicts the people's popular rebellion based on general dissatisfaction and, in particular, over the boring daily menu of manna. Moses has trouble handling the people and, right after this episode, God tells Moses to share the burden of his leadership with the seventy elders. During this period, when God's spirit has descended on the elders, Eldad and Medad also experience God's spirit and, unlike Aaron's sons (Nadav and Avihu, who were punished with death on a similar occasion), these latter-day prophets (possibly Moses' half-brothers according to one midrash)[6] are rewarded with Moses' protection and the famous statement, "Would that all the Lord's people were prophets!"

In chapter 13, we read the story of the twelve spies or scouts who went out on a reconnaissance mission to study the Land of Canaan, ten of whom come back with slanderous comments about the Land. The midrash connects the two texts (chapters 12 and 13) in its exposition of the passage: "Send thou men, that they may spy out" (Num 13:2):

> First we read, "And Miriam and Aaron spoke against Moses (12:1) and after that, "Send thou men." What reason had Scripture for saying, after the incident of Miriam, "Send thou men?" The fact is that the Holy One, blessed be He, foresaw that the spies would utter a slander about the Land. Said the Holy One, blessed be He: "They shall not say, 'We did not know the penalty for slander.'" The Holy One, blessed be He, therefore placed this section next to the other—for Miriam had spoken against her brother and had been smitten with leprosy—in order that all might know the penalty for slander, and that if people were tempted to speak slander they might reflect what had happened to Miriam. Nevertheless the spies did not want to learn.
>
> (Num *Rabbah* 16:6-7)

It is actually possible to connect the three texts (on Miriam, Eldad, and the spies), since anyone who speaks badly of God or his chosen is guilty of slander. According to the midrash (*Sifre Zuta* 12:1), it is through casual gossip that Miriam finds out from Tzipporah, Moses' wife, about the high price (Moses' failure to engage in marital relations) of being married to a public figure and, thus, there is a connection between slander and rebellion. At any rate, there are clearly others besides Miriam who prophesy together with Moses, or criticize him. Some of them are not punished but praised (like Eldad and Medad), while others, like the spies, are punished in that none of them (except for Caleb and Joshua) gets to the Promised Land. But this still does not explain why Miriam, and not Aaron, comes in for most of the criticism.

Let us recall the midrash where Miriam's father, Amram, is portrayed as a coward who stopped having intercourse with his wife, and divorced her after Pharaoh's decree to kill all the baby boys born to the Israelites. As a result of Miriam's advice, Amram took his wife back, and his example was followed by all the Israelites (Ex *Rabbah* 1:13). In this midrash, Miriam was praised for her assertiveness. Yet, in a midrash which has the same theme, and starts by portraying Miriam "as one who is concerned about the observance of the commandments and Jewish survival . . .",[7] Miriam is punished for the same act of assertiveness. In this midrash, Tzipporah complains to Miriam that, since her husband Moses was chosen by God, he no longer sleeps with her. Miriam consults with her brother, Aaron, and it turns out that although they, too, have received Divine revelations, they—unlike Moses—did not separate themselves from their mates. Furthermore, they claim that Moses abstains to show that he is better than they are and, in Miriam's view, Moses, rather than serving as a "model of the observance of the commandment concerning procreation",[8] abstains from conjugal joys out of pride.

Why did the rabbis go along with Miriam in the case of Amram her father, yet punish her here? The Rabbis themselves ask this question. The answer has to do with R. Judah b. Levi's saying:

> Anyone who is so arrogant as to speak against one greater than himself causes the plagues to attack him. And if you do not believe this, look to the pious Miriam as a warning to all slanderers.
>
> (Deut *Rabbah* 6:9)

In other words, one can stand for procreation as long as one does not attack the leader for not procreating! The leader is different; there are other criteria by which he is to be judged. Devora Steinmetz argues that the rabbis excused Moses from the commandment to "be fruitful and multiply," and agreed that it was correct for him to dedicate himself totally to God; and that to be an effective leader he had to separate himself from the people.

That is not Miriam's and Aaron's concept of what leadership should be, and, if one reads the Bible carefully, there are enough hints that Moses' distancing himself from the people may ultimately have been the cause of his downfall. However, the rabbis do accept the justice of punishment by leprosy, for that is what is ordained for those who speak ill of their neighbors. Presumably it would have been proper, or less objectionable, if Miriam had spoken about her concerns to Moses directly, rather than about him, behind his back.

According to the rabbis, Aaron became leprous as well, but only for a moment, because his sin was not as great. Why was Aaron's sin not considered as great a sin as Miriam's? Because Miriam was behind it all. On *that* the rabbis all seem to agree.[9] The rabbis explicate the passage, "Miriam and Aaron spoke against Moses . . ." in such a way that Aaron is a passive accessory rather than an active co-agent. They reason that malicious gossip is to be associated with women, who have nothing better to do with their time, as we see in a very revealing midrash:

> R. Isaac said: It is like the snake that bites everyone who passes by and it is surprising that anyone is willing to associate with it. So Moses said: "Miriam spoke slander against me; that I can understand since women as a rule are talkative. . . . "   (Deut *Rabbah* 6:11)

Another example of this bias against women, is the saying of R. Levi:

> Women possess the four following characteristics: They are greedy, inquisitive, envious and indolent. . . . The rabbis add two more characteristics: They are querulous and gossips. Whence do we know that they are gossips? For it is written, "And Miriam spoke."
> (Deut *Rabbah* 6:11)

The usual punishment associated with slander is leprosy because leprosy is also associated with quarantine, and lepers must be removed from the camp or city. One is in isolation—husband from wife, child from parent, friends from each other. This is also the effect of *lashon ha-ra'*, the evil tongue, which causes separation. *Lashon ha-ra'*, done often in secrecy, has the effect of isolating the victim from the rest of society, often without her or him even knowing why.

This sin was so egregious that the rabbis inserted two prayers about it into the daily silent recitation; one at the conclusion ("Keep my tongue from evil and my lips from speaking guile") and one a curse ("There shall be no hope for those who slander"). The rabbis think of slander as worse than rape, and equivalent to murder: The rapist must pay 50 *sela* to the victim, whereas whoever slanders must pay 100 *sela* to the slandered person (M. *Arakin* 3:5).

One might think that here is a case of overreaction: Surely the punishment for slander is not to be more severe than for rape. However, in the eyes of the rabbis, since the rapist also has to marry the victim and cannot ever divorce her, there is some kind of closure, whereas one never knows what the ripple effects of slander may be. The rabbis recognized the power of the spoken word to build or ruin human relationships, and considered the tongue the "elixir of life" (Lev *Rabbah* 16:2) and the primary source of good and evil (Lev *Rabbah* 33:1).

The rabbis tell us that the blame for *lashon ha-ra'* falls equally on those making their decisions on the basis of what they hear. And *lashon ha-ra'* is prohibited even when the remarks are true (Lev 19:16). It is written about those who utter slander: "They begin by speaking well of one and conclude by speaking ill" (Num. *Rabbah* 16:17).

The effects of slander (or what today we might want to call, character assassination) are deadly. They are like that of the "serpent who bites into one limb and whose poison travels to all the limbs. *Lashon ha-ra'* slays teller, listener and subject" (Lev *Rabbah* 26:2).

Character assassination of leaders or of God's chosen is, therefore, surely very serious—how serious can be seen in this final midrash, based on the passage: "Suffer not thy mouth to bring thy flesh into guilt" (Eccl 5:5).

> R. Manni interpreted the verse as alluding to Miriam. . . . Miriam spoke slander with her mouth, but all her limbs were punished. R. Joshua learnt: A word for a sela, but silence for two selas. Rabbi Judah Ha-Nasi said: Best of all is silence; as we have learnt in the Ethics of the Fathers: All my days I grew up among the Sages, and I have found nothing better for a person than silence (Eccl *Rabbah* 5:1).

Perhaps here lies the clue. Silence is a virtue; yet to women is attributed the gift of speech. It is said that of the ten measures of conversation that were given to the world, nine were given to women (B.T. *Kiddushin* 49b).[10] If silence is the supreme virtue, surely the nine measures of conversation are a dubious gift at best!

The punishment for *lashon ha-ra'* does not distinguish between men and women. However, the rabbis stack the decks against women. They predict that ninety percent of the time women will be doing the talking. This, then, leads the rabbis to expect the worst from women—even to assuming that when the Bible says that Miriam and Aaron spoke, it was principally Miriam who was at fault! Thus women's talk was viewed at best as worthless, at worst as dangerous. If women are naturally talkative, then silence, by contrast, will naturally be considered golden. The rabbis glorified Miriam when she asserted herself to defend the values of nurturance and motherhood, but disparaged her when she stepped out of line and spoke up to challenge Moses' authority.

Are rabbinic attitudes different today? Let us examine a fairly modern interpretation of the text, which glosses over the inequity of Miriam's punishment by minimizing it. Rabbi Gunter Plaut, in his commentary on the Torah, writes that it was Aaron who was more severely disciplined than Miriam. Though, to the ordinary reader of text, this goes against the grain of the *peshat* (the self-evident meaning), Plaut points out that Miriam is only punished corporally whereas Aaron is punished mentally, a suffering which is more intense. How so? First, because Aaron suffers guilt when he sees Miriam disfigured hideously, while he is let off free. Plaut writes: "The hurt of seeing a dear one suffer is often far greater than one's own physical agony" (p. 1101). Second, because Aaron has to humiliate himself before his younger brother by begging Moses' forgiveness, and by asking him to intercede with God on Miriam's behalf.[11]

Plaut asserts that Miriam's pain is short-lived and, like most physical ailments, quickly forgotten once she is healed, whereas Aaron's punishment probably leaves deep scars. He agrees that Miriam's leprosy is a warning to the people that slander and rebellion are evil, but argues that the sight of Aaron, the High Priest, bowing down before Moses and begging his pardon is a warning which was equally potent and "surely more memorable" (p. 1102). I am not arguing that Plaut's reading is wrong or even narrow-minded, but I hope it is clear that in emphasizing Aaron's pain it is minimizing Miriam's. Like all the jokes about the poor expectant father in the hospital waiting room, who suffers so from the traumatic experience while his wife is calmly going through the process of childbirth, Plaut's reading takes the limelight away from Miriam.

This type of modern interpretation assaults our sense of the meaning of the text by smoothing over the injustice inherent in the original story to make an apologetic statement. Can men and women who experience a conflict with those who continue to interpret the biblical text in such a biased manner, do anything about it? I think, yes! We can insist that the partnership model be considered as the traditional Jewish midrashic approach to text. Its starting point is that the Bible is a "sacred" text, but there is no monopoly on its interpretation. New insights are welcome, and the more diverse they are, the more the enrichment and understanding of God's purpose.

We must start imaginatively to re-engage with our sacred texts, by writing midrash.[12] Only in that way can *all* voices, not only a few, be part of the partnership. Then, we hope, different views will be voiced and will not be dismissed as just gossip or as *lashon ha-ra'*, but welcomed as the "beginning of moral inquiry . . . [and] self-understanding."[13]

NOTES

1. This article appeared first in *Judaism* (Spring, 1991), and in *A Feminist Companion to Exodus – Deuteronomy*, Ed. Athalya Brenner (Sheffield Academic Press, 1994).

2. *Tanakh: A New Translation of the Holy Scriptures* (Philadelphia: Jewish Publication Society, 1985).

3. Phyllis Trible, "Bringing Miriam Out of the Shadows," *Bible Review* 5/1, 1989, p. 179.

4. Deut *Rabbah* 6:14.

5. Edward Levinson and R. Zweiback, "Sexegesis: Miriam in the Desert," *Tikkun* 4/1 (Jan. Feb, 1989), p. 96.

6. Devora Steinmetz, "A Portrait of Miriam in the Rabbinic Midrash," *Prooftexts*, 1988, pp. 35-65. Eldad and Medad prophesy in the camp in contrast to Moses, who prophesies in the Tent of Meeting.

7. Norman J. Cohen, "Miriam's Song: A Modern Midrashic Reading," *Judaism* 33 (1984), p. 185.

8. Levenson, p. 96

9. This may remind the reader of the 'temptation' of Adam by Eve. Aaron, like his 'brother' Adam seems unable to say no. This is borne out by the text, since Aaron was the one who was 'dragged' into the episode of the Golden Calf. In all fairness to the rabbis, Miriam is depicted in some midrashim as refusing to give over the gold jewelry to Aaron, saving it for the creation of the Mishkan.

10. The context in the Talmud makes clear that this is a negative association.

11. Gunter Plaut, *The Torah: A Modern Commentary* (New York: Union of American Hebrew Congregations, 1981).

12. See introduction to my *S/He Created Them* (Professional Press, 1993), available from the author.

13. Phyllis Rose, *Parallel Lives* (New York: Vintage Books, 1983), page 9.

LETTER RE: SISTER MIRIAM
Davi Walders

So tell me, what more could she have done? Didn't she watch him night and day in that furnace of sun and dust, the buzz and bite of bugs her constant companions? Didn't she sit on that hard-packed earth, her back curved and aching, holding herself in fetal position through that humid cauldron of eternity, hiding, guarding, safekeeping, a sister alone? Didn't blood of her young womb, her own few, fragile eggs, spill there on those banks, her own body letting itself go, while she watched him, held him against all tides, waiting? Weren't her songs enough, carried like current through the reeds until the crying moment came, that terrible, frail, little wail that would change the world? Singing all the while, waiting for the right sunset, the right daughter, the right sandals to find the right bulrushes. Wasn't she clever enough, finding the best wetnurse to keep the thin thread of family tied through milk and nurturing? Did they not mold him meek and strong enough through his playful palace days and their long, tented nights? Don't you see . . . even angels sometimes bleed and tire and singers forget their songs can flood the banks.

So what was wrong? Didn't she say yes quickly enough when he asked, knowing that pillars of smoke and clouds of fire might not be enough? Of course she would go and take her timbrels along. Was she not a well holding his tears of frustration, a comfort through the nights and the days of their wandering? Yes, Aaron spoke for him when he stammered, fell to weeping from fatigue, when he was called away to the mountains. A brother spoke, but a sister listened, listened when his eyes glistened with pain, when his face turned crimson with rage, all the days as he lay sickened by blood on the floor. Didn't she let him bury his face in her robes when he had no where else to turn? And didn't the women know that, trusting, listening to the listener?

Would they have crossed? Tell me that. The men believed in miracles, saw an opening, marched on through. How quickly they went, pushing and tugging, lugging their arms behind them. But the women with infants in their arms, children hanging on to their skirts, sheep and goats mewing among them. They hesitated, gathering and counting, looking back. Commands could not hurry them. They saw the death waves rolling, echoing, "You shall not abhor an Egyptian." Were they not entitled to a moment's memory of other pharaohs, fertile communities, and long lost days of peace, confused that all that killing could have been Your will?

In that moment between moments, space between space, Miriam called to them, timbrel glinting at the sun. Curved, bronzed arms high above saffron robes, sandals dancing on the sand, she seduced them, sang them, danced them across. So many drowned, as they knew they would, and still Miriam sang, and the women sang, and Miriam danced, and the women danced, and they joined together with timbrels and dance, letting the waters let them go.

Was it any wonder that she got annoyed and said it? How many marriages did he need to learn to pick a bride he could trust, a woman he could talk to? The brother she raised, the one who talked to You, who led the people. So she said it, wondered what you two talked about and why, with all that talking, he couldn't get it straight. How many more of his rages would she have to listen to before the Promised Land, she, still so far from her own life?

All right, she shouldn't have said it. But she didn't disobey You. You weren't even talking to her then. She didn't' slay anyone, strike anything, throw tablets on the ground. Just words, she and Aaron were just talking. To give her leprosy, leave her outside the gates, skin oozing, fever raging, shivering and alone. And Aaron, not even a scratch, free to lament her rotting flesh. Moses, a moment's whiteness at his breast. But a sister, flesh burning, sores weeping for seven days. I know the people waited, would not move until she was healed, but all her suffering and all that long, long waiting.

Every parent knows these difficulties with siblings – jealousy, fights, feuding with each other. But loyalty, too, and look at the responsibilities those three had. So why, God, why Miriam, why all that time and suffering? Waiting . . . was that the point? Forgive me these days when I wonder again about all this, but I start thinking about rocks and insults and all the trouble women still have. So sometimes I wonder about waiting. And look, I checked a couple of encyclopedias just to read up on Miriam. She wasn't there, not one word. Don't you think it's time for a mention, even just a note, like "Hagar: see Ishmael"? But I already wrote you about that.

MIRIAM THE SPEECHWRITER
Janet Ruth Falon

Moses, awkward, chose to be mute
Aaron delivered
but it was Miriam who put words in the mouth
words that flowed like honey of bees that sting
sweet enough to make the message palatable
thick enough to spread through the crowd
sufficiently golden to reflect
     and remind of the calf.
Miriam the speechwriter is remembered most for dancing
but she was the one who gave voice
who swallowed the clouds and spit them out in letters
who translated God to People
and moved them to reconsider
     and to tears.
A woman's words, once again, ghostly and potent
A woman's voice, once again, silent and still.

MIRIAM THE BITTER
Naomi Graetz

She stands apart.
One of three.
Separate, different,
Sister to a priest.
Midwife (they say)
To the Leader.

The waters broke.
With song and delicacy
She pulled HIM out
And sweet water
From hard rocks.

As a child I knew
Blood, fear
Endless crying--
He was in my power.

I gave my all.

My reward:
HE has turned God against me,
Whiteness of skin,
Shielded from sun and friends
With no one to listen
To my prophecy.

"Has God not also spoken through us?"

MIRIAM THE REBEL

&

Miriam the Rebel hints at buried possibilities in Numbers 12, as Miriam calls for the right to speak for God, as Moses' equal and counterpart. In addition to references to bitterness and water, Miriam's name also contains a more subtle connection to the word *morim*, rebels. As Miriam makes the daring choice to confront Moses regarding leadership in the desert, she may be the first female since Lilith to challenge the status quo and demand equality. The talmudic sources highlight the rebellious nature of Miriam by embellishing the stories provided in the text. The rabbis portray Miriam beginning her revolutionary career in childhood. One of the best-known midrashim about Miriam describes her as a young girl challenging her father over his divorce of Yocheved. Amram and the other men divorced their wives to avoid Pharaoh's decree to kill male Hebrew babies. Miriam confronted him, stating that Amram's solution condemned the unborn female children, too, and also prophesied that her mother would bear a child who would bring about the liberation of the Hebrew slaves.[1]   According to some commentators, Miriam also resisted Pharaoh through refusing to kill the Hebrew babies through her practice of midwifery, as many commentators have linked Yocheved and Miriam with Shiprah and Puah, the midwives of the Exodus story.

Of course, Miriam's ultimate rebellion remains her challenge to Moses in Numbers 12, which is explored in depth in "If There Be a Prophet." Even the talmudic suggestion that Miriam was married to Caleb fits with this portrait of a rebellious Miriam, as Caleb rebelled against the counsel of the spies who were sent to scout the Promised Land. "Let the rebel come and take the rebel to wife," comment the rabbis.[2] Jill Hammer's poem, "The Names of Miriam," touches on all the different facets of Miriam's character, but has her clinging to her identity as rebel, challenging even God to find a name for her. In their essay, "Sister Miriam the Leper," Ita Sheres and Anne Blau argue that the Miriam story must be read through the context of Egypt, and give several new twists to Miriam's rebellion in Numbers 12. The "Covenant of Miriam" is a midrashic imagining of Miriam's life and exile in the desert, drawing on her outspoken nature and connecting her to the origins of Rosh Hodesh as a women's holiday.

NOTES

1. B.T. *Sotah* 12a.
2. Leviticus *Rabbah* 1:3, in Devora Steinmetz, "A Rabbinic Portrait of Miriam," *Prooftexts*, 1998, p. 56-7.

"IF THERE BE A PROPHET . . ."
Rebecca Schwartz

Feminist scholars have long turned to Numbers 12 searching for clues to the apparent injustice of Miriam's punishment. Questions abound: What did Miriam say to Moses? What did Tzipporah have to do with it? Was Aaron equally involved, and if so, why is Miriam alone punished? To explore these questions, I propose a different view of Numbers 12. Rather than moral weakness, we will see that Miriam might instead be demonstrating remarkable strength and courage as an advocate for the diminishing religious rights of women. What can we glean by reading between the lines? Let us begin with the text itself.

Numbers 12
And Miriam and Aaron spoke with Moses about the Cushite wife that he had married, because he had married a Cushite woman. And they said, "Is it only with Moses that God has spoken, has not God also spoken with us?" And God heard. And the man Moses was more humble than any other man, on the face of the earth. And God said suddenly to Moses and to Aaron and to Miriam, "Go out, you three, to the Tent of Meeting," and the three of them went out.

And God came down in a pillar of cloud and stood at the opening of the Tent. And he called "Aaron and Miriam," and the two of them went out. And he said, "Hear now my words: If there be a prophet among you, in a vision I will reveal myself, in a dream I will speak with him. Not so with my servant Moses. In all my house he is trusted, mouth to mouth I speak with him, with clear vision and not in riddles. Why did you not stand in reverence to speak with my servant, with Moses?" And God burned even more in them, and he left. The cloud departed from the tent and behold—

Miriam had *tzara'at* like snow. Aaron turned to Miriam and behold she had *tzara'at*.

Aaron said to Moses, "Please my lord, do not place sin on us for that which we have undertaken, if we have sinned. Do not let her be like one that comes forth from his mother's womb dead with half his flesh eaten."

And Moses cried out to God, saying, "Please God, please heal her."

And God said to Moses, "And if her father is spitting in her face, would she not be ashamed seven days? She will be shut outside the camp seven days and after brought back in."

And Miriam was shut outside the camp seven days and the people did not journey until Miriam was brought back in.[1]

Traditional Commentaries

By reviewing existing theories about this chapter we can trace the development of how such biblical passages have traditionally been read. One viewpoint holds that Miriam objected to Tzipporah's ethnicity, inferred by the reference to her origins as Cushite, or East African. Some say Miriam objected to the interfaith aspect of Moses and Tzipporah's marriage—a more plausible interpretation. However, I believe we can easily rule this out as well. Despite Judaism's strong preference for endogamy (in-group marriage), the "foreign wife" has been presented as an exemplary ancestress too many times. Beginning with Genesis we see Tamar, a Canaanite woman, held up as more righteous than Judah for following the Hebrew custom of the levirate marriage (Gen 38). Later the Book of Ruth appears as the classic tale of the non-Israelite woman who demonstrates her loyalty to the Hebrew God and community. Indeed, Tzipporah's own quick action (Ex 4:24-26) to circumcise her son in keeping with Israelite custom when Moses had neglected to do so speaks to her willingness as a "convert."

A common and accepted interpretation of this passage suggests that Miriam was punished for slander. The *halachic* position on *lashon ha'ra* (gossip or speaking ill about another) is unequivocal: to destroy a person's reputation is tantamount to murder (Lev *Rabbah* 26:2). If Miriam has indeed been guilty of slander then the punishment is well deserved. But if so, why Aaron's exemption? And do we really know that Miriam committed an act of gossip? The text says merely, "And Miriam and Aaron spoke with Moses about the Cushite wife that he had married . . . " We do not know that Miriam's comments about Tzipporah were critical in any way. In fact, we have even more reason to believe they were not.

Many commentators (including Rashi) have read this text with the view that Miriam spoke not *against* Moses' wife, but rather *on her behalf*. The rabbis viewed this passage as confirmation that Moses held himself physically apart from his wife at all times to remain ritually pure for contact with God. This is a logical supposition, since we know that to God's instruction at Mount Sinai "Be ready for the third day," Moses added a warning of his own: "Go not near a woman." Aside from the larger problem that Moses seems to be addressing only men here,[2] we can infer that to Moses the preparation to face God meant not touching a woman. Many have believed that he therefore refrained from sexual relations with his wife at all times. Miriam's complaint, then, on behalf of her sister-in-law, was to advocate for Tzipporah's conjugal rights. Traditional commentary still manages to put a negative twist on this version, claiming that Miriam and Aaron complained that Moses was being "too holy," since they did not need to keep apart from their own spouses. This is pure conjecture, of course, since the actual text nowhere mentions a husband for Miriam, or any comparison between them in the matter of marriage. Whether positive or negative, this possibility is at least consistent, and can be seen as paralleling Miriam's childhood attempt to reunite her father with his own wife and children following their separation. Indeed, Miriam is credited in the Talmud with reuniting all the Jewish men with their wives.[3] The rabbinic midrash states that Miriam called upon her father to perform his duties as a husband and father, to remarry his wife and produce children. By now trying to bring Moses and Tzipporah together in the marriage bed, Miriam advocates twice for family togetherness.

A New Perspective

But can we take this view, that Miriam spoke with Moses about the status of his sexual relationship with Tzipporah, currently accepted by mainstream scholars as a valid interpretation, yet one step further? Could Miriam have been confronting Moses about more than Tzipporah's sexual rights? We can posit that Tzipporah may well have been a priestess in her home nation of Midian. Briefly, what evidence do we have of this? Jethro, her father, served as the priest in Midian (Ex 3:1). We also look again to Tzipporah's circumcision of their son Gershom, during which she performs a ritual or cultic act involving a mysterious intercession with God, thereby saving Moses' life (Ex 4:24-26). Without digressing too far, we can legitimately propose the possibility that Tzipporah held some sort of cultic status, either in her own right, or as a result of her marriage to Moses. The text, oddly, reminds us twice in Numbers 12 that Moses has married a "Cushite woman." Since it remains unlikely that her national or ethnic origins formed the crux of the issue, why else is this significant? Did women of that region hold religious office, as did many women in surrounding communities during that era, a fact that would have been known to readers of the time? According to scholar Rita Burns, "Miriam belonged to a world where women commonly held positions which were priestly in character."[4] The text is unclear, but reading it fresh, without the echo of prior interpretations, we can find the possibility, even the likelihood, that Miriam is advocating for Tzipporah's *religious* rights.

Continuing along this road, could Miriam's challenge have wider implications than just her sister-in-law's marriage or even her religious status? Since the text offers no hint of any personal conflict between Miriam and Tzipporah, or between Miriam and any other wife of Moses, it seems logical that Miriam is raising a public issue and not a private one. We know from rabbinic teaching that Miriam served as an advocate for and leader of all the Israelite women. As a child she challenged Amram and the other men to remarry their divorced wives, in order to allow for the birth of baby girls.[5] She led the women in song and dance at the crossing of the Sea (Ex 15:20), and during her seven days of exile the entire community waited for her return before continuing the journey. The women respected and followed Miriam. Was she representing here the interests of the larger female community? As early as 1895 Elizabeth Cady Stanton noted that:

> In this narrative we see early woman's desire to take some part in government, though denied all share in its honor and dignity. Miriam, no doubt, saw the humiliating distinctions of sex in the Mosaic code and customs, and longed for the power to make the needed amendments.[6]

Stanton's suggestion remains just as plausible today, and we can look closely at the surrounding biblical passages to determine which amendments Miriam might have found necessary to implement.

One startling issue that comes into play just a few chapters earlier in the text is the trial of the *sotah*. Numbers 5 details an unusual ritual in which a husband who suspects his wife of infidelity but has no proof may take her to the priest at the temple. There she will be ordered to drink a bizarre concoction of dust from the temple floor and holy writings known as the "bitter waters." If the wife is guilty, the waters will cause her "loins to fall and belly to swell up"(Num 5:21), but if she is innocent she will suffer no ill consequence. Considering the closeness of the *sotah* discussion's placement in the text (seven chapters earlier) and the linguistic connection between drinking of "bitter waters" (*mei ha'marim*) and Miriam's name *(mar yam*—"bitter sea" or "bitter water")* we cannot ignore the issue entirely. Was Miriam really demanding female input into how wives were treated by their husbands? We have no reason to imagine that Tzipporah had anything to do with the *sotah* issue personally (there is no hint in the text that she was ever suspected of adultery). Perhaps Miriam had more than one reason to challenge Moses' authority; or else Tzipporah was a later excuse put in to diminish Miriam's cultic or religious role in the community.

Why else can we prefer this new interpretation? Immediately following the text's notice that Miriam spoke concerning Tzipporah, we read her question, "Has God indeed spoken only through Moses . . ." The fundamental issue here now has nothing to do with wives, Cushite or otherwise, but with the right to receive, interpret, and pass on the word of God. The fact that Miriam and Aaron join in the challenge adds weight to this theory. Miriam is commonly cited by the text as the sister of Aaron—putting her on a par with the high priest! Sisterhood in the ancient

Near East implies a higher or more nearly equal status for a woman than other family relationships.[7] By calling Miriam "the sister of Aaron" (Ex 15:20), the text informs us that she has a close relationship to the high priest, with a high status of her own. Let us take a moment to look at the institution of the priesthood at this time in Israel's early history. As the high priest of Israel, Aaron would be recognized as an intercessor for the divine word. The Levites were chosen from the other tribes (Num 8) for special priestly status, a very recent development coming closely before the passage in question. Might non-Levite religious leaders have taken offense at their sudden exclusion? Despite Moses' own cry, "Would that all the people could be God's prophets; would that God would put his spirit on all of them!"(Num 11:29) just a few lines earlier, this was clearly not to be the case. Immediately following our passage, the Korach rebellion and the distinction between the priestly duties of the "sons of Aaron" and the rest of the Levites come to pass. Religious leadership is limited to an increasingly narrow body.

Additionally, we must look specifically to the historic role of women in the Israelite priesthood. According to historian Susan Niditch, "That other threads in the tradition allowed for women priests is possible and even probable. . . ." [8] By sifting through the biblical text, what hints can we find that survived the editing process to support this view and highlight Miriam's role? We begin with the first mention of Miriam by name: at the Song of the Sea. Miriam's victory hymn at the sea, her dance and timbrel playing all reflect a cultic role in Israelite religion. Song, dance, and drum-beating by women appear in several places in the text (Jgs 11:34 ; 1 Sam 18:6), and in this instance mark a celebration of Israel's God as the Divine Warrior, in a specifically cultic or religious ritual and not merely in a spontaneous celebration. According to Burns, "The dance is not merely an aesthetic pursuit . . . it is the service of the god . . ." [9] Furthermore, if priestesses in the ancient Near East did not marry or bear children,[10] this is yet one more clue leading us to think of Miriam as a possible priestess. Otherwise, her status as unattached (in the text, if not in midrash) stands out as most unusual for a biblical woman. Carol Meyers cites the example of the women attendants at the Tent of Meeting (Ex 38) along with later references to women associated with oracular centers to conclude that women served a divinatory role in shrines in ancient Israel.[11] Other scholars have noted that since women commonly held priestly roles in surrounding cultures, it is likely that Miriam and other women may have in fact been priestesses, and their title changed to "prophetess" by later editors.[12] No Hebrew word for priestess (*kohenet*) survives, so if such a role in fact once existed it may have disappeared with the consolidation of religious power in the hands of the Levites, or at some point during the monarchy. Any trace of this tradition would have later been suppressed by the redactors of the Bible, just as they tried to suppress vestiges of idol worship and other traditions that were later condemned, or of which they disapproved. According to biblical historian Norman Gottwald, "It may be that the Miriam incident reflects a move for greater power by women within the confederacy."[13] Miriam, whose very name carries the whisper of rebellion,[14] speaks for fundamental issues going to the heart of the spiritual future of Israel. Has God, then, indeed spoken only through Moses?

The text informs us that God called to all three siblings, and the rabbis assure us that God spoke simultaneously, equally to all three when calling them into the Tent of Meeting, the holy place. [15] Miriam was not asked to wait outside during the divine conference, or called in after Moses and Aaron. God continues, saying, "If there be a *prophet* among you . . ." (emphasis mine). The Talmud clearly states that Miriam indeed received prophecy from God from the time that she was a small child. Exodus 15:20 directly names her *nevi'ah*, prophetess. So God's opening, "If there be a prophet . . ." is not a denial of Miriam and Aaron's challenge. We *know* there is a prophet among them, and she is Miriam. God seems to differentiate between prophecy, hearing God's voice in a dream, and face-to-face communication with Moses, such as atop Mount Sinai or at the burning bush. Moses is still God's chosen mouthpiece, but this does not mean that Miriam is not a prophet. The text undeniably names her so, and neither God nor Moses denies it here. Miriam is challenging Moses for some very powerful authority: the right to speak to the people on behalf of God.

Punishment vs. Reward

By most accepted interpretations, Miriam's challenge to Moses could not be allowed to go unpunished. Miriam is chastised more severely than Aaron for what was primarily a joint complaint. We cannot overlook an obvious reason for her more severe punishment. According to Cheryl Exum,[15] Miriam's claim threatens male hegemony, and her exclusion from the camp symbolizes woman's role as outsider in the power structure. Aaron poses no significant challenge to the symbolic order, and he remains within the camp. A woman challenging a man's leadership is more dangerous to the status quo than a conflict between two men, between equals. However, this has not always been so. Let's look for a moment at the rather common early biblical theme of female challenges to male authority. When women challenge men or male authority in the Torah, whether openly or through deceit, they frequently succeed, and do so with divine blessing. God tells Abraham to hearken to Sarah's voice when conflict arises over Hagar and the child she shares with Abraham (Gen

21:12). Rebekah deceives Isaac and causes him to bless their younger son, Jacob, instead of Esau as he had intended (Gen 27). A serious transgression indeed, but implemented as the outcome of her own divine revelation that "the elder shall serve the younger" (Gen 25:23). Tamar challenges her father-in-law Judah by impregnating herself with his child to chastise him for not following the levirate marriage custom (Gen 38) and she is proven worthy and righteous for doing so. Miriam herself successfully challenges authority throughout the text, beginning with her own father and his decision to lead the men in divorcing their wives, and soon thereafter by approaching the princess of Egypt to offer Yocheved as nursemaid to the baby Moses. When Miriam challenges Moses, the text implies she not only loses the challenge but also is punished for it. But the Torah honors the wisdom of women in its own way. A few feminist commentators have begun to hint that perhaps Miriam's "punishment" was in fact a later interpretation of the meaning of her separation from the traveling camp.

If we continue with our current presumptions, that Miriam served as priestess or prophetess to the Israelites, and that her challenge to Moses demanded recognition of that status, then we must see a different outcome than that usually found in traditional readings of Numbers 12. What if Miriam was not, in fact, punished at all? What if something else entirely is going on? Abraham and Sarah were told to leave their land to follow God; Rebekah left her family to enter the covenant as Isaac's bride; Jacob left his home to become Yisrael. In the tradition of her ancestors, Miriam is called forth to leave the security of home and family, ordered by divine will into the desert. Did God indeed speak to Miriam when she was alone, separated from her people? The text names her prophetess, *nevi'ah*, but nowhere in the biblical writing is she credited with actual prophecy. The rabbis assign much prophetic insight to her, most particularly the foretelling of Moses' birth. Could the tradition of Miriam as a prophet have originated with this passage from Numbers 12? Did God call Miriam out to the wilderness to speak to her?

The text calls Miriam leprous, using the Hebrew word *tzara'at*. The same term, the same form of leprosy, is used during Moses' conversation with God at the burning bush (Ex 4:7). When speaking to Moses for the first time, God chooses a physical sign, a transformation of the skin's outward appearance, as a symbol of divine communication. God chooses *tzara'at*. When Moses' hand turns white with leprosy, God is not punishing him, but choosing him for a special purpose. The physical change proves to his disbelieving eyes (and is intended to be a sign proving Moses' worthiness to the Israelites) that divine forces are at work in him. Why should it be impossible to believe that Miriam's *tzara'at* serves a similar purpose? The text states that Miriam's skin appears white *k'sheleg*, as snow. White or snow are metaphors for purity—could Miriam's *tzara'at* be an impurity that purifies? When Moses removes his hand from his robe at the burning bush, the text also notes that his *tzara'at* is *k'sheleg*, as snow. The book of Leviticus summarizes the laws concerning *tzara'at* and impurity: "If the *tzara'at* covers the entire skin . . . (the Kohen) shall declare the affliction to be pure; having turned completely white, it is pure (Lev 13:12-17). Miriam's skin is white as snow. If she is therefore purified and not impure, why her seclusion from the camp? We know she is a prophet and receives divine inspiration. The incident described in Numbers 12 initiates and validates that status. Seven days of separation for purification also remind us of the consecration of Aaron and his sons as priests, when they are instructed to remain secluded for seven days before their inauguration as *kohanim* (Lev 8). Was this then Miriam's consecration as a *kohenet*, a priest?

Most translations render Numbers 12:9 as "The wrath of God flared up against them." But the verb stem *charah* can be translated to mean simply "to burn or be kindled." The interpretation of God burning with anger is up to those who perceive anger within the context of this story. This sentence just as easily reads that "God was kindled more within them." If the spirit of God is kindled within Miriam following the declaration "If there be a prophet among you . . ." then clearly we are not reading about punishment. The "kindling of God" within Miriam seems to imply that she is receiving divine communication of some sort. The spirit of God burns within Miriam, and her skin glows pure white. Interestingly, the identical phrase, *"vayichar-af,"* appears immediately following Moses' leprosy of the hand as God appoints him to be the redeemer of the Hebrew nation (Ex 4:14). Also traditionally translated as "the wrath of God," here too we might interpret the phrase differently. [16]

Continuing with the text, the words "And if her father is spitting in her face would she not be ashamed seven days?" are problematic. Some scholars have suggested that two separate traditions come together here: one involving Miriam and Moses' Cushite wife, and a second tradition involving the struggle for oracular authority concerning the divine word. [17] Perhaps in this line we can also hear an echo of the midrashic story of Miriam's prophecy regarding Moses' birth, when her father hit her on the head as Moses was cast into the Nile. The Talmud teaches that Miriam's father praised her when she foretold of the liberator Moses' impending birth, but chastised her and hit her on the head when her prophecy seemed to fail with the casting out of the child onto the river. [18] Now Miriam is again justifying her prophecy—this time to Moses himself.

Aaron's plea, "Let her not be like one from the mother's womb . . ." continues the theme of childbirth found throughout the Exodus story and Miriam's life. Midwifery, deliverance, care for born and unborn generations; these are the overarching themes of Miriam's life. The image of stillbirth in this passage supports yet reverses this theme. By using the childbirth metaphor, Aaron recognizes Miriam's role as spiritual, if not literal, midwife to the Hebrews. Does Numbers 12 reflect a woman punished for speaking out of turn, or the consecration of a healer, midwife, and prophet as a priestess of Yahweh? Rabbinic midrash teaches that it was God, not Aaron or Moses, who declared Miriam once again ritually clean after the passing of the seven days of isolation.[19] God has indeed spoken to Miriam.

Conclusion

The final sentence of our text contains the carefully noted observation that the Israelites would not continue on their way to the Promised Land until Miriam had joined them again. The people for whom she spoke, the voices she represented, these remained loyal to her. Miriam the prophet went out into the desert to speak with God. What passed between God and Miriam during those seven days in the desert, however, must be left to the midrashists, for the text offers no more clues to follow.

We now read the entire story of Numbers 12 quite differently. From the rabbis' use of this tale to condemn Miriam and in fact all women as gossips (Deut *Rabbah* 6:11), we now have evidence pointing us toward a lost tradition of women as prophets and priests. Letting go of long-held images and interpretations of familiar biblical passages is never easy. But if ever a particular chapter cried out for review, it must be this one. Looking with fresh eyes and a feminist consciousness, suspending what we have always been told to be true, we see new and exciting implications arise from the ancient and esoteric texts of our ancestors. Miriam's rebellion may represent the last stand of disenfranchised Hebrew priestesses clinging to their way of life as a new hierarchy rose to power.

One remaining question: If this story reflects such a dangerous move for power by Israelite women that it needed to be altered, edited and reinterpreted, why has it survived at all? If we take the entire story literally, as the received word of God, then our concern is with the meaning of these events as they transpired. But if we read the Bible as the collective mythology of our people, written and shaped to transmit a culture, to teach ideas, to warn or inspire, then we must look one step further. As legends pass from generation to generation, embedded in the consciousness of an evolving society, the names and details change while the core of the story lives on. Despite the need to punish Miriam for her forthrightness, despite the danger of her claim, Miriam's story lives on. The real power of Miriam the prophet and the story of her rebellion is found in the fact that it has survived at all, even if turned on its head. But we can go back in time, to follow the instruction of the Haggadah, and "tell the story from the beginning."

NOTES

1. Translation mine, from the (massoretic) Hebrew, *The Stone Edition*, Mesorah Publications, 1996. All textual translations in this essay are the author's, unless otherwise noted.

2. See Judith Plaskow, *Standing Again at Sinai* (San Francisco: Harper & Row, 1990).

3. BT *Sotah*, 12a; also Ex *Rabbah* 1:13.

4. Rita Burns, *Has the Lord Indeed spoken only through Moses* (Atlanta: Scholars Press, 1987), page 98.

5. *Sotah* 12a.

6. Elizabeth Cady Stanton, *The Woman's Bible* (Boston: Northeastern University Press, 1993), p. 102

7. Savina Teubal, *Sarah the Priestess* (Ohio: Swallow Press, 1984), page 13.

8. Susan Niditch, Ancient Israelite Religion (Oxford University Press, 1997), page 91.

9. Burns, page 30.

10. Teubal, p. 78.

11. Carol Meyers, *Discovering Eve: Ancient Israelite Women in Context* (New York: Oxford University Press, 1988), page 160.

12. Carol Newsom and Sharon Ringe, eds. *The Women's Bible Commentary* (London: Westminster/John Knox Press, 1992).

13. Norman Gottwald, *The Hebrew Bible* (Philadelphia: Fortress Press, 1989), page 226.

14. The Hebrew word for rebels, *'morim,'* carries a linguistic similarity to Miriam's name.

15. Cheryl Exum, "Second Thoughts," in *Feminist Companion to Exodus-Deuteronomy*, ed. Athalya Brenner (Sheffield Academic Press, 1994), page 86.

16. *Dictionary of Biblical Hebrew*, Toyozo Nakarai (Philadelphia, Bookman Associates, 1951). There is some discrepancy between dictionaries for the phrase *"vayichar-af."* Most Biblical and modern dictionaries define the verb stem for *vayichar* as implying anger or wrath, or burning with anger. Only the above cited dictionary defined the term to mean *only* burn or kindle, without reference to anger. The word *"af,"* generally translated in modern Hebrew to mean 'nose,' in Biblical Hebrew generally means 'increasingly' or 'more so.' Admittedly, the joint phrase *"vayichar-af"* appears elsewhere in the text where it can only reasonably mean the wrath of God; see for example Numbers 32:13, as God condemns Israel to wander for forty years in the desert. It remains the most likely explanation that two separate traditions have been pasted together here by the redactors to change the tone of the orignial story.

17. Burns, 72

18. BT *Sotah* 12b-13a.

19. Deut *Rabbah* 6:9

THE NAMES OF MIRIAM
Jill Hammer

"You are known by many names. You received the
name Chelah when you fell ill (*cholah*) after marrying Caleb and
giving birth to Hur, the name Azuvah when Caleb deserted (*azov
otah*) you during your illness; Naarah when you regained your
health, became like a young woman (*na'arah*) again, and were
taken back by your husband; Yiriot because your face was like
the curtains (*yiriot*) of the Tabernacle; Efrat because Israel was
fruitful (*paru*) thanks to you; Zeret, because you rivaled (*tzarah*)
all other women; Tzohar because your face was as clear as noon
(*tzaharayim*); Etnan because all who saw you brought gifts
(*etnan*), and Akharhel, because all the women went out after you
with timbrels and dances (*akhar hol*)."
Ellen Frankel, *Five Books of Miriam*, p.113,
adapted from *Sotah 12a*.

ॐ

When I was born
I was Miriam,
beloved, bitter, rebel,
beloved in bitter times,
rebel against Pharaoh.
I was a stubborn toddler.
I did not want to be changed.

In my mother's home
I was the fruitful one.
My parents' bodies
lay separate, unfulfilled,
enslaved and frightened.
I sang to them my dreams:
the child that would come,
his fontanel pulsing with light.

When he was born,
I whispered him to sleep.
I packed a basket
with the seed of our redemption
and planted it by the water.

In the homes of Israelite women,
I was the blower of breath,
midwife at the birth,
hands ready
beneath the open womb.
I sang to mothers of trees,
of fragrant apple blossoms,
fresh, luxuriant, countless,
popping out into sunlight.
I wandered the caves of their longing.
When our enemies came hunting,
I blew them away.

At the shore of the sea, I was the one
they dance after.
I moved among the women
like the first wind moving on the water.
I was the antelope on the cliff,
the whirlwind descent of the sabbath,
the desert lightning.
I was the eye of the hurricane,
a galaxy of red and yellow skirts
spinning around me.
In my limbs was an alphabet of freedom.
When I stopped dancing, the people
had forgotten the word for slave.

At Mount Sinai,
God saw me and gave the Torah.
I was open to its first sound

as women are to first lovers.
At the middle, I became inventive,
climbing the crowns of the letters.
I smiled at the last utterance
as at an old beloved
who falls asleep while talking.
I pressed my fingers
into the hot sand of truth
and said yes.

In the Tabernacle, I was
the curtain-weaver.
I sat among the women spinning thread
to embroider tapestries with golden cherubim.
Together, we hemmed the Torah with silver bells
and pomegranates. I taught them to embroider
stories along the edges of the camp, to weave
tendrils of their mothers into the tentflaps.
While smiths made silver trumpets to summon wars,
we rooted the camp in two worlds.
Our stories spread, like tangled wisteria vines,
in ways we never expected.

One morning I grew into my rebellion.
As suddenly as night crowds over the ocean,
I became the one who rivaled Moses,
who demanded a place for my own prophecy.
When the God of Moses struck me down,
called me destroyer, demon, faithless daughter,
then I was the one who is lovesick,
who pants after justice.
I was sent outside the camp.
For seven days and nights,
I argued with God.

I was the abandoned one,
the one who walks where others do not look,
in places where bellies are swollen and books are locked,
in rooms where darkness has a footstool. I cannot say
I was not afraid, but I kept walking.
One morning I found my own God, her swollen belly
about to burst like milkweed. I reached out my hands
and a bird flew into my eyes. Turning, I saw empty pots
at my feet, children playing, the camp's well of water
brimming in the distance.

So I became a young girl again,
enchanted by seedlings and danger.
I gave birth to a daughter. I fell into time
again and found it sweet. When I passed in the street,
my cloak refused to be invisible.
I fed the nestlings I found in the underbrush
and I ground nuts for ink. I learned to heal
what had been wounded, replace what had been lost.

Now, at Kadesh, the holy place,
I have reached the day of my death.
I am radiant as noontime.
My light weaves and dances
like a flame floating in a cup.
I am waiting for the voice
as still as a pond.
What will you call me, God
of many names?

NARROW PLACES & OUTSTRETCHED ARMS
Aliza Shapiro

I tend to read *Tanach* (the Bible) as if I were watching a dance. I see the movement. In the book of Exodus, I am intrigued by a series of actions by women. This series is a high density appearance of the action "she took."[1] The very first taking by a woman in Tanach is Eve's taking of the fruit of the Tree.[2] What will transpire due to the takings of Exodus?

Before we delve in, let us set the stage. Movement occurs within a context. And significant movement is significant only in relation to the space in which it occurs. When the book of Exodus opens, the Children of Israel are in Egypt. The Hebrew word for Egypt, *Mitzrayim*, literally means "narrow places." In Egypt, the Children of Israel are fruitful, increasing abundantly, multiplying, and growing exceedingly mighty. They are filling the land. Pharaoh limits, presses, squeezes, and confines the Children of Israel through slavery. Through bondage he narrows their existence. And when this is not effective, Pharaoh attempts to diminish this population even more by charging that every son born "you shall cast into the River . . ."[3] Meanwhile, the Children of Israel are continuing to multiply, filling the land. The tension between Pharaoh's narrowing and the Children of Israel's expanding comes to a head.

With this setting of epic proportion, the narrative focuses on the response of a single woman. It is here that we first see a woman in Exodus take. The first segment of the story follows:

> And there was a man of the house of Levi,
> and took to wife a daughter of Levi. And

the woman [Yocheved] conceived, and bore a son: and when she saw that he was a goodly child, she hid him three months. And when she could no longer hide him, she <u>took</u> for him a box made of papyrus, and daubed it with slime and with pitch, and put the child in it: and she laid it in the rushes by the River's brink.   (Ex 2:1-3)

I often wonder at Yocheved's pivotal taking action. I imagine Yocheved watching her baby boy growing under Pharaoh's decree. What did she feel? How long was that papyrus box sitting there, near her, within reach? For how long had she glanced at it? A month? Three days? An afternoon? Perhaps she didn't even see it until that crucial moment. Suddenly the box, a piece of scenery in Pharaoh's narrow scheme became an instrument in her own scheme. Yocheved took the box and took the story line. And the story line broadened a bit, to one of possibility, no matter how slim.

Rather than allowing the context to dictate her actions, Yocheved altered it. And her action-taking seems to invite the coordination of others. We see this broadening of participation in the next segment of the story, with the next taking. For while Moses is living, he is quite vulnerable as he floats down the River. Again, our chances for redemption might have ended here, were it not for a woman's taking.

And [Moses'] sister [Miriam] stood afar off, to know what would be done to him. And the daughter of Pharaoh came down to wash herself at the River; and her maidens walked along by the River's side; and when she saw the box among the rushes, she sent her maid to <u>take</u> it. And when she had opened it, she saw the child: and behold, a weeping boy. And she had compassion on him, and said, This is one of the Hebrews' children.   (Ex 2:4-6)

The future of Moses and of the Children of Israel again pivoted on the taking of a woman. I keep wondering at this taking of Pharaoh's daughter (through her maid). She extended herself beyond the restrictions of the law, and indeed of her own father. I am reminded that narrowness is not just imposed by law, but also by family.

Back in our story, we are at a standstill. Moses could be murdered immediately. He could be adopted into the palace with no connection to his Hebrew home. Either way, the Children of Israel would have continued as slaves. Again, the narrative shifts through a woman's taking:

Then said his sister [Miriam] to Pharaoh's daughter, Shall I go and call thee a nurse of the Hebrew women, that she may nurse the child for thee? And Pharaoh's daughter said to her, Go. And the maid went and called the child's mother. And Pharaoh's daughter said to her, Take this child away and nurse it for me, and I will give thee thy wages. And the woman <u>took</u> the child, and nursed it. And the child grew, and she brought him to Pharaoh's daughter, and he became her son. And she called his name Moses.
(Ex 2:7-10)

Yocheved takes Moses to her bosom. Her personal space now houses a duet between herself and Moses. Her intimate realm has expanded.

This whirlwind of takings within a mere nine verses stuns me. Perhaps I am so struck because I pause to wonder at what it took for each woman to transform her self, and to transform her space. There is a traditional midrash in which the rabbis offer us some insight. Rooted in an idiosyncrasy in the Hebrew for "she sent her maid," the rabbis are split on whether Pharaoh's daughter sent forth her maid, or her own hand. From those who taught she sent her own hand we learn: "[She] now proceeded to do her own will. She stretched forth her arm, and although the ark was swimming at a distance of sixty ells, she succeeded in grasping it, because her arm was lengthened miraculously."[4]

This fantastic stretching teaches us about what is involved, essentially, in taking. To take, one must first stretch one's own self. One must first risk. One must reach past an edge and perhaps lose some balance. This is true whether one takes with her own hand or whether one sends an emissary to do it. This is true whether one is stretching sixty ells toward a foreign floating basket or six inches toward one's own papyrus basket. This is true for me and you stretching toward the people and things in our own lives that inhabit the space of our lives.

It may be interesting to note the rabbis' associations with Pharaoh's daughter's stretching action. *Midrash Hagadol*, a classic compilation of midrash, links this story to one from the Book of Esther. There, Esther finds favor with King Ahashuarus. And he in turn "held out . . . the golden scepter that was in his hand." In the midrash, the rabbis teach that the golden scepter miraculously lengthened.

This association of lengthenings lends Pharaoh's daughter vigor, potency, and lustiness. But I must say here that with Pharaoh's daughter, these qualities are strengthened by yet another. Pharaoh's daughter played a different role in her story than the King did in his. In

Pharaoh's daughter we witness a woman who has the gumption to be vigorous, potent, and lusty. We witness a woman who, in the midst of a confining edict, extends her hand.

The ability to extend oneself even within the narrow places may be one of the great struggles of humankind. At times we all find ourselves in narrow places. Sometimes these narrow places are even self-imposed. Often the narrow places clarify our existential aloneness.

These women of Exodus, in their narrow places, had the presence and grace to take issue, take initiative, take the bull by the horns, take charge, take a minute, take up space, take a stand, take to heart. Taking, as a process of stretching, transforming oneself, and transforming one's space may in itself be an act of exodus. Our exodus may not only have been bestowed on us by a God with an outstretched arm, but also seized by women with outstretched arms. (Although the Hebrew terms for God's outstretched arm and for the women's outstretched arms are completely different, I must juxtapose them. I see the movements in duet, one commenting on the other.) [5]

We return to the narrative with Moses now physically safe, living among the Egyptians and nurtured by his own Hebrew mother. We have discussed the events that brought about these changes in physical reality. But physical changes can be connected to changes in another dimension.

Women's takings that altered the human-God connection began with Eve. "And when the woman saw that the tree was good for food, and that it was a delight to the eyes, and a tree to be desired to make one wise, she took of its fruit . . ." (Gen 3:6). In this taking, Eve forever severs the existing connection between humankind and

God. In Exodus, Tzipporah reestablishes a connection between the Children of Israel and God.

As Tzipporah, Moses and their sons set out toward Pharaoh a strange event happened: [6]

> And it came to pass on the way, in the place where they spent the night, that the Lord met him and sought to kill him. Then Tzipporah took a sharp stone, and cut off the foreskin of her son . . . (Ex 4:24)

The story continues with no slaying.

While this episode is problematic, one thing is clear. Tzipporah had taken it into her own hands to reestablish the mitzvah connection that Moses had neglected. It may be that this mitzvah connection established the Children of Israel as God's children, ready to be redeemed from bondage and to accept God's Torah.

By this point, Yocheved, Pharaoh's daughter and Tzipporah have structured a narrative that places Moses and the Children of Israel in position for redemption. And this is exactly what happens. The Children of Israel break out of their physical and spiritual narrow places. They move through the Sea of Reeds. They are birthed as a nation. They sing the Song at the Sea:

> And with the blast of thy nostrils the waters were piled up,
> The floods stood upright like a heap,
> And the depths were congealed in the heart of the sea.
> . . . Who is like you, O Lord . . .? (Ex 15)

In the immediacy of this grandness, the narrative again focuses on a single woman. This woman at this moment performs an utterly simple and clear action. We read, "... and <u>took</u> Miriam, the prophetess, sister of Aharon ..." (15:20).

What is this revisiting of "she took" at this moment of miracle? We are in the expanses now, and connected to God. What is this taking? It is about neither physical nor spiritual survival. Miriam is taking a timbrel to exalt and rejoice. This is a stretching out and a transforming within the expanses. How different it feels! How different it looks!

Yet this expansive taking is in no sense a solo. In this moment of miracle, the earlier takings are evoked. It is as if choreographically we are reminded that the gumption to take even within the narrow places may be part of the miracle. With the rhythm of the hand-drum, all the takings reverberate. Miriam echoes the earlier takings. And in turn, "all the women followed her with timbrels and with dances."

NOTES

1. 'She took' (*vatikach*) appears only seven times in Genesis and five times in Exodus. After Exodus, this verb in this form does not appear again in Torah. Women in Prophets then continue the transformative takings, for example: Rahav <u>taking</u> the spies in to hide them (Joshua 2:4), Yael <u>taking</u> a tent peg to drive into Sisera's temple (Judges 4:21) and Michal <u>taking</u> *teraphim*, enabling David to escape (I Samuel 19:13).
2. For more on this, see my article "On Choreographies of Taking from the Tree" in *Living Text* #6.
3. All translations are from the Koren edition of *The Holy Scriptures*. A few alterations, however, have been made. The spellings of some names have been changed. In one instance, "you" has been substituted for "thee." In one instance, "take" has been substituted for "fetch." In one instance, word order has been changed, and in the final sentence "followed" has been substituted for "went out after."
4. This translation is from Louis Ginzberg's *The Legends of the Jews* (Philadelphia, Jewish Publication Society, 1911).

5.   In the Passover Haggadah, we read that God brought us out of Egypt with a strong hand and an outstretched arm. Outstretched arm is *zroa n'tuyah*. The Torah depicts the daughter of Pharaoh as sending her maid with *vatishlach et amata*. The Rabbis discuss the lengthening of the daughter of Pharaoh's hand with the terms *na'aseh arucha* and *nimshcha v'nitmcha*.

6. For context, read Exodus 4:22-26.

PARASHAT BEHA'ALOTECHA: THE SILENCING OF MIRIAM
Ruth H. Sohn

"And Miriam and Aaron spoke against Moses because of the Cushite woman whom he had married; for he had married a Cushite woman."
(Numbers 12:1)

৵

Perhaps there is no woman from the Bible who inspires women today more than Miriam. Even more than any of the matriarchs, Miriam has been embraced and celebrated by Jewish women in Rosh Hodesh rituals, Miriam's cups at Seder tables, and in modern midrash, poetry, and song. The figure of Miriam standing at the Sea with timbrel in hand, leading the women in dance and song, is the most powerful image of her which the Torah presents. It suggests that Miriam was a true leader among the Israelites, a point supported in the text by the prophet Micah: ". . . I redeemed you from the house of bondage and I sent before you Moses, Aaron and Miriam" (Mi 6:4). Miriam's Well, which, according to traditional midrash, accompanied the Israelites through their desert wanderings, providing the Israelites with sorely needed water and, symbolically, spiritual sustenance, has continued to inspire Jews in both ritual and lore.[1] Yet Miriam is mentioned only five times in the Torah, with two of those references consisting of only a single verse. The longest narrative involving Miriam as a key figure comes at the end of our *parashah*. This is not the most well-known story about Miriam, largely because it is such a complex and troubling narrative. It is a narrative that leaves us with more questions than answers about who Miriam was and how her role among the Israelites— indeed how the role of women as a group—should be understood.

The opening verse of our story raises many questions, among which the first is, Who is this Cushite woman? It could be Tzipporah, the Midianite woman whom Moses had married years before, whose father is referred to earlier in our *parashah*. But perhaps this reference is to a second wife. Miriam and Aaron are upset, yet the text is not clear as to why. Was it because this was a foreign wife, or because she was a second wife? And finally, the verse begins with the verb *"vatedaber"* which means "she spoke," yet it is both Miriam and Aaron who speak out against Moses. The text grammatically implicates Miriam but not her brother. Why?

The second verse, rather than providing answers, only raises more questions. Numbers 12:2 continues, "They said 'Has Adonai spoken only through Moses? Has God not spoken through us as well?'" Here, it seems Miriam and Aaron are questioning Moses' position as the primary leader of the Israelites, rather than his choice of a spouse. It is as prophets that they compare themselves to Moses. They ask, rhetorically, whether they aren't also prophets. What is behind this challenge to Moses' authority? What grievance on Miriam and Aaron's part leads to these words? And how is this complaint related to the previous verse about the Cushite woman?

As the narrative continues to unfold, God responds in anger to Miriam and Aaron for daring to question Moses' singular role as prophet of Israel. God tells Miriam and Aaron that Moses is indeed in a category by himself as one who speaks to God directly, *peh el peh*, "mouth to mouth." But even God's response leads to more questions. Why is there no reference here or anywhere else in the chapter to the Cushite woman of verse one? God departs in anger and Miriam is stricken with *tzara'at*, a scaly white skin disease. Miriam is singled out for harsh punishment and ultimately shut out from the camp for seven days, but

Aaron is not punished at all. Again, we are forced to ask why?

Several modern scholars suggest that the apparent lack of connection between verses one and two may be explained by the fact that these opening verses are actually fragments of different traditions pieced together.[2] Some scholars also note that God's response in verses 6-8, which begins, "Hear now My words," is a distinct literary unit, more poetic in form, which might also have originated in a different context:[3]

> Hear now My words: When a prophet of God arises among you, I make Myself known to him in a vision, I speak with him in a dream. Not so with My servant Moses; he is trusted throughout My household. With him I speak mouth to mouth, plainly and not in riddles and he beholds the likeness of God. How then did you not shrink from speaking against My servant Moses!
>
> (Numbers 12:6-8)

This response from God never mentions Miriam or Aaron by name and could well have been uttered originally to a whole group of people. If we accept this theory of different textual traditions woven together, the murmuring against Moses and subsequent defense in this narrative may be evidence of a whole body of tradition that, in different ways, challenges Moses' behavior and exercise of power. These narrative fragments all question how other leaders and potential leaders were able to function alongside Moses. Set against the backdrop of our *parashah*, which begins with the consecration of the Levites and a delineation of their duties, and with the rebellion of Korach reported a few chapters later, Numbers 12 opens a window on the challenges threatening Moses' seemingly unchallenged, singular leadership.

How Moses exercised and shared leadership is in fact a subject treated more broadly in our *parashah*. At first reading, the Torah emphasizes Moses' humility and ability to share the stage with others. In Numbers 11, it is Moses who turns to God and asks that the burden of solitary leadership be eased. When God suggests that Moses delegate power and responsibility among seventy elders, Moses very willingly agrees. These elders begin to prophesy after God transfers some of the *ruach* (spirit) from Moses to them, and afterwards, two men, Eldad and Medad, remain prophesying in the camp. When Joshua and another young man run and report this to Moses in alarm, Moses responds, "Are you wrought up on my account? Would that all God's people were prophets, that God would put the Divine spirit upon them!" When others view Eldad's and Medad's behavior as a possible affront to their leader, Moses appears humble and ready to share leadership with as many others as would present themselves.

But Numbers 12 presents a more complex picture. On the one hand, we have the narrator's words, "Moses was a very humble man, more so than any other man on earth," immediately following Miriam and Aaron's complaints against Moses. These words support the previous chapters' description of Moses. And in Numbers 12 itself, it is not Moses who rebukes Miriam and Aaron, but God. Yet, on the other hand, in this same chapter, Miriam and Aaron question Moses' behavior and their own respective roles as prophets. When they do so, they are soundly rebuked by God and Miriam is singled out for harsh punishment. Were Miriam and Aaron forgetting their place and overstepping reasonable limits on their authority, or were they voicing legitimate complaints about Moses' exercise of power? Their complaints could well represent a larger faction of discontent. Perhaps the question of leadership among the Israelites during the wilderness period is more complex than we thought.

The punishment of Miriam stands out in particular as a challenge to the notion that anyone who was willing and worthy could lead. If Aaron rather than Miriam had spoken, would he have been punished in the same way? It is hard to escape the conclusion that it is as a woman challenging male authority that Miriam is so sharply rebuked and singled out for punishment. Miriam's punishment, in its severity, would have been a clear warning to her and to all other women to remember their place. God's sentence—the scaly white skin affliction and the requirement that Miriam be shut out of the camp for seven days—demanded that Miriam symbolically act out her own death. Aaron's words to Moses "let her not be as one dead," say no less. Miriam's words against Moses were, in a sense, her last. They are the last words we hear from her in the Torah. The next mention of Miriam is her death in Numbers 20.

Miriam's treatment in Numbers 12 is symbolic of her treatment in the Torah as a whole. The prophet Micah tells us that Miriam was a principal leader of the Israelites along with Moses and Aaron. Where in the Torah are the narratives that detail her leadership? Miriam was a prophetess, we learn in Exodus. Why, in the entire Torah, do we have not a single example of her prophecy? Miriam has been all but silenced and banished from the narrative. All we are left with is shards, fragments of a tale, hints of a reality we are left to ponder and dream.

Why was Miriam silenced? Was there conflict over Miriam's leadership in her own day? Were there Israelites who claimed her as their leader while others contested her right to lead? Perhaps she served as a leader of the women. The fact that the people would not move on without Miriam while she was healing from her skin ailment suggests that she had quite a loyal following.

Bible scholar Ilana Pardes suggests "[I]n Moses' day a woman with the gift of prophecy would have had to be silenced and then buried in the wilderness for daring to demand a central cultural position."4 According to Pardes, Moses and Miriam's world was not ready for a woman with the gift of prophecy. Miriam was silenced by the Israelites of her own time, who were unwilling to have a woman in such a high position.

But perhaps there is another explanation for Miriam's silence in the Torah. Perhaps in her own day Miriam *was* a prophet and leader, and it was later generations who, in retelling the tales, silenced Miriam and all but banished her from the text. Perhaps it was later generations who were not willing to have a woman with the gift of prophecy standing strong, inspiring the women of their own day to seek public roles and voice demands for themselves. This would better explain the shards, the fragments of the tale which we do have—the various references to Miriam as leader and prophet without the detailed narratives that would flesh out these claims. It would also explain Numbers 12, which cryptically suggests Miriam's fate in the Torah as a whole: a woman who did rise to power who was subsequently denied that power and silenced.

Where modern scholarship asks us to take a step back and view the Torah narrative from afar, traditional midrash invites us to jump into the text from a particular perspective. Both approaches seek to fill in the gaps in the Torah text—the questions which are raised by the text without apparent answers—through attention to the details in the text, and creative reconstruction; one from without and the other from within. We have explored some of the possibilities of looking at the text in new ways from without. Now let us reenter the text from the inside, with midrash as our guide.

One midrashic tradition identifies the Cushite woman of Numbers 12:1 as Tzipporah and maintains that Miriam's complaint in verse 1 about Moses' marriage to a Cushite woman is actually a complaint on behalf of Tzipporah, who had a serious grievance against her husband.[5] The starting point for this midrash is in the narrative immediately preceding our own, Numbers 11, where Eldad and Medad were discovered to be prophesying. When the young man ran and told Moses, Tzipporah said "Woe to the wives of those men!" When Miriam heard this she realized that Moses was neglecting Tzipporah, and she then spoke about the matter with Aaron.

Another midrash provides us with the details of the conversation that took place between Miriam and Aaron. "Miriam said, 'The Word was upon me but I did not keep away from my husband.' Aaron said, 'The Word was upon me but I did not keep away from my wife.'"[6] Miriam and Aaron question why Moses' role as a prophet exempts him from his duties as a husband. The midrashim further explain that it was because Miriam spoke *lashon hara*, gossip about Moses to Aaron, that she was punished, even though her intent was ultimately for the purpose of seeing him fulfill his duties to Tzipporah. Miriam should have known better, the midrashim seem to be saying. She should have acted as Tzipporah's advocate by taking the matter directly to Moses.

These midrashim artfully link the challenges raised in Numbers 12:1 and 12:2 about the Cushite woman and Moses' role as prophet compared to Miriam and Aaron's, which on first reading seem disjointed and unrelated. They also raise several issues of interest to women and feminists. First, these midrashim suggest that Miriam may have occasionally or regularly acted as an advocate for other women. It is not hard to imagine that Miriam's particular leadership role was as a leader of the Israelite women. Exodus 15, where Miriam leads the women in song and dance, suggests the same. As a leader of women, Miriam would have played a major role during the desert wanderings.

Second, with the suggestion that Moses, in fulfilling his responsibilities as a prophet neglected his wife Tzipporah, these midrashim raise the question of how an intense spiritual life can coexist with an intimate relationship with another human being. Do these two relationships enhance one another or are they in tension? What is the relationship between sexuality and spirituality? Many traditions, including our own, are ambivalent about bringing the two together. From the separation of men and women at Sinai to the traditional separation of men and women in Jewish prayer settings, a sense of the conflict between sexuality and spirituality has been expressed through the ages. Some other religious traditions require celibacy of their most devoted members, those who will be dedicating themselves most fully to a relationship with God. Is this how we can explain Moses' behavior and God's defense of him? Did Moses' role as prophet demand that he be "on call" for God and preclude any other intimate relationship, particularly a sexual one? Or did the intensity of his relationship with God lead Moses away from full engagement with people? Even if this was required of Moses, is it required of the rest of us? We ought to be cultivating a spiritual life that leads us back into life, back into deeper relationships with others.

The two approaches, looking at the text from without and within, utilizing the tools of critical scholarship and traditional midrash, both yield rich insights. We need not choose between them, but we can weave together the insights we gain from the two approaches. We mourn for the Miriam who was silenced and banished in Numbers 12 and from the Torah generally. Our anger and sense of loss is real. But so too is the inspiration we draw from this woman who had to struggle and still struggles to be heard. Miriam of the Torah and the midrash invites us to be prophets ourselves, to speak from the heart of our own visions and dreams. She invites us to be our sisters' advocates and to be direct in our advocacy, not to get sidetracked in simply ventilating our grievances to other parties. Finally, the figure of Miriam urges us to be brave enough to raise those issues that are of vital concern to women and men today, but about which no one seems willing to speak.

Miriam's banishment and silence stand out in stark relief against a textual tradition that puts so much emphasis on words. Who was Miriam? What words did she speak to the women of her day, to the men of her day, and to God? What would her words from so long ago say to us today if they had been preserved? The figure of Miriam calls out to women today to bring forth her voice in poetry, midrash, dance and song.

NOTES

1. See for example *Sifrei Bamidbar* #106, *Mekhilta d'Rabbi Ishmael, VaYassa Parashah* 5, Babylonian Talmud Shabbat 35a.

2. See for example, the ideas of George Coats, W.R. Smith and M. Noth as discussed by Rita Burns in her published dissertation, *Has the Lord Indeed Spoken Only Through Moses? A Study of the Biblical Portrait of Miriam* (Atlanta: Scholars Press, 1987) pp.61-71.

3. Rita Burns, pp. 51-61.

4. Ilana Pardes, *Countertraditions in the Bible: A Feminist Approach* (Cambridge, Massachusetts: Harvard University Press, 1992) p.10.

5. *Sifrei Bamidbar* #99, *Tanhuma Tsav* 13 and *Avot d'Rabbi Natan* A.9 for example.

6. *Avot d'Rabbi Natan* A.9

SISTER MIRIAM THE LEPER
Ita Sheres & Anne. K. Blau

Miriam, the "sister" of Moses and Aaron and the "prophetess" of the song of the sea (Ex 15), is a named woman in a text that often avoids naming women or giving a voice to the few named. Her voice is discovered to be joyous, celebratory and influential. Other women join her as she leads the singing and dancing. Miriam's voice can also be problematic when it both complains and demands (Num 12).

This essay will address the above episodes and attempt to respond to political and family issues related to Miriam and her "brothers." These issues will then be placed within the larger cultural, social, and political frameworks. The reader should remember that these episodes occurred in an Egyptian framework that historians consider unique.

Out of Egypt

The exodus from Egypt is ambiguously chronicled in the Book of Exodus. The ambiguity is not in the ultimate mythical and historical impact of that event; rather, it is in the way the story unfolds and the manner in which the characters are finally presented to the reader. While the initial few chapters (1-3) are dedicated to an exploration of the character of Moses and those who surround him, the emphasis is clearly dual; namely, it repeatedly shifts between Hebraic and Egyptian frameworks. Exodus retells the Genesis narrative of Joseph and his brothers, who came to Egypt following a severe drought in Canaan. The text reminds us that the Hebrews' sojourn to Egypt occurred in a patriarchal past linked with the family of Jacob/Israel and, specifically, Joseph.

The Exodus story describes a decisive moment in Israelite history, literature, psychology, and culture. It defines the character of the nation emerging from that upheaval and forever changed the conversation about slavery, freedom, leadership, revolution, and redemption. It also changed the role of women and furthered the process of marginalization. The story introduces a hero who is beholden to both the past and the future—a leader with extraordinary and charismatic qualities that united a people as they undertook spiritual and political journey that would produce individual and cultural changes.[1]

The Exodus is also related to notions of spring, seasonal renewal, and fertility (both human and natural), as well as to ideas of purification and worthiness— concepts that involve humans attempting to get close to the Divine. For the first time in human experience, a God speaks loudly and clearly about choice and hope, about dignity, and about the flight of the soul from bondage. Moreover, that God speaks to a whole community, daring it to reject what He offers and presenting a host of choices underlining His commitment to a new order. This order will equalize and open up the channels of purity, once reserved for an elite priesthood, to masses of people who ultimately say, "We will do and hear!"[2] The rabbis have already noted that the Israelites, on that occasion, were ready to "do" first and "hear" later—they seem to have been enchanted with the new program![3] Purification became the group's marker, and it enabled those who adhered to the new ideology to rally around the sign of male circumcision.[4]

And then there are the unforgettable symbols— water, the serpent and the rod, the well of betrothal, the plagues and famines, circumcision of the flesh, songs of redemption as well as the motif of "strangers," and more. All of these signify a departure from the old and an onset of the new; all surround events of heroic proportion; all focus as much as possible on men and their accomplishments, men and their deeds, men and their power, men and their God. There are the male "children of Israel" who went down to Egypt four hundred years before it all happened, and who became enslaved to a new Pharaoh who did not know (remember) Joseph and the protection he afforded his people (Ex 1:8). Joseph was the beloved son of Jacob and Rachel, the one who received his father's blessing (and inheritance) and who invoked the ire of his brothers at the end of the Book of Genesis. Joseph was brought down to Egypt by "Ishmaelites" (Midianites?) who bought and sold him. As it is told in Genesis, Joseph kindled the desire of Potiphar's wife and landed in jail (another "well," or pit) because of his purity, virginity, or innocence. Maybe there is more to this tale related to Joseph being a stranger and aspiring to inherit the power of Potiphar? After all, it is Potiphar's wife who referred to him, contemptuously, as a strange Hebrew man[5] who came to their house to "play with her" (in the sexual sense) and not vice-versa.[6] Maybe there is a reference here to some mixing with the Hyksos, kings of the shepherds, foreigners or strangers who ruled Egypt along with their allied princes or "Lords" (1665-1557 BCE);[7] their last Pharaoh was named Osarsiph (Kendrick, 268-269)—a Joseph-like name.

At first glance the Egyptian sojourn cycles seem to begin with Joseph, who "removed" (Gen 30:22) his mother's shame of barrenness, who was Jacob's beloved son and who wore that special "tunic of many colors" (37:3). This unusual robe may have been indicative of some priestly or royal bearing. And did not this special son born of a special mother and a unique birth have to travel down to the pit and the dark well (there is irony in the later use of Miriam's well as a symbol of regeneration and life[8]) before assuming his special priestly duties? Was not his journey the typical, privileged one that designated a hero as "chosen" for a particular fate and duty? Those dreams of Joseph's—they all focus on agricultural cycles: the sun and the moon as well as wheat and corn—all associated with the duty of a priest/ess, all related to the grain center of the ancient Mediterranean world, Egypt. But this is not the first memory of Egypt. The relentless march of Joseph is part of the ultimate Egyptian experience which really began with Abraham and Sarah who first went down to Egypt (during a famine) as brother and "sister." (Gen 12:13)[9] We may also recall that Sarah's maidservant was an Egyptian named Hagar who gave birth to Ishmael (Abraham's firstborn); was Hagar one of those "gifts" offered to Sarai (and Abraham) as a token of appreciation by the Pharaoh?[10] In any case, the emotional story of the barren wife who gave her husband another woman as a surrogate mother for herself (Sarah),[11] becomes a story of the mixing of blood between Abraham and an Egyptian woman—Hagar. Ishmael, who is the product of this "mixing," not accidentally is rejected by the biblical tradition in favor of the son of Sarah, Isaac.[12]

To summarize: There appears to be a long Hebraic tradition intimately involved with Egypt, one that may even indicate the mixing of blood as well as of culture. The main point is that the "Mosaic way" attempts to refine that relationship, both the physical and the spiritual, and sort out that which is truly distinctive in the way that gold and silver are refined to remove all impurities (Mal 3:3). This is not to say that there are no root or experiential connections with Mesopotamia or even with Canaan itself, but we believe Egypt to be the major source of this revolutionary legacy.[13]

Purity & Tzara'at

The crucial notion here is purity, both in a real and in a symbolic context: purity in the heart and mind, and even more, purity in the body, and its preservation for posterity. Disease, contagion, spiritual pollution and impurity as well as other misfortunes seem to plague the Israelites and are directly linked with an angry God who sends a signal to an individual, but even more, to a whole group about how much (or, how little) God is dissatisfied. The image of Job sitting on the ground and miserably scratching himself, due to a severe skin affliction, supposedly because of God's action (or inaction) still haunts all of those who read the book and wonder about the suffering "ways of God with man." The Pharaoh and the Egyptians are punished with "blood in the Nile" and various other agricultural/economic disasters, including boils on the skin, which point to their "evil ways" and finally enable the Israelites and an *"erev rav"*[14] to depart from Egypt towards a new life and a radical redemption.[15] The issue of impurity of mind and body comes to full fruition here and lays the foundation for what is to follow in the desert.

The story of the Exodus, from start to finish, is governed by imagery which singles out "strangers," impurities, and what today we might call ethnic cleansing (the Pharaoh's desire to rid himself of the Hebrews is only one example). It is entirely possible that, historically speaking, the Habiru of the Delta regions could be associated with the *"erev rav"* (the rabble) who are indeed the "impure ones" among the "Asiatics" or Hyksos. In the same context then, the inscription on Queen Hatshepsut's Temple is telling: "Asiatics were in the midst of Avaris of the Northland and *vagabonds* (emphasis ours) were in the midst of them overthrowing that which had been made."[16] The Pharaohs wanted to remove these polluted ones.[17] There is a serious complaint about illegal immigrants in the Delta: "Foreigners have become people everywhere. There are no Egyptians anywhere."[18] Also, we find that Mantho, the Ptolemaic historian, is quoted by Josephus as saying that Moses himself was a leper as were the Children of Israel. Josephus further says that this made him smile because it was the Egyptian who was cursed with plagues.[19]

Wherever the historical truth lies, the tremendous emphasis on purity, various sources of pollution, and rules of separation become deeply embedded in Jewish ritual as well as in its theology. Skin disease, *tzara'at*, possibly leprosy with its white and sometimes reddish spots and deformities, or other venereal diseases with skin manifestations, stand out visibly as a most dreaded, disgusting pathology. Whether the disease of *tzara'at* was leprosy or not, the intense consciousness of danger and fears (maybe for the children borne by the Israelites, too) is so strong that purification by water, by circumcision, by fire, by separation of all sorts, including shunning dangerous persons, characterize the Mosaic code. In fact, Moses is associated with a decree pronouncing that such infected people be separated out as if they were dead; and they must cry out "unclean, unclean" and wander beyond the settlements (Lev 13:45). The association of white with *tzara'at* and death, the white shroud, as well as with unrighteousness, spiritual death, and Godly punishment are evident here as well as in other stories of afflicted individuals.[20]

Quite curious, and of great interest to us, is the incident in the Moses tradition when Miriam is struck with "white leprosy." She receives this punishment from God for questioning and complaining about Moses' Cushite wife (Num 12:1-15, Deut 24:9). But she is healed fairly quickly once her "brother," the priest Aaron, intercedes on her behalf with her other "brother," Moses (elsewhere in the Exodus tradition associated with his double-snake rod of healing),[21] who, in turn, asks God to remove the curse. What then is the point of this episode? What is the text teaching? Or, better still, what is it remembering? Maybe the metaphor tells us about impurity, fear of "white"—death being the ultimate separation and purification, bone white—and political dissent (if not spiritual rebellion), more than about the medical condition of Miriam. In other words, we can learn more about the concerns of the three major political (and spiritual) operatives of this episode than about medicine. Moreover, the impact and intent of the story is political and spiritual, revealing some of the tensions between Moses, Miriam, and Aaron, and between these leaders and the community they were trying to serve and influence.[22]

We suggest that Miriam's objection to the marriage of Moses (and the "Cushite woman") is justified because it is based on the rules of her past and her possible position as a priestess of Egypt.[23] Indeed, it may have been her prerogative to marry Moses in a traditional "brother-sister" ritual marriage. The message in her punishment, her skin turning white, is clear: Her way of action is no longer acceptable; it is dead for the Hebrews. Not only that, but Moses is assigned her song of protection—the Song of the Sea. Strongly associated with a chant to the waters of Osiris, it is sung by "Moses and the Children of Israel" (Ex 15:1) as they cross over the boundary and into the desert and a new life.[24]

To investigate this admittedly unorthodox interpretation, we turn to a more complete analysis of the somewhat cryptic story about Miriam, Aaron, and Moses in the desert. Our emphasis will be on the use of leprosy or some comparable disease as indicative of supernatural punishment in conjunction with the color white. This white leprosy denotes not just simple "jealousy" (and punishment for that jealousy) on the part of Miriam and Aaron (specifically Miriam[25]), but a whole array of political and spiritual concerns that are raised, with growing desperation, by those who remain in the minority.

The context of the story has to be addressed first. It is typical of the whole book of Numbers, which is filled with stories about confrontations between Moses and various individual Israelites, between Moses and other leaders (or, those who seem to be leaders), and finally, between Moses and presumably his own family. The Miriam episode comes sandwiched between various examples of dissatisfaction and discontent, even open revolt. If Moses was leading a revolutionary movement, which brought freedom to the slaves, it was not a grassroots revolution, neither was it accomplished peacefully. All the stories in the desert are fairly bloody and contentious; those who may have held power before were not ready to surrender it so quickly, and those who emerged as new leaders in the desert and disagreed with Moses' ideology were not about to back down either.

The Priestess Way

The Miriam-Moses confrontation occurs at the end of the Torah portion, which begins with the seven candles and the menorah that are part of the priestly ritual associated with Aaron. In fact, the first few verses of the chapter (Num 8) ease the reader into a "bright" godly framework which fits the "house (tent) of God" and the altar which was built for God. The traditional number seven is a part of the ceremony and the light of fire suggests spirituality, purification, and commitment. This introduction leads us into a cleansing ceremony which involves the Levites who are the "firstborn," dedicated to God's service. The Exodus from Egypt is briefly remembered with its specific connection to "firstborns" and "plagues" (8:17-19). The chapter thus sets the tone for what will follow; specifically, it prepares us quite carefully for a discussion related to the political event of the Exodus, and to certain roles within this new society that is formed in the desert.

Chapter 9 describes the Passover festival which is "performed" ('sa) by the children of Israel (b'nei Yisrael) with an emphasis again on "purity." Only those who are pure can "do" the pesach; those who wish to join the congregation and are not pure must undergo a purification/sacrificial ritual before attempting to be like the others. The cloud and fire associated with the tent of the tabernacle are the symbols of spirituality and purity in this chapter.

Chapter 10 is fully ritualized with trumpets and tribal recognition and a certain order, which are crucial for a community in the making. The emphasis is on the "new way," with male symbols taking over. The women are less and less of a factor here, and there is only a vague reference to Tzipporah, the wife of Moses, via an elusive description of Hovav and his role in the community of the Exodus. Interestingly, the text continues with the "strangers" motif by placing the Midianites (who are fairly close to the Egyptians and their culture) in the center of the Israelite experience.

Chapter 11 is stormy! The traditional food images that are equated with Egypt, its culture and history, are brought fully to bear. The people, including the "asafsuf" (riff raff),[26] desire the Egyptian diet, particularly the meat! Manna, the supposed "soul and holy food" of Yahweh, is entirely rejected here and Moses is distressed, as is Yahweh (11:10). When the final episode of chapter 11 is fully narrated we find ourselves in the midst of a political and spiritual crisis which may or may not have been related to Hovav's presence or absence. Moses' spiritual leadership is under attack and it is not absolutely clear that he can survive it. He attempts to pacify all parties by sounding humble and compromising, but at the end of the day there are dead bodies all over the desert floor (v.33b).

Those who perish because of "Yahweh's anger" are finally buried in what are called "the tombs of desire" (v. 34). Desire is associated with food, which must be seen as ritually important as well as psychologically comforting. The people are described as uncomfortable with Moses' diet and they are looking for a way out.

At this point the more "familial" rebellion occurs, and is introduced as follows:

> And Miriam and Aaron spoke about Moses about the Cushite woman whom he had taken because it was a Cushite woman that he took (12:1).

There is no question about the centrality of the concept "Cushite" in this verse. The woman is not named (unlike the three characters involved in the episode), neither is she present when it all takes place. Is the subject Tzipporah? Our literary sensibilities indicate it is not, because she is not named; we have already been introduced to Tzipporah, and we have seen her perform what the text describes as an extraordinary act of courage (circumcision) that saved her son and maybe her husband (Ex 4:25). Tzipporah the priestess performs a ritual that is fully identified with the Hebrews' covenant with Yahweh. But it is also an Egyptian cleansing ritual. Is she then attempting to legitimize the revolution, and does she thus give it her stamp of approval?[27] Moreover, as already noted, Tzipporah was a Midianite (not a Cushite). We propose that the troubling story about Miriam (also involving her two "brothers") focuses specifically on the Cushite woman and her roots, which go back to Egypt in a more concrete sense than the Hebrew tradition allows. Miriam may have been an Egyptian-styled priestess (the text in Exodus 15 refers to her as "prophetess"). Her role then explains why she objected to Moses' marriage, as well as why Moses' reaction to her was so damning. We may remember that the Egyptian theology called for a virgin to perform a sacred brother-sister marriage to address the fertility needs of the people. We may also recall that fertility encompassed agricultural success as well as human reproduction. Both aspects were part of a program of maintaining and regenerating life; this was particularly important to elite circles with divine connections and obligations.[28] In that context, Miriam should have been the designated wife of the leader, not the outsider/foreigner/Cushite he chose. But in line with the rest of the Mosaic program, Miriam becomes "leprous"; she is now fully and completely dead (white).

Ultimately, Moses usurps her role for himself, including her water magic (parting the sea, as well as producing water from the rock [Ex 14 ; Num 20]). It is also very important to bear in mind that "sister" or "brother" designations are titles, not necessarily kin relationships. The name "Miriam," which in Hebrew already has water allusions, may derive from a more ancient Egyptian source linked with pure water.[29] In any case, Miriam's life-giving well follows the Israelites through the desert, and serves them well when they triumph over the Egyptians (see the Song of the Sea), until her death. Miriam's traditions reflected in popular culture indicate to us that the Mosaic way was never able to fully suppress something that Miriam the Egyptian-Hebrew woman represented.

Is there a connection between the death of Miriam, the loss of water, and the rebellion that occurs in Numbers 20? Yes. Moses is not to enter the land at the end. Possibly, this is where he is killed. Also, the "speech" to the rock as opposed to "hitting" the rock and extracting water point to a connection: brute force versus the traditional, priestess, woman way. Miriam is not just "leprous," she is now fully and completely dead ("white") and does not provide the community with any water. The new source of water and the new way is Yahwistic, associated with brutality and death. The chapter comes to full closure with the death of Aaron, the "brother" of Miriam and the transfer of power to his son, Eleazar ("God helped"). Thus comes to an end a complex chapter in Israelite culture and tradition. It is associated with the past, Egypt and its bounty, its food and priestly promises which provided for men and women, with priestesses guarding the springs of water. Although Miriam's role is not absolutely coherent (in fact it is evasive and deliberately vague), she does appear to have inherent powers that are accepted by a community reluctant to depart without her, and which finally mourns the death of her brother for thirty days (20:29).

NOTES

1. The fact that the birth and survival myth of Moses was told in a reversed manner only elevated the ultimate impact of the Exodus itself. In other words, if Moses, the slave-turned-prince, could reach godly heights, so could any one who finds him or her self in a low position.

2. Egyptian purity was reserved for only priests; this new purity designates the Hebrews as "A kingdom of priests and a holy nation;" they were all "passed over" by the avenging angel and thus became a literal "house of life."

3. We wish to emphasize the communal nature of this political and spiritual agenda; indeed, in Egyptian chronicles, only priests and pharaohs have access to channels of purification.

4. The flag in this context is both literal (e.g. war against those who wish to harm the group) and conceptual.

5. There is thus some good reason to assume that the *sitz um leben* of this story is the period of the Hyksos who were seen as the Asiatic, foreigners who penetrated Egypt and its power structure in devastating fashion. Presumably, Joseph could have gained the power he did only because of the presence of the Hyksos who were less sensitive to strangers in their midst. By the same token, when the text in Exodus suggests that the

Pharaoh did not "know" Joseph, we are to assume that a more "pure" Egyptian political establishment was back in place and foreigners were frowned upon.

6. It is not our intent to analyze the story of Joseph and Potiphar's wife, merely to point to a few peculiarities that we believe are significant: first, regardless of the general traditional consensus that J really tells a story about an anonymous officer of the Pharaoh and that the name, Potiphar, is somewhat irrelevant (after all, the rest of the narrative does not mention this name anymore) and unimportant, we think that since he is named Potiphar, a name which can easily be confused (if not identified) with Potiphera, a man of the sun (Aseneth's father and the priest of On, Heliopolis), he has to be viewed as an important character in the overall story. Second, the Masoretic text describes Potiphar as a "eunuch of Pharaoh" (37:38, 39:1) who thus has a special relationship with the main source of Egyptian power and may have some priestly connections too. If he is a "eunuch", Potiphar's "wife" is certainly in a special position because she cannot have children with him and if she is to have a family, she must look for it somewhere else, maybe with Joseph. Possibly also she is a special "wife" who has her own agenda and loyalties in the house of Pharaoh. Third, Joseph ends up exactly where he should be after the episode is over and indeed he does become the most powerful man in Egypt.

We should also emphasize that re-working the tale of the two brothers into the story of Joseph is certainly interesting but one should not ignore the Hebrew flavor here and the ultimate point that J is trying to make, not only about Joseph but about redemption and the plans of Yahweh for his people's redemption.

7. John Van Seters. 1966. *The Hyksos: A New Investigation.*

8. According to midrashic tradition, the well of Miriam which assisted the Israelites throughout their wilderness travels, was created on the second day of creation.

9. We have already elaborated on the Sarai/Abram episode in relation to the DSS and its perception of Sarai as the "virginal" mother who attracts men of power and who may have "saved" Egypt from the famine. See, Ita Sheres & Anne K. Blau. 1995. *The Truth About the Virgin: Sex and Ritual in the Dead Sea Scrolls,* p. 38.

10. Rashi and other commentators thought so and there are various legends to that effect.

11. The future born of Hagar is described as Sarah's son, not Abraham's. The story evolves in a manner that frustrates Sarah who is "angered" against Abraham who seems not to adhere to the original plan struck between the two of them.

12. We should note here that Abraham loves Ishmael.

13. There is an array of books, essays and articles that deal with this legacy and we will not summarize them here; this task is too daunting; when appropriate we will quote and make reference. Our contribution is as indicated within the body of our paper and we will continue to focus on images that we believe tell us a strikingly human story that pays homage to power and people's attempts to keep it within their grasp.

14. The "erev rav" (rabble) may have included the Israelites who were not necessarily a totally cohesive group at the time.

15. The ten plagues have been interpreted in a myriad of ways and the one that suits us the best is symbolically political. See Ita Sheres, "Moses, Mao and the Messiah: The Politics of Redemption." *The Centennial Review*.

16. Van Seters, p. 172.

17. Breasted, p. 215.

18. Van Seters, 116.

19. Antiquities, III: xi.

20. Naaman the Syrian, another stranger, imports the disease, in a rather obscure episode which involves "an Israelite girl" who leads Naaman to a Hebrew king and prophet (was she the source of that *tzara'at*?) Gehazi, the servant of Elisha is a greedy turncoat who eventually dies of the disease. (2 Kings 5) King Uzziah is a righteous warrior king gone bad and he carries the mark of the disease on his forehead for the rest of his life. (2 Chron 26:19-21). See also Donald Ortner, "What Bones Tell Us," *Biblical Archeological Review*, August 1966, p. 52. Ortner indicates that leprosy, as well as tuberculosis, was prevalent during the Bronze Age in the Jordan area. See also *Encyclopedia Judaica* about lepers and leprosy and the existence of enclosed ruins and houses for lepers in Gaza. It is also possible that bodies of lepers were burned for purification reasons. More references and

discussion of the above can be found in the Tosefta 6:1 and Lev 14:34-53.

21. Heka, the Egyptian magician-god's emblem, showing his two fertility goddesses crossed over his chest (Shaked, 205 and Ritner, 4 and 25).

22. Commentaries about this story abound, and the most classical ones have to do with "gossip and bad-mouthing" of either Tzipporah or a second wife of Moses', who was looked down upon by Moses' God who afflicts Miriam with the disease. It is also connected in commentators' minds with Moses' humility as compared with that of Miriam and Aaron, who in the same episode seem to be questioning Moses' authority.

23. We should remember that even the Hebrew text assigns her the title "prophetess" while describing her engaged in a ritual of triumphant celebration after the Exodus (Ex 15).

24. Osiris' birth place was so honored by the Love Priestesses of Isis. According to Egyptian theology Isis "artificially" inseminated herself with the seed of her dead husband, Osiris, to produce the savior, Horus. (Delta, Middle Kingdom Coffin Texts, pp. 183-4).

Additionally, Theraputae choirs (male and female) of Ptolemaic Egypt were reported to have sung the song of Miriam and Moses (*Judaica*, Vol. 15, p. 112). At last, Moses' mouth is opened, so to speak, and his "speech impediment" (stuttering?) disappears.

25. The story clearly relates to Miriam rather than to Aaron; he is there, as the priest, in order to reinforce the impurity concept and to more concretely become associated with her as a holy woman.

26. The reference is similar to *"erev rav"* which signifies the position of those who left Egypt. The discontent of those who have nothing to lose, be they slaves or poor, uprooted people, is well summarized in the sociological concept *"erev rav,"* a multitude of people. Those who left Egypt are not just Israelites, and Moses has an extremely difficult task in "converting" all to his radical Yahwistic ideology.

27. In another essay we discuss that obscure episode in Exodus (4:24-26).

28. Important symbols and rituals included the *ankh*, water baptism, healings, chants/psalms, the marking of agricultural cycles, star knowledge, etc.

29. Miriam's name is not used in other Hebrew Biblical materials and is resurrected only in the Second Temple period where Miriam becomes a most popular aristocratic name and is particularly significant for the Dead Sea Scrolls sectarians.

THE COVENANT OF MIRIAM
Rose Z. Novick

We had been scheduled to leave and continue on our journey. But for the seven days during which I remained in exile from the camp, none of the people moved, holding fast to their positions to await my return. The women of each family understood that, in a way, their own futures went with me into the desert. Through my seven-day separation I bore the punishment of rebellion for each of them, and no woman would prepare her household for travel until I had returned.

I headed west into the hills, envisioning in my mind's eye the desert walk of first menstruation, part of the womanhood initiation, a ritual I and the other girls of my generation had been unable to fully complete during our enslavement in Egypt. As I made my way across the desert, I imagined I could see the drops of first blood, soaking into the ground as I walked. I visualized the blood on the sand, concentrating on its burnt red color and texture with every step. The hills rose above me, and the coarse sand burned my bare feet. The sun penetrated my skin, and I walked with eyes closed to shut out the brightness of the light. I remembered the tightening of my womb from the years of my youth when my blood would surge at dark of each moon. I felt the warm sticky wetness on my thighs, and could actually smell the acrid odor. I opened my eyes, and looking down at my body saw blood coming from between my legs. I had not shed womanblood in more than thirty years; I felt touched by God, like Sarah, who miraculously conceived at ninety. This transformation of my body, the leprous appearance of my skin and the flowing of my blood, could only presage a deeper transformation of the spirit. As I recited the blessing over menstruation, I knew that the greatest revelation still lay before me. Memories of my life floated before my eyes like a bird circling on a downwind. How far I had come to reach this particular journey . . .

✍

My mother woke me before sunrise and instructed me to come with her quietly. She took the baby and several items in a large basket, and together we stole down to the Nile bank and hid ourselves among the tall reeds. My mother placed the infant in an ark she had woven, and sealed it with pitch to keep out the water. As she set the basket afloat I saw tears well up in her eyes and begin to fall. "El Shaddai protect you, my son," she whispered. When she could stand the sight no longer, she turned her back to the river. "Go after him, Miriam," Yocheved pleaded with me, "watch over him." Crying openly, she returned to the Hebrew camp.

I waded into the murky water, feeling my cotton dress clinging to my legs, the reeds pricking my feet, and hid myself behind leafy fronds hanging from the bank. Peeking through, I kept my eyes on the floating basket. I waited while the sun rose, and feared for my discovery as the golden rays illuminated my hiding place. I thought of my baby brother, and remembered how I would crawl to my mother's bed at night and sit up with her just to watch her nurse. The miracle of her life-sustaining breasts, which never failed to quiet and soothe him, never failed to enthrall me. Now his life was at the mercy of the Nile, and the waters of the river must sustain him. In the next moment I saw a procession of Egyptian women approaching the river from the direction of the palace, and I hid myself deeper in the blanket of the earth. These were women as I had never seen. Young, not far past their first womanblood, their hair hanging down in beaded braids, they wore dresses dyed all the colors of the rainbow. Thick bands of gold encircled their necks and arms; their eyes were painted black and their lips bright red. The Princess Thermutis and her waiting-ladies assembled on a grassy spot not far from where I crouched. As the young ladies prepared the princess for her bath they kept a watchful eye for any males, Hebrew or Egyptian, who might come to spy on the princess as she disrobed.

"What is that?" one of them shouted, pointing.

"Where?" asked the princess, re-fastening her gown and looking about. Her eye fell on the basket and, her curiosity aroused, she sent two of her women to enter the water and fetch it for her. As they brought the basket to the princess I feared for my brother's safety. If discovered by Pharaoh he would surely be killed. At that moment the baby began to cry, a pitiable wail that carried with it all the sorrow and loneliness of an orphan.

"Poor thing," said the princess softly, shaking her head as she peered into the basket, "This must be one of the Hebrew children."

Hearing her compassion and sensing opportunity I stepped forward to approach the women. I knew that if I took no action my brother would be lost to us forever. But since many Hebrew women with stillborn or murdered babes had been called to the palace as wet-nurses for offspring of the royal harem, I knew the princess might be searching for just what my mother and I needed as well. Bowing low before the princess, I took a risk.

"Forgive my intrusion, Your Highness. With your permission I can send for one of the Hebrew women to nurse him for you." I hoped that she could not hear the quavering in my voice. The princess looked me over, a six-year-old barefoot child in the dress of a slave. At first she seemed to wonder where I had come from, and just stared as if I were some ghostly apparition. Then slowly she smiled, figuring out what had transpired to place the infant on the river, with me as his unlikely guardian.

"Go," she said gently. I ran back to find my mother as fast as I could, before the princess changed her mind and disappeared back into the palace with the baby. I found my mother with several other women in the barley field, and panting for breath I told her quickly what had happened. We returned together to the riverbank, where the princess awaited our return. She had dismissed all but one of her servants, who held the empty ark while the princess herself carried my brother. She turned to Yocheved, who bowed deeply.

"Will you nurse this child?" Thermutis asked simply, betraying none of her knowledge of who we really were.

"If you will it, your Highness, it would be my privilege to serve you," Yocheved answered, keeping her head low.

"Look at me," the Pharaoh's daughter commanded. My mother raised her head and her gaze met the other woman's. As their eyes met they both acknowledged the depth of what took place here. It was an act of secrecy, daring and courage. A moment later the princess looked away and spoke in the tone of one accustomed to being obeyed.

"Take this child to the palace and nurse it. You will be assigned living quarters, and I will pay you two silver coins each month until he is weaned." Never again, by word or glance, did either of them hint at the true nature of the relationship between the adopted prince and his nurse. To do so would go against the Pharaoh's personal decree, and even his own daughter was not exempt from the law.

"I worship the Goddess Isis," said the princess, and this time she seemed to speak to me, although her eyes faced the tents of the Hebrew slaves behind me. "The

Goddess mourns the death of her brother and husband, Osiris. She birthed her own son Horus in secret, and hid him among the marshes. The mother Goddess understands life and loss, and would never decree the slaughter of so many innocent babes. Even the offspring of slaves."

Now she looked down at the child in her arms and said, "I take you for my own, and I call your name Moses, because I drew you from the water."

Handing the baby now to Yocheved she sent us all back to the palace with her servant to take our places there. As we climbed the steps of the massive structure I looked back toward the river, and in the distance I saw the princess still standing where we had left her, staring into the water. As I grew older I heard the whispered stories of what the Egyptians thought had happened that day. Some said the princess had borne the boy herself, out of wedlock, and invented the story of the basket on the river to hide the identity of her Hebrew lover. Others clucked with pity as they recounted the princess' barren state, a curse to any woman, and how in desperation she had adopted the son of one of her slaves. Still others merely shook their heads, noting that nothing good could ever come of a slave reared to manhood by the daughter of a king.

My mother received her own room in the servants' wing, hardly luxurious to an Egyptian, but far more comfortable than our own tents, while I moved back and forth between the two worlds. Some nights I spent in my father Amram's tent, in the morning weaving cloth with the old Hebrew women. Other nights I would sleep with my mother in her bed, and if Moses cried during the night I would sit up with her and we would talk as she nursed. On these nights my mother would recite the stories of our ancestors, entertaining me with tales of the beautiful and strong-willed Rivkah, or the young Joseph who knew from an early age that his destiny would be different from his brothers'. I believe my mother told me these stories not just to pass the time, but to help me see my own place in the history of our people. When I think back on my mother, I don't remember the bent old woman with the lines around her forehead and eyes, who didn't live to see our freedom. I recall the beautiful face, hands, and body that held and loved me, and the jasmine smell of her hair as I nestled against her shoulder, wrapped in the soft cotton bedclothes, listening to the soothing sound of her voice.

I was a female child, and adults hardly noticed me; I could sit unobserved on the floor and learn much about the world around me. At my aunt Serach's loom I learned about the suffering of my people. I carried the skeins of undyed wool back and forth while the old women traded stories: A son had been whipped for talking back; a friend put to death by stoning for stealing food—the swift and unequal justice of the Pharaoh's guards In the servants' quarters of the palace I heard the whispered tales of royal intrigue—who thirsted for power and whose star had fallen, who had taken a lover and who had seen them together. The jarring difference between the two universes I inhabited tore at me, and increasingly I turned to my own world, my dreams, and the Voice that spoke to me within them. I came to cherish that secret and mysterious Voice that came to me only at night, and whispered of promises yet unfulfilled.

On the day that Moses was weaned, in the spring following his third winter, my mother said a prayer for his well-being, clothed him in his finest robe, and instructed him to be brave. Yocheved took him by one hand and I held the other as we walked through the maze of passageways to the princess' chambers. She met us as arranged at her courtyard gate, looking just as I remembered her from the river. Pharaoh's daughter would be a beautiful woman even without her adornment, paint and jewels, but she appeared before us dressed befitting a royal princess.

"How fares the child?" she asked Yocheved, inviting us both to enter her private chambers. As they discussed my brother's eating and sleeping habits I examined the room. Tapestries of exquisite color and design hung from every wall, and gold statuettes graced intricately carved pedestals. In one corner stood an image of a large seated cat of black onyx with sapphire eyes; the Egyptian goddess Bastet, I learned much later. Then the princess' words caught my attention.

"Things will become worse for your people before they get any better," she was saying quietly. "I love the king, for he is my father. But he can be a cruel tyrant, especially when he is afraid for his power. The Pharaoh would be Ra, the sun god himself, and destroy any perceived threat, no matter how small. Even as small as an infant . . ." her voice trailed off. "The child will be safe here, and well cared for," she continued. The princess was rising now, signaling that our royal audience had concluded.

"I thank you for your duty," the princess said rather formally, pressing a single gold coin into my mother's hand. Turning around to leave I noticed a statue that I had missed when we came in—a woman, seated on a throne with the sun disc behind her head and an infant at her breast. She had wings growing from her shoulders, and her eyes held both wisdom and compassion. This must be Isis, I realized, the goddess of whom she spoke at the river.

The princess' faith served her well. Beyond hospitality and mercy she had displayed moral courage, for even if she did not speak out publicly against Pharaoh's injustice, she undermined him at every turn. Saving Moses was just one act of very personal resistance.

Over the years, for as long as I could remember, there had been Egyptian women who came regularly into the Hebrew camp bringing baskets of food and healing herbs, and occasionally small coins or cloth. Having spent time in the palace I now recognized these women as the personal attendants of the princess, undoubtedly following her orders, at no small risk to themselves.

My mother's face wore no expression as we walked together out of the palace gates, but I knew her well enough to read the pain behind her eyes. She had abandoned this child of her flesh for the second time.

"At least he will live," she said quietly, taking my hand and walking faster as we approached our tents.

Over the years one of the princess' women with her baskets of medications and clothing would occasionally enclose a note for my mother, a thin sheet of papyrus saying only, "The child fares well," or "The child is now a man." By now I too had grown, having passed my initiation with my first womanblood at age thirteen.

The ceremony had been simple, with a gathering of our female relatives and a few of my mother's and my friends. Yocheved prepared a traditional feast of foods from the earth, especially foods that grow on trees, symbolizing life and fertility. I drank a cup of milk, to symbolize the ability of my body not only to create but to nurture and sustain life. We broke bread together, and my mother recited the blessing of our ancestors.

> Let us praise Yah, the glorious One
> Who causes the moon blood to flow.
> El Shaddai, You have gifted woman with the
> ability to bear life.
> Our blood, like the moon, returns, returns,
> like night into day into night;
> like life into death into life.

Since I had come of age my father Amram had wanted to find a suitable husband for me. But I had dreams beyond cooking pots and childbearing, and I asked my parents not to arrange a marriage for me. Disappointed but understanding, they agreed. My mother sent me instead to Shifrah the midwife to train as a healer. She began with simple herbal preparations for relief of common illnesses and symptoms, particularly the concerns of women. She taught me to identify and gather the plants, grasses and flowers to ease a woman's menstrual flow or bring on labor. As I grew older, she taught me the secrets of those herbs which could inhibit conception or bring an end to an unwanted pregnancy. I studied the properties of sage and hyssop, and learned to treat fever and heal open wounds. From Shifrah the midwife I learned many things: proper delivery of the infant and care of the new mother, as expected, but also courage, faith and dignity. Shifrah taught me pride in the craft of midwifery, and a respect for this science that belonged so completely to women.

As I grew older, the customs and rituals of the Hebrew women became my passion, but under the harsh rule of Pharaoh our community too often overlooked them. Many rituals are unique to the women. Men do not practice our dances, nor do they use the sistrum or cherish the *teraphim*. Over the coming generations male priests would outlaw the *teraphim*, time and again, but centuries would pass before their use finally faded away; no birth I attended was ever without their presence. Timbrels, chants and amulets—these were the threads that wove my life, and I spent my days teaching women and girls to read and write and play music, and fostering their love of the women's sacred dances.

Two or three times a year I would make contact with one of Princess Thermutis' waiting-ladies. They would warn the families of someone about to be punished, and on more than one occasion they would help a luckless Hebrew who had committed some unpardonable sin against the throne of Egypt to escape into the desert. Some of these servants I remembered from my childhood years in the palace; others were new, and younger than I. I don't know how the princess found them, or secured their fast loyalty, but through them she took the roughest edges off her father's, and later her brother's, harsh rule. Once I dreamed that I stood before a small pool of sparkling water, seeing the reflection of the moon imposed upon my own face. The dual images of moon and water appeared often in my dreams, especially when the Voice whispered to me, and somehow I knew that both would come to play a part in my future.

The next morning just after dawn word swept through the Hebrew camp like a sandstorm across the open plains: The prince Moses had killed an Egyptian overseer! Moses had fled the palace and headed south into the desert.

Banishment, exile, murder—the words hung heavy in the air as we breathed them in. My mother would not be consoled; all her hopes for this hidden son now vanished with him. Moses was lost to her for the third time. Despair over this news brought us low; the morale of the Hebrew slaves sank even further. That evening I walked down to the river, remembering Moses' birth, the basket, the sunrise, and the princess. I stood there, lost in prayer and meditation, staring into the depths of the river.

"Speak to me," I pleaded in an urgent whisper. I had never before called upon the voice of my dreams, but had let it come to me. Now I had nowhere else to turn. "El Shaddai, Protector of Israel, Shekhinah, guide me now. Impart your wisdom, and I will do your bidding."

"Miriam," answered the familiar and by now beloved voice, "do you not see my plans unfolding? The same faith that led you to seek me out must see you through this time of fear. As I come to you now through the medium of water, so shall I speak to your brother Moses through fire. The two of you shall complement each other, as brother and sister, and neither alone without the other will bring the redemption of Israel. When Moses returns from the desert, the hour will be at hand, and at that time you will prepare the women. Believe in your strength. I am with you." As the Voice drifted away I noticed a light shimmering in the water. It was the reflection of the moon, which had risen while I stood praying. I lifted my eyes to the heavens. The moon was full.

Toward sunset the next evening as I headed back from my day of tending the ill and teaching music a sudden fear gripped my heart, and I turned toward my mother's tent. Since Amram's death several years before I had kept close to Yocheved. She was forever changed by his loss, although she kept busy with cookery and teaching weaving to the young wives. My feet had stones weighing them down as I slowly approached her tent, dreading each step but forcing myself to continue. Entering Yocheved's tent I found her as I expected, lying on her bed with eyes closed, and a peaceful stillness in the air. I knelt at my mother's side, took her hand and placed a gentle kiss on her forehead. Softly I heard, "Weep not child, for the one who birthed you is now at rest." From that moment on, whenever I heard the Voice, it was Yocheved's.

My mother was buried the following day in a simple cotton shroud, in a ceremony attended by the entire Hebrew camp. Aaron and I together performed the burial rites, and I placed my hands on her head for a final blessing.

El Shaddai, who nurtured and suckled
Yocheved the Levite,
Take her again into Your womb.

Bring comfort and peace to her soul.
Praised is the One who creates life out of the Earth.
This life is returned to You.

᪥

In the desert, I set up my campsite in a cave that wind and time had carved out of the hillside, alone, for the first time since childhood when I hid myself in the Nile marshes. I was surrounded daily by women seeking my skills and young girls questioning me and wanting advice. This new and unfamiliar silence enveloped me like a womb, and I could hear my own thoughts as if someone else spoke them aloud. As I laid down my blanket I removed a round manna cake from my bag, and began to murmur a blessing of thanksgiving. Before I could take a bite, the Voice rose up out of the earth, and washed over me like a warm bath.

"Miriam," spoke the Divine Presence, in Yocheved's comforting and gentle speech, "do not eat, nor drink. You asked your brother Moses, the chosen shepherd of My flock, whether I have not also spoken to you. The voice you have heard since childhood through your dreams is Mine. You are indeed My prophetess, and I reveal to you now a vision of the world as it shall be long after you have left it. I have brought you into the wilderness, apart from the others, to speak with you of the world to come."

I bowed my head and breathed deeply. "Holy One who brought us out of Egypt, I await your word as I have always done. Blessed is El Shaddai."

"Miriam," She continued. "As the moon grows large and then wanes and disappears, awaiting rebirth once again, so will the light of women wane and fade. The voice of woman on this earth will fall silent, her songs and stories grown dim, as man comes to fear her power. I made covenants with each of your ancestors, and today I make one with you. Your promise, the Covenant of Miriam, is that after the turning of many years and the passage of countless generations of darkness, women will re-emerge like the shining crescent of the new moon, wax and grow bright, once again filling the universe with luminescent glory.

"This shall be the message and the meaning of the new moon. Because you led your women followers away from the idolatry of the golden bull, and danced in the desert singing my praises, I give to you and to all women the holiday of Rosh Hodesh. Each lunar cycle the reappearance of the new moon shall serve as a reminder of My covenant to you, just as the rainbow marked My covenant with Noah. As the light of women reappears, men will also come to perceive the light, and then both will grow and flourish. When women and men together celebrate the joy of life in harmony and peace, and worship together My holy Shekhinah which fills creation, the hour of humanity's redemption will be at hand."

The next morning I began this journal, as one would light a candle to burn through the long dark night ahead. I set to parchment the words, the steps, the notes of all our sacred songs and dances, and all the secrets of healing taught to me so many years ago by Shifrah the midwife. Perhaps when the light returns, one of those daughters of the far distant future will read my story and discover the lost knowledge and traditions of her ancestors. I wrote all day for the rest of my days of separation, and on the morning of the seventh day I awoke to a new consciousness, a feeling that I had completed my life's work and would soon be returning to the womb of El Shaddai.

∽

Years passed. Pharaoh died, and his son, the brother of the princess who still appeared so often in my thoughts, became the new king. His reign was even more cruel and more oppressive than his predecessor's. Day after day we cried out to the God of Abraham and Sarah, pleading for mercy. One night Aaron announced that he had heard the voice of God calling him to go out into the desert to meet Moses, in exile.

"I don't know what will happen when we return," he said, "but have faith in God's plan, and be ready for us."

The following morning before dawn, Aaron left to meet Moses.

And all of Egypt knew when they had returned.

The battle raged between my brother and Pharaoh. The great Nile ran red with blood and there was no water to drink. The cotton and wheat fields were overrun by frogs, and the animals and children were infested with lice. Plagues and disease swept the villages, and still the king would not yield. Months passed. One day toward the end of a year a terrible darkness descended upon the land, and the sun did not rise, nor the moon. A palace messenger found me at home, lighting incense and baking bread.

"You are summoned to the palace," she said brusquely, with none of the warmth I remembered in the woman who had brought baskets to the ill and needy of our people.

Retracing my steps up to the palace gate behind the servant of the princess I was thrust back into childhood, remembering my fear and awe the first time I had walked this path. Now I was a mature woman, a lifetime of experiences behind me since leaving the palace with my mother when Moses was weaned, decades ago.

The servant led me to an anteroom lit by torches, and left me there to wait. My eye fell on a great urn in one corner of the room, bearing a painting of the cat goddess Bastet. "I remember you," I said to the cat, hearing gentle footsteps behind me.

"And I remember you," said the princess, now a very old woman indeed. We studied each other a moment. Gone were her bangles and beads, and the painted lips and eyes. She wore a simple white gown, of the softest linen, with a single piece of jewelry, a large amulet representing Isis, around her neck. I curtseyed low before the princess, as much out of genuine respect as obedience to the law.

"I am glad to see you are well, your Highness."

"Still alive, you mean?" she chuckled now with a twinkle in her eye. "You must wonder why I have sent for you after all these years," she added, motioning me to a long, cushioned bench. "Sit with me. We are neither of us so young anymore."

We sat together, two old women silently comparing wrinkles and counting gray hairs. She remembered a precocious child, and I, a great beauty. We talked of the changes in our lives and in the land. The princess, it seemed, had greater concerns even than the plagues that had befallen Egypt. She believed that the gods were punishing her people not only for the enslavement of the Hebrews, but for their abandonment of the old ways of worship.

"My people are dying, losing their crops, their livelihoods. The heavens storm with anger, but the king does not yield. Legend tells us that in the days of the Old Dynasties the priestesses made all religious decisions, and that women held dominion over their husbands in economic and social matters. Isis, my own patroness, and Nut, the Great Creator of all, ruled supreme in the heavens. Today it is no longer so. Women serve in the temples only as musicians, and the crown passes to the sons of the royal house and not to the daughters. We rule with and are ruled by the sword. But you Hebrews worship only a male god, the warrior Yahweh. Miriam, you are a great priestess, yet you do not hold the Goddess in your heart? How can this be?"

"I have heard of the old days, when the world was such as you describe," I answered. "The Voice I hear is strong, but with the strength of a mother, not a warrior. The words and their meaning are what matter. Woman's role in the sacred mysteries is changing, and oddly it comforts me to know you share my distress. Here we are not queen and slave, but two women of faith mourning the loss of our era."

Footsteps and male voices sounded in the halls behind us, and the princess began to hurry. "It is time for your people to be leaving Egypt," she whispered. "My father was a ruthless king, and my brother is no better. I know he has agreed to your freedom and then repented of it twice. The longer my brother resists yours, the worse will be everyone's fate."

"You speak the truth, as I have always known you to do," I answered her. "But with whom are you asking me to intervene? God, or Pharaoh?"

"Neither, Miriam. I am asking you to take your people and go. I have spoken with Moses, pleaded with him as a mother to a son, since he will always be that in my heart. But he insists he only follows his god's instructions. One month ago I consulted with the priestess at the high temple, who foretold the death of many Egyptians, including innocent children. If you leave now under this blinding darkness the soldiers will be unable to pursue you, and lives on both sides may be spared."

"I will speak to my brother, and do what I can," I promised her.

"And I will do likewise with mine. Together we once saved Moses' life from Pharaoh's decree; now I must save Egyptian lives from Moses' decree. Perhaps, together, we can avert disaster a second time."

I took my leave of this great lady, never to see her again. I tried to do as she requested, but God had sealed the fate of Egypt. At midnight the tenth and final plague came to pass: the death of the firstborn son in every Egyptian family. In a gruesome parallel to Pharaoh's ruling condemning Hebrew babies, his own son now lay dead in the royal chamber. But we had little time to contemplate this turn; we needed to move, and quickly. While the men gathered the herds, the women piled clothing, cooking pots, ritual objects and food high on our carts and animals. All this we gathered in the hurried hours before our escape. The bread dough that had been prepared for the day's baking had not yet risen, so we gathered the flat dough to bring with us. Each woman took her frame drum or sistrum, and laid it carefully in a special basket with incense, amulets and *teraphim*. These we wrapped in our best scarves, and we laid the unrisen dough on top, to bake in the sun.

Our journey had begun, and we were not alone, because in each heart beat faith in our divine Midwife who would deliver us forth to freedom. I stepped away from the camp to look at the moon. It shone brightly, full and round.

"Savior of Israel," I spoke to the heavens, "I pray to you this night that in the morning we will be safely borne out of slavery. As a mother protects her children, keep us safe, and be with us on our journey. Bring us home to the land of Sarah and Rachel, that we your daughters may keep their traditions alive."

◈

Returning from my cave retreat, I made my way back to camp where I was greeted with much rejoicing by the women, and with relief by my brothers who had feared for my health during my absence. We were all three of us quite old, I realized. In these final weeks of my life I have tried to draw inward, reflecting on my accomplishments and the meaning of the revelation I experienced. As we journeyed onward to Kadesh, I gathered my friends around me to say goodbye. With these closing words I pass this journal to the safekeeping of one of the younger women, with a request that she bury it in the Promised Land, when they arrive.

> *Let the name of Shekhinah be forever praised.*
> *When the world is strange and dim*
> *Her light will shine forth.*
> *As sure as the moon reawakens to its place in the*
> *   heavens*
> *Will all humankind come to praise the glory of the One.*
>
> *To my daughters of the future, I leave you my legacy.*
> *Tell my story to your daughters, that they may always*
> *   remember*
> *That their grandmothers danced barefoot at the shores*
> *   of the Sea,*
> *And they shall be the crescent moon which will light our*
> *   way Home.*

"... and there was no water for the community ..."

MIRIAM'S WELL

∽

Miriam's Well draws out the mystical possibilities of Miriam, the new connections and rituals she has inspired, and the new wave of Judaism created by the women who follow her. Here she moves out of the realm of historical personage, and onto the symbolic plane. Miriam is sometimes compared to Elijah, and the new rituals invoking her name call her healer and redeemer. The Torah acknowledges Miriam's death with a brief note, immediately followed by the information that there was no water for the congregation. From this the rabbis deduced that the water that had miraculously followed Israel through the desert existed solely for the merit of Miriam, and dried up with her death. Talmudic lore granted the Well magical healing properties, and feminists today look to the symbol of Miriam's Well as a source of lost women's traditions.

Through the songs, Haggadot, and rituals honoring and invoking her, we see that the women of Israel are still following Miriam. Several pieces call for increased inclusion of Miriam at Passover: Debbie Findling's review of historical Passover observance, and Yael Katz's study of placing fish on the seder plate in honor of Miriam. Susan Schnur looks at Miriam from an anthropological perspective, exploring her possible origins as a goddess figure. Reprinted here is Matia Angelou's ritual for Miriam's Cup, which sparked the trend that is now so popular.

A number of very personal pieces bring the spirit of Miriam into the authors' and readers' own lives. With Miriam's centrality in Jewish observance continuing to grow, the coming years will see new songs, rituals and midrash, as we continue to draw from the wisdom of Miriam's Well.

PLACING A COOKED FOOD ON THE SEDER TABLE
IN COMMEMORATION OF MIRIAM[1]
Yael Levine Katz

In a compendium of responsa which has come down to us in the name of Rav Sherira Gaon (Gaon of Pumbedita from 986 – 1006. He was responding to questions posed to him by Jews of Kairouan, North Africa), we learn of a custom designating a special cooked food on the seder table in commemoration of Miriam. This compendium, which includes additional responsa related to Passover as well, has been preserved in the work *Ma'aseh Roke'ah* by Rabbi Eleazar of Worms (c. 1165-1230). The actual manuscript that served as the source for the printed edition was destroyed by fire in 1791, and the published work is a third copying. It is possible, therefore, that the copyists introduced various changes.

> And they further asked concerning the two cooked foods and he replied that they were in memory of the two emissaries, Moses and Aaron, that the Holy One, blessed be He, sent in Egypt. And there are those who put an additional cooked food in memory of Miriam, as it says, "And I sent before you Moses, Aaron, and Miriam" (Mi 6:4). And those three cooked foods are fish, meat, and an egg, corresponding to the foods that Israel will eat in the Time to Come, fish corresponding to Leviathan, egg to Ziz of the field, meat corresponding to Shor ha-Bar (wild bull).[2]

Two customs are mentioned in this passage, one concerning the placement of two cooked foods in commemoration of the two emissaries, Moses and Aaron, and another according to which an additional cooked food was placed in commemoration of Miriam. No specification is provided as to the cooked foods that should be placed for the former. By contrast, with regard to the second custom, there is a detailed enumeration concerning the three foods: they are fish, meat, and an egg. They contain symbolic significance—they correspond to the foods that Israel will eat in the Time to Come.

The three cooked foods are mentioned twice in the text. In the first instance it is stated "fish, meat, and an egg." The order in the second appearance is, however, different: "fish . . . egg . . . meat." It is, therefore, unclear which of the foods correspond, in actuality, to each of the personalities.

The custom concerning the placement of a cooked food in commemoration of Miriam is introduced with the articulation, "And there are those who put an additional cooked food," and we may, thus, conclude that it was not as widespread as the practice of placing the two cooked foods. It is possible that it was a relatively new custom at that time, and had not yet taken root. It is also conceivable that this custom did not become widely accepted owing to economic conditions.

It should be mentioned that in the time of Rav Sherira Gaon no official seder plate was in use. This came into being in the time of the *rishonim* (c. 1050 – 1500 CE).[3]

This source appears in variation in ms. Oxford Bodleian 2343 (Opp. Add. 4⁰ 127), which is a work of compilations from Provence, and was apparently copied from the *Ma'aseh Roke'ah.*

And they further asked concerning the matter of the two cooked foods. And he replied that they were in memory of the two emissaries that the Holy One, blessed be He, sent in Egypt, Moses and Aaron. And there are those who are more stringent and add to these another cooked food in memory of Miriam, as it says, "And I sent before you Moses, Aaron, and

Miriam." And those foods are fish, and an egg, and meat, corresponding to the three types of cooked foods that the inhabitants of the exile will [   ][4]

From this source we hear that the custom concerning Miriam was considered a stringency, in its positive connotation, in relation to the first custom. The order in which the foods are brought, "fish, and an egg, and meat," which corresponds to the first time these foods are mentioned in the *Ma'aseh Roke'ah*, is the same as that which appears the second time in the latter work.

The closing portion of the text is illegible. One possibility is that its reading was similar to that of the text of the *Ma'aseh Roke'ah*. Whereas in the latter it says, "that Israel will eat in the Time to Come," it is possible that the original reading in the Oxford manuscript was, "that the inhabitants of the exile will eat." However, it is also possible to point to a connection to the commentary of Abraham Ibn Ezra (1089-1164) on Daniel 12:2: "Many of those that sleep in the dust of the earth will awake, some to eternal life, others to reproaches, to everlasting abhorrence." In his commentary he mentions, *inter alia*, that the righteous who die in the exile will come to life in the time of the Messiah, and will then rejoice in Leviathan, Ziz, and Behemoth, and will die once again and be resurrected in the resurrection of the dead. It is possible to surmise that the ending of the text in the manuscript read "that the inhabitants of the exile will live in the Time to Come and rejoice in Leviathan, Ziz of the field, and Behemoth," and reflects a source or concept similar to that of Ibn Ezra.

We will presently refer to the animals mentioned in Rav Sherira's responsum: Behemoth, Leviathan, and Ziz of the field. It is beyond the scope of this paper to refer to all the aspects pertaining to them, and we will focus on the motif present in the responsum concerning these animals as food for the righteous in the Time to Come. Behemoth, Leviathan, and Ziz of the field are each mentioned in the bible separately.[5] Behemoth resides on the earth, the place of the Leviathan is the sea, and Ziz of the field is a type of bird. All these animals are depicted in the sources as being of enormous size.

Much additional information concerning these animals is contained in the Apocrypha and in the talmudic and post-talmudic literature. In 1 Enoch, from the second century B.C.E., it is stated that the female of the *tannin* (sea monster) is called Leviathan and the male Behemoth, and that they would serve as food in "the garden of the righteous ones."[6] In the work *Hazon Ezra* (The Vision of Ezra), of the first century C.E., it is mentioned that the two *tanninim* live apart, Behemoth resides on the earth and Leviathan in the sea. "And you preserved them to be eaten by whom you wish, and when you wish.[7] It is not specified which persons will eat them. In *Hazon Baruch*, of the first century C.E. as well, it says that Behemoth and Leviathan will be kept until a future time, and will serve as nourishment for those who are left.[8]

The meal of the righteous in the Time to Come is referred to in various sources in the talmudic and post-talmudic literature. Leviticus *Rabbah* mentions that Behemoth and Leviathan will engage in a wild-beast contest before the righteous in the Time to Come. Behemoth will, with its horns, pull Leviathan down and rend it; Leviathan will, with its fins, pull Behemoth down and pierce it through. Their meat will be the food of the righteous, without *shehitah* (ritual slaughtering), as a temporary ruling.[9] This motif appears in variation in the parallel sources to this passage.[10] In the continuation of Leviticus *Rabbah* a statement is brought whereby the Holy One, blessed be He, will make a banquet in the Time to

Come for the righteous who have not eaten meat that has not been ritually slaughtered.[11]

In Tanhuma ed. Buber it is mentioned in the name of the Holy One, blessed be He, that in this world Israel ate the manna through the merit of their forefathers, but in the Time to Come He will feed them Behemoth, Ziz, and Leviathan through their own merit.[12]

The basic sources concerning the two cooked foods on the seder table are found in the Babylonian and Jerusalem Talmuds. From its context, we may deduce that these served as the actual foods eaten at the meal, and that at that time had not yet assumed a symbolic nature.[13]

> What are the two dishes? Rav Huna said beets and rice . . . Hezekiah said: Even a fish and an egg on it. Rav Joseph said: Two kinds of meat are necessary, one in memory of the Passover offering and one in memory of the *hagigah*. Ravina said: Even a bone and broth.

What is of significance in this source is that all three foods mentioned in the responsum of Rav Sherira; fish, an egg, and meat, appear in the Babylonian Talmud as possibilities for the dishes on the seder night.

In the Jerusalem Talmud the source appears as a *baraita* ("outside" Mishnah): "It was learnt: And outside the Temple two cooked foods are necessary, one in memory of the Passover offering and one in memory of the *hagigah*" (Jerusalem Talmud *Pesahim* 10:3, 37d).

Apart from the responsum attributed to Rav Sherira, from the writings of Rav Sa'adyah Gaon we learn that the number of dishes at the seder wasn't fixed, and that it was possible to add to or subtract from it, or that this was the actual practice. "And one should put two types or three or four, beets, and rice, and something salty, and eggs, and save all of this until the night of the fifteenth of Nisan."[14] In practice, though, we do not find in sources other than the talmudic text and later sources derivative from the tradition that connect the foods placed on the seder table with the foods that Israel will eat in the Time to Come, that fish was indeed placed on the seder table as one of the cooked foods.

The responsum of Rav Sherira, which mentions the custom concerning Miriam, contains three threefold components: three cooked foods, three persons, and three animals. The majority of later medieval sources mention two elements: two cooked foods, Moses and Aaron, and two animals.[15] However, some of the sources from the fourteenth century onwards speak anew of three foods corresponding to the three animals, but the three emissaries do not figure in them.[16]

As mentioned, the responsum attributed to Rabbi Sherira appears in the *Ma'aseh Roke'ah* by Rabbi Eleazar of Worms. It is therefore of interest to note that in the work *Sefer ha-Roke'ah* by the same author, as well as in his commentary to the Haggadah of Passover, we hear only of the tradition of placing two foods in commemoration of Moses and Aaron. "Two cooked foods in memory of the *hagigah* and the Passover offering, and some say in memory of Moses and Aaron."[17]

Whereas, according to the source attributed to Rav Sherira and as stated by some of the later sources, the cooked foods correspond to the foods that Israel will eat in the Time to Come, this motif is expanded in several later sources to include the entire seder meal. We thus find in *Shenei Luhot ha-Berit* by Rabbi Isaiah Horowitz (c. 1565-1630) that one should "think that the meal is like a spiritual meal . . . and an example and an allusion to the banquets of the Leviathan."[18]

Rabbi Hayyim Palache (1788-1869) wrote in his work *Mo'ed le-Kohl Hai* that on the first night of Passover, apart from the foods that are placed on the seder plate, one should eat beets, one of the examples offered in the Babylonian Talmud for the two dishes, as well as fish. This should be accompanied by short recitations.

> It is befitting to eat on the first night of Passover beets and to offer thanksgiving to the Lord that he removed our enemies and adversaries and it is also proper to eat fish and to say "May it be Your will that You merit us to eat from the banquet of Leviathan."[19]

Rabbi Rahamim Nissim Isaac Palache (1813-1907), son of Rabbi Hayyim Palache, made mention of the custom to eat fish on the Passover holiday, adducing support for his view from the midrashim in the Babylonian Talmud *Sotah* 11b and in Exodus *Rabbah* chapter 1, concerning the righteous women in Egypt. These sources commence with the well-known statement, "As the reward for the righteous women who were in that generation the Israelites were redeemed from Egypt." They continue to relate that when the women went to draw water, the Holy One, blessed be He, arranged that small fish would enter their pitchers, and they drew up half water and half fish and carried them to their husbands in the field. They set two pots on the fire, one for hot water and the other for the fish, and they washed their husbands, anointed and fed them, gave them to drink, and cohabited with them between the mounds in the field. Rabbi Palache concluded by saying that by virtue of the fish that the women used to feed their husbands they were redeemed from Egypt, and he, subsequently, deemed it worthy to eat fish on Passover in commemoration of the Exodus. He further stated an additional reasoning for the eating of fish, which was to signify that the Egyptians cast the children of Israel into the Nile, and fish ate them.[20]

The frame of reference in Rabbi Palache's work is to the eating of fish on Passover, and it appears that he was of the opinion that one should eat fish not at the seder meal alone, but at the meal eaten during the day as well.[21]

Rabbi Simeon Sofer (1820-1883), known from his work *Mikhtav Sofer*, explained in his commentary to the Passover Haggadah, with reference to this midrash, that the righteous women fed their husbands fish knowing that fish are pure, and do not require ritual slaughtering.[22]

Practical Aspects of Renewing the Custom

The custom concerning the placement of an additional cooked food in commemoration of Miriam pays tribute to the role that she fulfilled in the redemption from Egypt.

We are not aware of the precise circumstances that brought the custom into being; whether it was the initiation of a group of women or men or families, or, perhaps, of Sages. The custom, as depicted in the source attributed to Rav Sherira, took place within a family context, and in that respect its portrayal in the source is not feminist.

In time, this custom has fallen into oblivion. It is unclear in what period this occurred and what the precise circumstances were that effected the loss of this tradition. It is likewise possible to point to a custom concerning Miriam's Well that has fallen into disuse. Several medieval sources, amongst them the anonymous halakhic work *Kol Bo* (written at the end of the thirteenth or beginning of the fourteenth century), state that women would draw water immediately on *motza'ei Shabbat* (Saturday after sundown), following the recitation of *Barekhu*, the opening call of the evening service. Miriam's Well, it is stated, is situated in the Sea of Tiberias, and every *motza'ei Shabbat* water is drawn from all springs and wells, and anyone who is sick and chances upon that water and drinks from it, even if his entire body is afflicted with boils, will immediately be cured.[23] This custom was prevalent in the circles of the disciples of the Maharam of Rothenburg (c. 1215-1293) at the beginning of the fourteenth century, and most probably fell into oblivion sometime near the middle of the fourteenth century.[24]

The custom of designating a cooked food on the seder table as a commemoration of Miriam is worthy of renewal in our time, in recognition of the crucial role she and the other righteous women played in the Exodus. This custom was brought down and sanctioned by one of the greatest figures of the geonic period, which should be borne in mind as we contemplate its reinstitution.

According to the practice in most communities today, the two cooked foods are the *zero'a* (bone) and *betzah* (egg).[25] It would appear, then, that fish should be brought in commemoration of Miriam.

There is no specification in the source attributed to Rav Sherira as to the type of fish that should be used. In *Shibbolei ha-Leket*, for instance, two types of meat are mentioned: roasted and cooked[26]. The talmudic text itself does not, however, include any such details. Since the *zero'a* and *betzah*, which according to our present-day custom represent the two cooked foods, retain their natural form, it would seem that one should place baked or cooked fish rather than gefilte fish, for instance. It would also appear that a whole fish with head and tail intact should be used, much as the *zero'a* is, according to many customs, an entire neck, and the *betzah* a whole egg. In the sources concerning the righteous women in tractate *Sotah* and Exodus *Rabbah*, it is stated that they brought their husbands small fish, and this size fish would seem appropriate and suitable to those of the *zero'a* and *betzah*.[27]

Vegetarians or vegans might choose to replace the fish with other produce of the sea, such as sea grasses.

Another consideration that should be borne in mind has to do with the actual location of the fish on the seder plate. It should first, however, be stressed that all the foods, including the fish in commemoration of Miriam, should be on the seder plate, and not in a separate place on the table. In the Babylonian Talmud *Pesahim* 115b we learn that it was customary to move the entire table from its place so that the children should inquire concerning the differing customs of the seder night in relation to the rest of the year. However, it is stated in the commentary of *tosafot ad loc.* (s. v. *lama*) that this was the former practice, since the tables at that time were small. However, since tables were currently large, it was customary to move the seder plate from its place, and not the table itself. So one may deduce that all the foods should be on one and the same plate.

Different *shitot* (halakhic opinions) exist concerning the arrangement of the foodstuffs on the seder plate. According to Rabbi Jacob Moellin, known by the acronym Maharil (c. 1360-1427), the foods eaten first are placed closest to the person conducting the seder, the underlying principle being that "one must not forego the occasion for performing the precepts."[28] The *matzot* themselves are put near the plate.[29] The Vilna Gaon (1720-1797) was of the view that the two *matzot* are placed in the center, the *maror* and *haroset* above them and the *zero'a* and *betzah* below them.[30]

In all cases the *betzah* and *zero'a*, representing the two cooked foods, are on the same level. The question is whether the fish should be placed on that row, and if so, precisely where, or on a separate row. A consideration to bear in mind is whether the fish could be placed directly adjacent to the *zero'a*, or whether there should be a separation between them in space by placing one of them, perhaps the fish, in a separate utensil on the seder plate (owing to the custom of not eating meat and fish together). In this context it should be stated that one should differentiate between cooking the two together, eating these two foods together when cooked separately, and eating them one following the other. The initial prohibition brought down in the Talmud is that of roasting fish together with meat (*Pesahim* 76b). This was brought down by some *rishonim*, but not by all. Some mentioned that it also pertains to cooking. The prohibition of eating fish and meat that were not cooked together is post-talmudic, brought down first in some *rishonim*; likewise the proscription of eating meat following fish, though some are of the opinion that there is no injunction here.[31]

With time, and as more and more persons take upon themselves this custom anew, it is probable that a permanent place for the cooked food will be determined, and subsequently, a new seder plate will have to be designed reflecting the change.

No text for recitation accompanies the source attributed to Rav Sherira, but it would seem advisable to make mention during the seder of the reason for the additional food. As stated, Rabbi Hayyim Palache recommended saying a short prayer, when eating the fish at the meal, in which the hope is expressed that one will merit to eat from the banquet of the Leviathan.

Another possible passage for recitation both in connection with the fish placed on the seder plate in commemoration of Miriam and the fish eaten at the meal, might be from *Perek Shirah*, an anonymous collection of hymns of praise to the Creator placed in the mouths of the heavenly bodies, the earth, animals, birds, and vegetation. The precise dating of the work is unknown. It is alluded to in the Talmud, and an earlier version was known in the geonic period. The majority of the hymns are, in fact, scriptural verses, mostly from Psalms. *Perek Shirah* was intended to be a liturgical text, and was included in the early Ashkenazi manuscripts of *mahzorim*. Its later inclusion in printed siddurim had to do with the influence of Safed kabbalists.

Perek Shirah includes, *inter alia*, recitations by the Leviathan and fish.[32] "Leviathan what does he say? 'Praise the Lord, for He is good, His steadfast love is eternal' (Ps[s] 118, 1).[33] Fish what do they say? 'The voice of the Lord is over the waters; the God of glory thunders, the Lord, over the mighty waters'" (Ps[s] 29:3).[34] It would seem that since, according to Rav Sherira, the Leviathan corresponds to the fish, and since the fish represents, according to the present-day custom, Miriam, the verses that both the Leviathan and the fish said, according to *Perek Shirah*, are suitable to be recited. The first verse appears several times in Psalms, including in the Hallel, which is recited, apart from the first day of the holiday, on the first night of Passover as well, according to many customs, and portions of it are included in the Haggadah itself. The second verse, which speaks of God's connection to the sea, is especially appropriate for recitation on the night commemorating the Exodus.

In the Babylonian Talmud *Pesahim* 118b a midrash having to do with the Exodus is brought concerning the fish of the sea who recited the words "And the faithfulness of the Lord endures forever" (Ps[s] 117:2).[35] It is related that the Israelites of the generation of the Exodus were of little faith, were rebellious at the Red Sea, and said: "Just as we ascend at one side of the sea so, too, the Egyptians ascend from another side." The Holy One, blessed be He, ordered the Prince of the Sea to deliver them on the dry land, and Israel came and saw them, as it says, "Israel saw the Egyptians dead on the shore of the sea" (Ex 14:30). The Prince of the Sea voiced a complaint, claiming "Does a master offer a gift to his servant and then take it back?"

That is, the nourishment of the fish was taken from them. The Holy one, blessed be He, replied by saying that he would give them one and a half times their number; the chariots of Sisera were nine hundred in number whereas those of Pharaoh were six hundred. The Prince of the Sea then said, "Master of the Universe, can a servant claim a debt from his Master?" The Holy One, blessed be He, responded by saying that the brook of Kishon would serve as a surety. When Sisera and his people came to wage war against Israel they went down to cool themselves from the heat in the brook of Kishon. The Holy One, blessed be He, said to the brook, "Go and deliver your pledge." The brook immediately swept out and cast them into the sea, as it says, "The brook Kishon swept them away, the ancient brook" (Jgs 5:21). At that hour the fish in the sea opened their mouths and exclaimed, "And the faithfulness of the Lord endures forever."

The wider context of the biblical words is as follows: "Praise the Lord, all you nations; extol him, all you peoples, for great is His steadfast love toward us; the faithfulness of the Lord endures forever. Hallelujah" (Ps[s] 117:1-2). These two verses, which compose chapter 117 of Psalms, are also included in the Hallel which is read on the Eve of Passover, and they, therefore, seem appropriate for recitation in connection with the fish in commemoration of Miriam as well as with the fish eaten at the meal.

Some may also wish specifically to address Miriam as part of a recitation for the eating of the fish. It might feel appropriate to read passages from the Torah about Miriam, or tell the story of the Well and discuss Miriam's traditional connection with water.

NOTES

1. This essay is an abridged version of a more extensive article to appear in *Jewish Legal Studies by Women* (Urim Publications, 2001) Micah D. Halpern and Chana Safrai, editors.
2. Eleazar of Worms. 1912. *Ma'aseh Roke'ah*, Sanok, Paragraph 59, p. 17. See further Simcha Emanuel. 1993. *The Lost Halakhic Books of the Tosaphists* (Hebrew). Dissertation, Hebrew University, pp. 169-200.
3. See: Tosafot to *Pesahim* 115b, s.v. *lama*; Zedekiah ben Abraham Anav. 1886. *Shibbolei ha-Leket ha-Shalem*, ed. Solomon Buber. Vilna: Re'em, Chapter 218, p. 181.
4. Chapter 691, 100b. (reel 21407 at the Institute of Microfilmed Hebrew Manuscripts). On this manuscript see also: *Catalogue of the Hebrew Manuscripts in the Bodleian Library, Supplement of Addenda and Corrigenda to Vol. I (A. Neubauer's Catalogue)*. 1994. Compiled under the direction of Malachi Beit-Arié, Edited by R. A. May. Oxford: Clarendon Press, pp. 456-457.
5. Behemoth: Joel 1:20; 2:22; Psalms 8:8; 49:13; 21; 50:10;. 73:22; Job 12:7; 35:11; 40:15; Leviathan: Isaiah 27:1; Psalms 74:14; 104:26; Job 3:8; 40:25; Ziz of the field: Psalms 50:11; 80:14.
6. I Hanokh. 1937. *ha-Sefarim ha-Hizonim*, ed. Abraham Kahana. Tel Aviv: Mekorot, Volume 1, 60,7; 60, 23, pp. 56, 58.
7. Hazon Ezra. 1937. *ha-Sefarim ha-Hizonim*, ed. Abraham Kahana. Tel Aviv: Mekorot, Volume 1, Book 2, 4,49-52, p. 625.
8. Hazon Baruch. 1937. *ha-Sefarim ha-Hizonim*, ed. Abraham Kahana. Tel Aviv: Mekorot, Volume 1, Book 2, 1, 29, 4, pp. 379-380.
9. *Midrash Va-Yikra Rabbah*, ed. Mordecai Margulies. 1993. New York: The Jewish Theological Seminary, 13,3, pp. 277-278.
10. See, *inter alia*: Tanhuma, Shemini 7; *Pesikta de-Rav Kahana*, ed. Bernard Mandelbaum, 1987[2]. New York: The Jewish Theological Seminary, p. 456.
11. *Midrash Va-Yikra Rabbah*, ed. Mordecai Margulies. 13,3, pp. 278-279.
12. *Midrash Tanhuma ha-Kadum ve-ha-Yashan*, ed. Solomon Buber. 1885. Vilna, Be-Shallah, 24, p. 68.

13. Yosef Tabory, *The Passover Ritual Throughout the Generations* (Hebrew). 1996. Tel Aviv: Hakibbutz Hameuchad, pp. 105-122.

14. I. Davidson, S. Assaf and B. I. Joel. 1941. *Siddur Rav Sa'adyah Ga'on*, Jerusalem: Mekize Nirdamim, p. 135.

15. *Sefer Da'at Zekenim*, Livorno. 1783. Shemot 12,8, 34a; "Sefer Amarkal: The Halakhoth of Passover," ed. Michael Higger. 1950. *Alexander Marx Jubilee Volume*, New York: The Jewish Theological Seminary, Hebrew Section, p. 163.

16. See, *inter alia*: Ms. Parma 1147 (unpaginated) (reel 13154 at the Institute of Microfilmed Hebrew Manuscripts); Jewish Theological Seminary ms. Mic. 8279, 14b (reel 40108 at the Institute of Microfilmed Hebrew Manuscripts); Ms. Budapest - Kaufmann 427, 9a (reel 15151 at the Institute of Microfilmed Hebrew Manuscripts); Ms. 8⁰ 5492 of The Department of Manuscripts of the Jewish National and University Library, Jerusalem, 321a; Haggadah, Soncino 1486 (unpaginated).

17. Eleazar of Worms, *Sefer ha-Roke'ah*, Fano, 1505, Chapter 283 (unpaginated); Rabbi Eleazar of Worms, *Roke'ah*. 1984. *A Commentary on the Passover Haggadah* (Hebrew), Edited by Rabbi Moshe Hershler. Jerusalem: Beit Hamidrash Latorah, Regensberg Institute, p. 43.

18. Isaiah Horowitz. 1649. *Shenei Luhot ha-Berit*, Amsterdam, 165a.

19. Hayyim Palache. 1861. *Mo'ed le-Khol Hai*, Izmir, Chapter 4, 24b.

20. Rahamim Nissim Isaac Palache. 1876. *Yafeh la-Lev*, Part 2, Izmir, 38b, 39c; *Midrash Shemot Rabbah, Chapters I-XIV*, ed. Avigdor Shinan, Jerusalem: Dvir, 1984, 1,12(2), pp. 54-55. Parallel source: "*Mahadura Hadasha shel ha-Tanhuma al Shemot, Va-Eyra*", *Ginzei Schechter*, ed. Louis Ginzberg. 1928. Volume 1, New York: The Jewish Theological Seminary, p. 64. According to a parallel source in Tanhuma, Pekudei, 9, the women did not actually feed their husbands the fish, but they would sell them, and buy wine with their worth, and cook with it. According to Deuteronomy Rabbah (*Devarim Rabbah*, ed. Saul Lieberman. 1974.³ Jerusalem: Wahrmann Books, *Parashat Devarim*, 15, p. 15) they bought wine and oil. Compare *Yalkut Shimoni*, *Shemot*, 163, in the name of *Midrash Avkir* where is it stated that they brought their husbands "every food and drink." In *Midrash ha-Gadol* it says that they

brought them hot food (Rabbi David Adani. 1956. *Midrash ha-Gadol, Sefer Shemot*, ed. Mordecai Margulies, Jerusalem: Mossad ha-Rav Kook, to *Shemot* 1,12, p. 15).

21. One is required to eat only two meals on the holiday, in contrast to the Sabbath where three meals are eaten. See *Shulhan Arukh, Orah Hayyim*, 529, 1.

22. Simeon Sofer. 1995. *Haggadah shel Pesah Mikhtav Sofer*, Bene-Berak, p. 70.

23. Kol Bo, ed. David Abraham. 1990. Part 2, Jerusalem, p. 258. For the complete range of sources see: Israel M. Ta-Shma, 1999³· *Early Franco-German Ritual and Custom* (Hebrew), Jerusalem: Magnes Press, pp. 214-216.

24. Ta-Shma, pp. 215-216. Daniel Sperber, 1991, in the second volume of his work *Minhagei Yisrael*, Jerusalem: Mossad ha-Rav Kook, pp. 234-239, referred to the disappearance of various customs mentioned in halakhic works in general and brought several examples to illustrate this phenomenon.

25. See, *inter alia, Sefer ha-Minhagot*, 1935. *Sifran shel Rishonim*, ed. Simcha Assaf, Jerusalem: Mekize Nirdamim, p. 156; *Shulhan Arukh, Orah Hayyim* 473,4.

26. See *supra*, note 3.

27. Compare Genesis *Rabbah*, where the scripture "And the fat of the earth" (Genesis 27:28) is interpreted as alluding to the well that brought up various kinds of exceedingly fat fish (*Midrash Bereshit Rabbah*, ed. Julius Theodor and Hanokh Albeck.1965.² Jerusalem: Wahrmann Books, 66, 3, p. 747.)

28. On this concept in the Babylonian Talmud see: *Pesahim* 64b; Yoma 33a; 58b; 70a.

29. *The Book of Maharil: Customs by Rabbi Yaacov Mulin* (Hebrew), ed. Shlomoh J. Spitzer. 1989. Jerusalem, pp. 94-95; Rema to *Shulhan Arukh, Orah Hayyim*, 473, 4.

30. Issachar Baer ben Tanhum. 1990.² *Ma'aseh Rav: Minhagei ha-Gra*, Jerusalem, pp. 214, 216.

31. *"Dagim."* 1987. *Talmudic Encyclopedia*, Volume VII, Jerusalem: Yad Harav Herzog, pp. 224-226.

32. See in detail: Malachi Beit-Arié. 1967. *Perek Shirah: Introductions and Critical Edition*, Dissertation, Hebrew University; idem. 1972. "Perek Shirah", *Encyclopedia Judaica*, Jerusalem, Volume 13, pp. 273-275.

33. This verse appears in additional places in the Holy Scriptures as well: Psalms 106:1; 107:1; 118:29; 136:1; 1 Chronicles 16:34.

34. Malachi Beit-Arié. 1967. *Perek Shirah: Introductions and Critical Edition*, Dissertation, Hebrew University, Volume 2, pp. 31, 33.

35. The first portion of the midrash appears in Babylonian Talmud Arakhin 15a as well.

PASS(ED) OVER: MIRIAM AND THE HAGGADAH
Debbie Findling

I can still recall the taste of my mother's chopped liver. My mother cooked for days preparing our annual family seder. And chopped liver was just the beginning. She'd stand over the hot stove a full day just to make gefilte fish. And another day for the chicken soup with matzah balls too big for the delicate gold-rimmed china bowls. For my mother, preparation for Passover actually began weeks before anyone tasted the first bite of matzah. Like many women, my mother scrubbed and cleaned the house weeks before she even planned the seder menu.

Passover seder was a joyous, mysterious, enchanting evening and a culinary feast for the hordes of family and friends who squeezed into our tiny dining room, made smaller by the added card table and folding chairs extending into the hallway. My father sat at the head of the table, like a king on his throne, leading his flock through the Haggadah; my mother perched at the opposite end, close to the kitchen so she could serve the meal and clear the dishes. Although my mother glowed from happiness at seeing her family together, she also had a look of exhaustion—dark circles forming around her weary eyes, throbbing legs from long hours of standing in front of the stove. Years later, as I cook and clean preparing seder for my own family, I know her exhaustion.

Jewish tradition teaches that Passover is the season of our freedom from the metaphoric house of bondage. Yet, for many women by the time we sit down to the seder table we are completely exhausted—not free at all, but rather enslaved by cooking and cleaning. What's more, the story of our people's exodus from Egypt is packed with legends about heroic men who devoted their hearts to God and risked their lives to save the Israelite nation. The Haggadah bursts with wondrous stories of hope, redemption and renewal—yet stories about women are significantly absent. A friend recently joked that women are missing from the Haggadah because like today, they were too busy cooking and cleaning.

Although the stories of women are noticeably missing from the Haggadah, the Torah and Talmud are replete with stories about Miriam and her contribution to the Exodus from Egypt. Jewish texts portray Miriam as a central figure in the Exodus story. She held key leadership roles during the Hebrew enslavement in Egypt and throughout the journey in the desert. This essay examines some of the traditional Jewish texts and commentaries that document Miriam's merits as a courageous leader and wise prophetess, and suggests some modern practices for including her story in a prominent place at the seder table.

The Torah teaches that Miriam is the sister of Aaron and Moses and the only daughter of Amram and Yocheved (Num 26:59; 1 Chr 5:29). Her name, Miriam, is associated with the Hebrew words *mar* and *maror*, meaning bitterness, because her birth coincided with the enslavement of the Children of Israel in Egypt (Cohen, 1992, 129). Yet Miriam's legacy is the antithesis of bitterness. Viewed another way, her birth symbolizes the end of enslavement and marks the beginning of freedom.

Many of the lesser-known stories about Miriam bestow her with chutzpah uncharacteristic of women at that time. For example, the Talmud (*Sotah* 11b; 12a-13a; BB 120a) teaches that as a young girl Miriam brazenly challenged her father's defiance of Pharaoh's wrath. Pharaoh's astrologers had warned him that the savior of the Jews was about to be born. In response, Pharaoh ordered the death of all Hebrew male infants. As an act of resistance to Pharaoh's proclamation, Amram, who was head of the Jewish court, divorced his wife and encouraged all the men of Israel to do the same to avoid siring children who would be killed. Young Miriam argued with her father about his decision. She eventually convinced him that his decree was worse than Pharaoh's because although Pharaoh stopped Hebrew boys from being born, Amram's response stopped both boys and girls from being born, thereby thwarting the possibility of an Israelite future. Amram recognized the validity of Miriam's plea and reversed his decision.

The midrash teaches that sometime later Miriam had a prophetic dream. In it a man clothed in fine linen came to her and said, "Tell your parents that a son will be born to them who will be cast into the waters. The waters will become dry, and wonders and miracles will be performed through him. He will save My people Israel, and be their leader forever." Miriam told her parents of her prophetic dream and indeed Yocheved gave birth to a son, whom she hid for three months before placing him in a basket in the Nile River.

The basket was not left unguarded, however. Miriam hid nearby to discover whether her prophecy would be fulfilled. When Pharaoh's daughter (called Thermutis in the midrash) found the basket floating in the river Miriam stepped out of her hiding place and offered to find a Hebrew woman to nurse him. "Thermutis therefore bade Miriam fetch a Hebrew woman, and with winged steps, speeding like a vigorous youth, she hastened and brought back her own mother, the child's mother." Miriam's prophecy began to unfold with the birth of Moses and was fully realized when the Israelites escaped from Egypt through the parting or "drying" of the Red Sea.

Miriam is again honored with prophetic status once the Israelites cross the sea to freedom. On this occasion Miriam is not merely described as having a prophetic dream, but rather she is directly called a prophetess by the text. The Torah (Ex 15:20-21) says that after crossing the Red Sea Miriam led the women in celebration and dance. "Miriam the prophetess . . . took her drum in her hand and all the women went forth after her with drums and with dances. Miriam spoke up to them, 'Sing to God for He is exalted above the arrogant, having hurled horse with its rider into the sea.'" It was an Israelite custom for women to welcome the men home from battle with dance and song, and Miriam the prophetess is given the lead role at this most prominent and auspicious celebration (Jgs 11:34; 1 Sam 18:6-7; Ps[s] 68:26).

Miriam's virtues during the Israelites' sojourn in the desert are also well documented in Jewish texts. Miriam is mentioned with Moses and Aaron as one of the three who led Israel out of Egypt (Mi 6:4). Further, it is said that due to Miriam's merits, a miraculous well of water, created during the twilight on the eve of the first Sabbath, accompanied the Israelites in the desert (*Avot* 5:6; *Ta'an* 9a). When Miriam died the water stopped flowing and the Israelites cried out to Moses that they would rather be slaves in Egypt than wander in the desert without water (Num 20:1-5).

Miriam's death is further expanded upon in the Talmud (*Baba Batra* 17a), which states that like Moses and Aaron, Miriam died by the kiss of God since the angel of death had no power over her. In addition, although in the text Miriam remains unmarried and childless, she is so highly honored that some Talmudic commentators hold that even King David was descended from her (*Sifre* Num 78; Exodus *Rabbah* 48:304).

It is evident that Miriam is praiseworthy and significant to the Exodus story. She was instrumental in saving her brother, Moses, from Pharaoh's harsh decree to kill Hebrew male infants; she risked her life by hiding by the riverside to ensure that Moses would be rescued, and arranged for her own mother to be his nurse. She led the

Israelite women in praise of God after they safely crossed the Red Sea. She is influential in the leadership of the Israelite community in the desert, and is blessed by God.

Yet, when we read the dramatic Exodus story from a traditional Haggadah each Passover, Miriam is entirely absent. Women, however, are not completely missing from the Haggadah. Three women are mentioned: Pharaoh's daughter, and the Egyptian midwives, Shifrah and Puah, who defied Pharaoh's decree to kill Hebrew boys. It is unclear why these three women are mentioned and why Miriam is not. However, a brief history of the evolution of the Passover seder sheds some light on the mystery of Miriam's absence.

The Haggadah and the Passover ritual evolved over thousands of years of Jewish history. The first Passover, called *Pesach mitzrayim* was held during the Hebrews' last night as Pharaoh's slaves in Egypt, with the sacrifice of a lamb (Ex 12:1-20). From the time the Children of Israel entered the Promised Land, observance of the Passover sacrificial offering became a national ceremony with service and cooking performed by the *kohanim* (priests) in the Temple (2 Chr 30:21-22). During the Roman Empire, in response to the destruction of the Temple and the need to reinvent Temple-related observances, the same rabbis who gave us the Talmud, midrash, and *siddur*, developed the elaborate home-study Passover seder that we still practice today. Much of the seder was modeled after the Roman banquet rituals observed at the time when these rabbis lived. Miriam's exclusion from the Haggadah is most likely based on omissions of the rabbis who were not overly concerned with lauding the heroic acts of women.

It is time for women to come out of the kitchen and reclaim Miriam as a symbol of women's strength and significance in Judaism. Although Miriam's story and those of other women were excluded from the traditional

Haggadah and the Exodus story, it is not too late to bring their voices to our seders.

Some women host third-night seders for women only, while others opt to express God's name in gender-neutral or feminine forms. One new ritual parallels Elijah's cup with Miriam's cup—by placing a cup of water on the seder table in honor of Miriam's Well. Other Haggadot propose placing an orange on the seder plate in tribute to Susannah Heschel, who in the 1970s was at a gathering of Jewish leaders in Florida. Heschel made a plea for involving women in Jewish leadership positions. In response, a hostile listener shouted out, "Women belong in positions of Jewish authority just as much as an orange belongs on a seder plate!" Since then it has become the custom at some Passover seders to place an orange either on the table or on the seder plate to signify that women's participation in Judaism represents transformation, not transgression (Cohen, 1997).

I suggest including Miriam in the telling of the story. The Mishnah teaches that one of the required Passover rituals is to tell the Exodus story. We are not required, however, to read the story verbatim from the Haggadah. Tell Miriam's story, and in doing so we tell the story of all the matriarchs in Jewish history, of all the mothers, the sisters, and daughters, whose stories were lost, or forgotten, or never told while they were too busy cooking in the kitchen to tell them.

REFERENCES

Brown, F., *A Hebrew and English Lexicon of the Old Testament.* Trans. by Edward Robinson (Oxford: Oxford University Press, 1951).

Cohen, J., *101 Questions and Answers on Pesach.* (Northvale, New Jersey: Jason-Aronson, Inc., 1992).

Cohen, T., Elwell, S., Friedman, D., & Horn, R., *The Journey Continues*. (New York: Ma'ayan: The Jewish Women's Project, JCC of the Upper West Side, 1997).

Ginzberg, L., *Legends of the Bible* (New York: Jewish Publication Society, 1992).

Henry, S., & Taitz, E, *Written Out of History* (New York: Biblio Press, 1990).

Jewish Publication Society, *Tanakh: The Holy Scriptures*. (New York: Jewish Publication Society, 1985).

Orenstein, D., & Litman, J., eds, *Lifecycles: Jewish Women on Biblical Themes in Contemporary Life*, Vol. 2. (Woodstock, VT: Jewish Lights Publishing, 1997).

Stern, E., "Miriam" in *Encyclopedia Judaica*. (Jerusalem: Keter Publishing House Jerusalem Ltd, 1972).

ALL THE WOMEN FOLLOWED HER

D'VAR TORAH: PARASHAT CHUKKAT
Randi S. Brenowitz
on the occasion of her *bat mitzvah* at age 46

∽

Water plays a central role in today's parashah. Rabbi Akiva likened the Torah to water, saying:

Just as rain comes with thunder and lightning, we received the Torah with thunder and lightning: "There was thunder and lightning and a thick cloud upon the mountain and the voice of a horn (Shofar) exceeding loud and all the people trembled..."
(Ex 19:16)

Just as water cleanses the body, Torah cleanses the soul.

Just as water comes in drops and helps raise the level of streams and rivers, the same is true of Torah. Just a little bit of study can make a difference.

Just as water is appreciated when a person is thirsty, Torah is appreciated when one has a spiritual thirst.

∽

The study of *Parashat Chukkat* frequently concentrates on the story of the red heifer and the rituals of purification. This morning, however, we are going to concentrate on just five words in the *parashah*: "*v'tamot shom Miriam, v'tikavere shom*"— "Miriam died there and was buried there." Later, in verse 29, when Aaron dies, we are told, "The whole community knew that Aaron had breathed his last. All the house of Israel bewailed Aaron thirty days." Now that's still not a lot of words, but it is a few more—and at least Aaron gets thirty days of wailing.

My first reaction was one of anger. Here we go, I thought, yet another time when the women simply don't get counted. Yet when I started reading the commentary, I discovered that some of the rabbis were also concerned about why there was so little mention of Miriam's death. One suggested that it was because she did not suffer pain. Another hypothesized that the water dried up because the people did not shed tears for Miriam as they did for Moses and Aaron. Although none of the explanations satisfied me, they did make me wonder. Why were the rabbis concerned about the small notice given to Miriam's death? Certainly, other women had died and not been mourned. In fact, we all know that there are many cases where women's voices are not heard, where the women are not even named. So why this concern over Miriam?

Miriam is the only woman in the Torah who is a prophet in her own right. All other women are important because they are somebody's mother, wife, or daughter. Remember that Ruth and Esther come much later and their stories are not in the Torah. Even Sarah, the mother of us all, is considered important in the Torah because she is Abraham's wife and Isaac's mother. In fact, Miriam does not actually get named when she is first referenced early in Exodus. She is merely called "*achoto*"—Moses' sister. Only later, during the trek in the wilderness, she is referred to as "Miriam, the prophet, the sister of Aaron."

Regardless of her designation, Miriam exhibits her first act of courage when she is six years old. It's early in *Shemot* (Exodus) and Pharaoh has decreed that all male Jewish babies will be killed. When Pharaoh's decree is announced, Miriam's father Amram divorces his wife Yocheved and encourages his peers to do the same. Miriam is reported to have said, "Your decree is worse than Pharaoh's. Pharaoh only decreed against boys, but you decree against both boys and girls. Pharaoh's decree concerns this world, but your decree concerns this world and the world to come. Besides, since Pharaoh is wicked, his decree may not be fulfilled, but since you are righteous, your decree will certainly be fulfilled." When Amram hears the logic of his six-year-old daughter, he remarries Yocheved, and all the Jewish men again follow his example, returning to their wives (from the midrash).

A little over nine months later Miriam watches while her baby brother floats down the Nile in the direction of Pharaoh's daughter . . . and again, it is Miriam who arranges to have Yocheved appointed Moses' wet nurse. All of this before her tenth birthday!

When the Jews have finally left Egypt, pursued by Pharaoh's army of chariots that are drowned in the Sea of Reeds, Exodus 15:20 tells us that "Miriam the prophet, the sister of Aaron, took the timbrel in her hand, and all the women went out after her, with timbrels and with dancing. And Miriam led them in song." Now, here's where it starts to get interesting. Miriam's song as reported in the Torah is a mere half verse. It is not only truncated, it is simply a repetition of the first lines of the Song of the Sea, which was led by Moses. Scholars have long suspected that either the complete song was somehow suppressed or that the Song of the Sea was originally Miriam's song and only later was put into the mouth of her brother Moses. In 1994, fragment 4Q365 of the Dead Sea Scrolls was translated. It suggests that Miriam did indeed have her own song, different from the Song of the Sea, and that this song was known as late as 50 BCE. In the first century CE, the Jewish philosopher Philo, who lived in Alexandria, described a group called the "Egyptian Essenes" who as part of the Passover celebration had the men and women form separate choruses and sing different songs about the events at the Red Sea. This and other documents have led some modern scholars to believe that there might be many cases in which, when Moses was speaking to and directing the men, Miriam was doing the same with the women—and that when the rabbis compiled the Torah, they only documented the male activities.

Returning to the biblical narrative, in Numbers, chapter 12, Miriam and Aaron speak against Moses because of the Cushite woman he had married. In punishment for this, Miriam is turned into a leper and is secluded from the camp until Moses speaks to God on her behalf and she is healed. What's interesting is that generally, when someone had to be secluded, they just traveled separately from the camp. In Miriam's case, however, the entire nation comes to a standstill and does not move on until she is ready to go. Rashi says that this was her reward for having watched over Moses in the Nile. It is also clear that this indicates her status as a leader.

Let us now turn to Miriam's Well. The "well" was a rock, shaped like a beehive, and wherever Miriam journeyed, the rock rolled along with her. When the people made camp, the well settled opposite the Tent of Meeting. The midrash says that the head of each tribe would touch the rock with his staff, and that water would then stream out toward that tribe's camp. The image here is of a sieve-shaped rock with twelve streams of water coming out of it. You can imagine why the people panicked when the water dried up and the rock settled in among the other rocks. Commentators believe that later, when God tells Moses to speak to the boulder and that water will come forth from it, God is referring to THAT rock, not just any old rock. Legend teaches that the rock eventually settled in Lake Tiberias, where the healing waters are still to be found today. Whether we believe this or not, the imagery is quite beautiful.

The well itself nourished the Israelites because of Miriam's merits. To a people traveling in the desert, the person entrusted with the water supply certainly takes on unparalleled importance. It seems to me that a God who will entrust the water of life to a woman cannot be a God who does not count women, who does not hear their voices, and who considers them "less than." This God must be one who trusts women, and who believes that they can play a responsible leadership role in the community.

What the rabbis of the Sanhedrin in the first century of the Common Era decided when they compiled, documented, and edited the history is another story. I will have to decide what kind of relationship I can have with their work. But I can have a relationship with this God of the Jews—this God who honors the merits of women and trusts their judgment. This God can be my God, and I trust that my voice will be heard and my accomplishments will be recognized.

REFERENCES

Antonelli, J.S., *In the Image of God: A Feminist Commentary on the Torah* (Northvale, NJ: Jason Aronson Inc., 1995).

Brooke, G., "Power to the Powerless: A Long-Lost Song of Miriam," *Biblical Archaeology Review*, May/June 1994, 62-65.

Fox, E., *The Five Books of Moses* (New York, NY: Schocken Books, 1995).

Leibowitz, N., *Studies in Bamidbar* (Jerusalem: Eliner Library, 1993).

Plaut, W.G., *The Torah: A Modern Commentary* (New York, NY: Union of American Hebrew Congregations, 1981).

THE BIRTHING OF COMMUNITY: SOCIAL RESPONSIBILITY AND THE WOMEN OF EARLY EXODUS[1]
Marsha Pravder Mirkin

It was past midnight when I received a phone call from Jill,[2] then twelve years old. She was calling from a phone booth in a dilapidated, crime-ridden part of town. She knew me, although she rarely had a friendly word to say to me, because I supervised the residence where her brother and sister lived. Months earlier, an evaluation had determined that Jill would continue to live at home, and now she, too, found herself on the streets after a fight with her mother. Both had been drunk at the time.

When I found Jill, her usual bravado was as shattered as the beer bottles whose shards lined the streets. Scared and vulnerable, Jill felt desperate enough to call me and to allow me into her world. We hung out on the broken steps of the community church for a long time, Jill talking, me quietly listening. As dawn approached, she agreed that, following the directions of the family's social work agency, I would drive Jill to the designated emergency shelter. When I walked in with her, a warm, friendly young man with a long ponytail greeted us and started to introduce Jill to the other staff members. I felt Jill tug at my arm and pull me aside. "I don't want to stay here. They're a bunch of hippies," she whispered frantically. I was surprised. I perceived the warmth of the young staff members and the caring atmosphere of the shelter, and I was taken aback by how differently Jill experienced the situation. The urgency in Jill's whisper was palpable, her fear just under the surface. Legally, I could leave her at this shelter. She would be safe. But is there something going on beyond physical safety? What about her soul? What about mine? As we will see in this story of early Exodus, to fulfill the teachings of our Torah, I was responsible for something more than her physical survival.

In early Exodus, we meet Hebrew women and Egyptian women who not only defied Pharaoh at great personal risk, but went much further to insure the survival of the bodies and souls of Hebrew babies. What is the power in the story that makes it worthy to be remembered across centuries, and allows it to guide our lives today? How did this story teach me to leave the shelter with Jill, and join others in finding an alternative place for her to spend the night?

As we open to the beginning of Exodus, we know something remarkable is about to happen: A nation will struggle to be born. A nation that will be committed to a covenant with God and guided by God's commandments is about to emerge. Interestingly, the chapter begins with a struggle about another birth, the birth of Moses. It is not a coincidence that we meet Moses before he is born. His birth is a template for the greater story about the birth of a nation. We learn the ingredients for the birth of a nation by learning how this child survived in a hostile world. Survival in this story is not autonomous or independently achieved. Survival is possible when a group of people come together in a mutually supportive, empathic manner to develop a relational community.

Just as in Genesis we learned about how to develop family relationships, in Exodus we are given the task of developing a relational community. A relational community is mutually supportive and looks out for the welfare of even its weakest members. We learn the groundwork for developing this community from five women in the first two chapters of Exodus: Shifra, Puah, Yocheved, Miriam, and Pharaoh's daughter. It is not a coincidence that the protagonists of early Exodus are all women. Women give birth to babies and are socialized to nurture them into adulthood and teach them about care and commitment. They therefore are fitting models for Moses, who will help birth a nation that moves toward a commitment with God. These women are archetypes of righteousness and rebellion, of courage in relationship. In fact, our Talmud tells us that "on account of the righteous women of that generation was Israel redeemed from Egypt.[3]"

Exodus begins with a genealogy. We are told the names of the twelve sons of Jacob (there is no mention of Jacob's daughter), and of the seventy souls composing Jacob's family who originally entered Egypt. When I was younger, I skipped the genealogy. I found it boring. Last month, as I found myself in the national archives tracing my grandparents and great-grandparents in the 1920 census, I reflected more on the meaning of genealogy. I was again impressed with the wisdom of our Torah in highlighting where we came from before tackling where we're going. The first step in forming our new nation is remembering our common history.

These first few lines give us another message as well. It wasn't simply seventy people who came to Egypt, it was seventy *souls*. We first hear about *nefesh* (soul) in Genesis 2:7 when God breathes into us and we become living souls, and again in Genesis 12:5 when Avram sets out on God's mission. After years and years of slavery, how important it is to be reminded that the breath of God is in us, and that there is a possibility of life beyond servitude to Pharaoh. Remembering our connection with God, with what can be and not simply with what is, propels us forward as we attempt to form this new nation.

Curiously, in early Exodus we don't hear the voice of God and God's name is mentioned only once. This story is a template for human action, for human behavior. It is a story of what you and I and everyone else need to do to make this a better world. In doing so, we become models of living in God's image, acknowledging that the responsibility for behaving ethically in this world belongs to each of us.

With this introduction, we enter the story of early Exodus. We find out that Pharaoh ordered the midwives to kill newborn Hebrew boys. In the first recorded example of spiritual resistance to tyranny[4], the midwives, Shifra and Puah secretly refuse to carry out Pharaoh's decree.

Who are these women? They are described as Hebrew midwives. Does that mean that they are Hebrews or that they are midwives for the Hebrews? We don't know.[5] My preference is to think of them as non-Hebrews, as the first example of righteous gentiles. In our Torah, we often meet non-Hebrews who are wise and ethical, demonstrating that the battle for justice has no ethnic or religious bounds. The Torah may also be telling us that we are responsible for the human race, and not only for other Jews. If two non-Hebrew women can risk their lives by resisting Pharaoh, then what is our responsibility when we see pictures of starving children in the United States, or children in lands devastated by floods, famine and war? What is our responsibility right here back home, when a child is in distress who is not our child?

When a child is at risk, each of us has a responsibility toward that child. Long ago, a phrase emerged from Africa that "it takes a village to raise a child". Puah and Shifra, two African women, understood that, and passed it on to us. If we want to create a sacred community, we need to push beyond ourselves, and like Shifra and Puah, hazard reaching out to others.

Torah tells us that Shifra and Puah not only disobeyed Pharaoh but also kept the baby boys alive. This sentence is ripe for interpretation. Why are we told both that they disobeyed Pharaoh and that they kept the baby boys alive when Torah is never redundant? Perhaps "disobeying Pharaoh" is a comment about their spiritual resistance—they disobeyed Pharaoh by listening to what God would have wanted from them. "Keeping the boys alive" might refer to their physical resistance by refusing to kill these children. Our midrash tells us that Shifra and Puah did more than simply disobey Pharaoh by not killing the babies. They also helped sustain the babies by feeding and clothing them [6]. The midrash is teaching us that refusing to participate in an immoral activity is necessary but not sufficient—we also have to take action to counter the impact of the immoral activity.

My daughter and I recently finished reading "Jacob's Rescue,"[7] the story of two Jewish brothers who were hidden and lovingly attended to during the Holocaust by a Polish Catholic couple, Alex and Mela. As I read the story, I was moved to tears not only by the courage shown by Alex, Mela, and their children, but also because Alex went further than hiding Jacob. What touched the very core of my being was the love he extended to the helpless boy. He gave Jacob their extra food when the boy was ill, he sneaked him into a hospital when he needed an operation, he held Jacob when the child was frightened. This was not only defying Hitler by hiding the child. Alex and his family went beyond this to a relational heroism, a heroism that fought to insure the survival not only of Jacob's body, but also of Jacob's soul. Alex's acts of resistance, courage, and love hearken back to Shifra and Puah in Exodus.

The obligation to care for the soul, and not just the physical being, of those who are hurt arises in our everyday lives when we aren't encountering personal risk. It guided me to listen to Jill's fear and leave the shelter together. We were able to make arrangements for Jill to spend the next day with me at a familiar residence. Shifra and Puah would have told me that it wasn't enough to leave Jill in a safe shelter, that I had to help care for her emotional as well as her physical needs.

Of course, Shifra and Puah were found out. Pharaoh called to the midwives and asked them why they saved the babies. They answered that the Hebrew women were unlike the Egyptian women—they were so hardy that the babies were already delivered before the midwives could get there! Pharaoh believed this ludicrous story, thus teaching us a great deal about prejudice. When we are prejudiced against another, we reduce the other to something non-human. If we truly saw each other as human beings all created in God's image, it would be hard to be so destructive toward each other. Pharaoh had to dehumanize the Hebrews in order to abuse them. Because they were already reduced to animals in his mind, it wasn't strange to think they could give birth quickly and not follow the same rules as human mothers do in the birth process.

When I was seventeen, I spent a summer month learning French in a Swiss international school. There were only three Jews in this school. One day, a Norwegian friend started playing with my hair. His look was so intent that I knew his action wasn't flirtatious—instead, it appeared that he was looking for something. When I asked, he blushed and told me that he was looking for my horns. He was raised in a community where there were no Jews. Jews had been reduced to something other than human, making it feasible to imagine us with horns. Yet, he knew me and liked me. So, he began to see me as more human and to question what he had learned. Furtively, he tried to check it out, and when he realized that of course I didn't have horns, he was embarrassed. The embarrassment, I believe, came from a self-conscious recognition that he was treating me as other than human, and that this behavior was wrong. Pharaoh certainly didn't have the self-reflective potential that my friend displayed. Pharaoh believed the midwives.

Once Pharaoh realized that the baby boys were surviving he ordered all Egyptians to throw Hebrew baby boys into the Nile. Every daughter was allowed to live. What irony! Pharaoh thought that by killing the males, he'd be safe from Hebrews. Instead, a community of relationally courageous women made it possible for Moses to survive and for the Hebrew Exodus to occur. The story continues as we meet Yocheved, Miriam, and Pharaoh's daughter who continue to demonstrate how we can support the birth and development of a sacred community.

Right after Pharaoh declared that the Egyptians must drown Hebrew baby boys, we meet a Hebrew couple. We are not told their names. We know only that they are of the house of Levi, the third son of our foreparents Jacob and Leah. The anonymity allows this Levite couple to be any of us. If we were immediately told that this is Moses' family, they would seem larger than life and out of our reach. But Torah doesn't name them at first, perhaps allowing us to see that ordinary people can rise to the most extraordinary of occasions. They are us.

In Exodus 2:2 we find out that this woman, later referred to as Yocheved, gave birth to a son. ". . .when she saw that he was a goodly child [*vate'eray oto ki tov*], she hid him . . ." The only other time we hear the words "*ki tov*" is during creation. When God noticed the divine creations actualizing their potential, God said, "It is good."[8] When earth brought forth grass and trees and fruit, God commented that "it is good," and when Yocheved gave birth to Moses, she saw that he, too, was good. Perhaps we are being shown that the birth of a child (and the metaphoric birth of a nation) is a creation as worthy of the "*ki tov*" as the beginning creations of God. The awesome holiness of birth reminds us each time it happens of the miracle of God and creation, and of our co-participation in the continued creation of the world. My first response to seeing my newborn daughter was to cry—what else could I do confronted by the indescribable awe of that moment?

Yocheved, in recognizing her son as "good," through the use of the same words as in the creation verse, names herself a participant in continued creation. As such, it is unthinkable to sit passively and await the murder of her son. So she hid him until he was too big to hide. Then, she placed him in a *teva*, an ark, much like Noah's in miniature. She placed the ark at the brink of the Nile, and left. Her daughter, Miriam, stayed to observe what would happen.

As Rabbi Ullman points out,[9] Noah's ark was rectangular. It can't be steered by humans. Placing Moses in a rectangular ark in the Nile meant that Yocheved had to have faith. She had to believe that God would steer this little boat. At the same time, faith is not the same as abandonment of human responsibility, so Miriam remained nearby. That intricate balance between being there and letting go, staying connected and allowing movement that doesn't include us, is played out in this scene by the Nile.

We all know that moment of letting our children go while still staying in connection. I remember dropping our younger daughter off at day care. She was two and began crying as soon as I said goodbye. I left her in the arms of a teacher. In order for me to leave, I had to have faith that she would be nurtured and supported for the next six hours. At the same time, especially at the beginning, I would drop by to peek in and be assured that the staff was relating to my daughter in a loving, responsible way. I was trying to find that balance between knowing I couldn't steer the ark, but still waiting in the bulrushes.

As our children grow older, they spend more time with their peers and are more and more influenced by the larger society. Any parent who has allowed a child to go off with friends or go to a party recognizes that we can't steer the ark. We have to let our children grow up and we have to have faith that our experiences together and their inner sense of themselves will steer them in the right direction. And we may have someone waiting nearby. The first times that our daughter baby-sat, my husband and I stayed home so that she could call us if she needed help. We certainly trusted her, but we knew that there are circumstances bigger than she is. We couldn't go with her, but we could wait out of sight in case she needed us.

But Yocheved's decision to place the ark in the Nile has meaning beyond its application to individual families. There are also lessons here about community. If Yocheved hadn't known that there was a community of resistance to Pharaoh, could she have left her child there in an ark? Could she have taken a child whom she saw as good, and left him in a river overflowing with the blood of Hebrew baby boys? The leap of faith was more possible because Yocheved had already encountered Shifra and Puah, two members of this community of resisters. They demonstrated to us that part of forming a sacred community is joining together to raise a child by nonviolently resisting spiritual and physical tyranny.

In the story "Jacob's Rescue," his aunt sneaked out of the Warsaw Ghetto with Jacob, but she didn't just leave Jacob vulnerable and exposed in Nazi-occupied Poland. She knew that a sympathetic person would be waiting on the other side. Even though it was a risk, it wasn't an abandonment of the child. It was a calculated risk, hinging on the assumption that someone else cared enough to take the boy and protect him. In our lives today, in order for me to leave my child at day care, I needed to know there were teachers who would take care of her physically and emotionally. One of the most hurtful contemporary issues in our society is that mothers on welfare are being told to go to work for substandard wages; they are also asked to allow their babies to float in an ark down a river without the assurance that a loving childcare environment is available to care for the bodies and souls of their little ones. As we will see in this story, it is a community, and not just a nuclear family, responsibility to care for our children.

Let us now meet the woman from "the other side": Pharaoh's daughter. In Exodus 2:5 we are told that Pharaoh's daughter went to bathe in the Nile, accompanied by her servants. Bathe in the Nile? The same river into which Hebrew baby boys were thrown and drowned? Why would anyone want to bathe in a river full of dead babies? Couldn't a princess bathe in the palace?

Perhaps this is a metaphoric washing. Going to the Nile River, looking at the perversity and horror, could be a conscious, deliberate act on the part of the princess. Perhaps she needed to see with her own eyes what her father was doing. However, Pharaoh's daughter didn't see only dead babies. There was a live baby crying in an ark in the river. Once she saw him, she couldn't turn around, go back to the palace, and resume her sheltered life. Once she saw him, she needed to wash the blood of this deed off of her own soul by taking action. Once she saw what her father was doing, she would hold herself complicit if she turned away and left the crying baby to die in the Nile.

We all know those moments of decision. Several years ago, our daughters enjoyed playing with a particular toy. We heard rumors that the toy was made by exploited laborers. I made several phone calls, but couldn't determine whether the rumors were true. Yet, when I tried to buy one of the toys, there was a gnawing inside of me. The toy was very inexpensive, given its quality. What if the rumors were true? What if I was supporting exploited labor? Our family couldn't ignore what we saw in front of us, and we couldn't buy those particular toys anymore.

Pharaoh's daughter asked her servants to fetch the ark, and when she saw the crying baby, she felt compassion and announced that this was a Hebrew baby. She didn't only refrain from killing the baby by noticing the Hebrew child and then walking away. Just like Shifra and Puah, she went a step further: She adopted the baby. She could be at tremendous risk if her father found out that she had adopted a Hebrew boy. She could have pretended that this child was an unwanted Egyptian baby who was deserted by his parents and in need of a new family. She didn't have to put herself at risk of someone reporting to her father that she saved a Hebrew child. But, she chose to go public with an ethical stance. She committed herself publicly to not only renounce the rule decreeing death to Hebrew boys, but also to take action to undermine it. Pharaoh's daughter, the child of the oppressor, teaches the nation that is about to be born that being silent in the face of injustice is being an accomplice to that injustice. Similarly our Talmud teaches us that saving one life is like saving the world. Indeed, saving this life was like saving our world. This child was destined to lead our people out of Egypt and into a covenant with God.

As the princess announced her discovery of the baby, a young Hebrew girl stepped out of her hiding place and approached the daughter of Pharaoh. Miriam, a simple slave, proceeded to ask the most powerful woman in Egypt whether she needed a Hebrew woman to nurse the baby. In a conspiracy of resistance, of refusal to yield to the immoral rule of Pharaoh, the princess agreed and Miriam introduced Yocheved as the baby's nurse. Pharaoh's daughter goes even further than simply allowing Yocheved to nurse her son. In a remarkable act of lovingkindness, the princess chose to pay Yocheved to take care of her own child! Our Torah honors this noble Egyptian by giving her the privilege of naming the child. This baby, the product of a relational community and resistance to an ethic other than God's, is named Moses.

This Egyptian heroine is not named in Torah, but she is given the name "Batya" in our midrash. In this legend, God speaks to Pharaoh's daughter saying, "You adopted a child that was not your own, calling him your son. In return, I shall call you My daughter."[10] Batya means "daughter of God," and indeed, she does demonstrate to us what it means to be a child of the Eternal One. It means going that extra step, going beyond what would be considered the right thing to do and leaping to the most empathic, compassionate stance we can take. And, it often means working with others in our community to right the wrongs, to offer emotional and spiritual as well as physical sustenance. The woman honored with this name is not a Hebrew, and again our Torah teaches us that we all belong to a larger community of people, all made in the image of God, and some aspiring to live up to that image.

Several years ago, I went to the Bat Mitzvah of my daughter's friend. She is a loving, smart, warm young woman whose mother died when she was a young child. Her father remarried a few years later and her dad and adoptive mom, whom I'll call Cynthia, have raised her and her sister. Cynthia was not Jewish but went out of her way to raise this child as a Jew. Just like Batya, she made sure that this child was nurtured by the values of her biological mother. At the Bat Mitzvah, I was moved to tears by Cynthia's beautiful words. She said that her daughter would always have two moms who both love her and who both admire the young woman she is, that the presence of her first mom would be with her forever, and that both moms would be at her side whenever she needed them. Like Batya, Cynthia did not respond only to the physical needs of the child, but went a step further by keeping Yocheved present in her daughter's life. While so many people in our culture fight for the singular right to a child, this family shows us a sacred community. Batya and

Yocheved could both raise Moses, and what a son they raised!

Not long afterwards, I was at a Bat Mitzvah of a daughter of a friend who recently died. Her father called up all her mother's friends so that we could say the Torah blessing together. All of us women huddled close around the Bat Mitzvah girl, with one larger *tallit* covering us so that we truly felt we were standing under the wings of the Shechinah.[11] That was as close as I ever came to feeling a sacred community. We were wrapped together, all deeply committed to the physical, emotional and spiritual well-being of this one special teenager, who was radiant at her Bat Mitzvah. I felt my friend's presence with us at that moment. I felt Yocheved smiling at us.

There is a strong cultural pull in the United States to "mind your own business," to give people "space," to "stay out." I believe our Torah tells us the opposite: that we are part of something larger than ourselves, and as members of a community, we have a responsibility to each other. When someone is in need, we are encouraged to offer our support and take that extra step. When my daughter was in fifth grade, I had planned to drive her and her friends home from school. On my way to meet them, I got a flat tire and it was clear that it would be a long time before I could get to the school. Sheepishly, I called the mother of two of the girls. This mother had recently had twins, and I can only imagine how exhausted she must have been feeling. She could have picked up her daughters and let the other two wait at school. She agreed to pick up the four girls. Then, she went even further and took care of all of them until I returned. This is a beautiful example of the mutual caring and responsibility that early Exodus portrays. This "going beyond" in order to take care of the larger needs of our children and our community is demonstrated in her exemplary actions. I hope she also believes that other parents will come through for her children. A friend of mine[12] brought up the critical point that if that mother had been tired or busy, it would also have been exemplary had she called another parent and asked him or her to pick up and take care of the girls. The underlying issue is for us to be engaged members of a community where we have mutual responsibility for each other and our children. We do not have to feel that we are "superwomen" with responsibility to independently take care of everything that comes our way. Batya didn't act alone, and neither did Miriam or any of the other women of Exodus. They acted in a community of mutual caring and mutual responsibility. Together, they birthed a child who would eventually help birth a nation.

The story of Exodus is the story of the birth of a nation, and starts with the midwives, in the service of God, resisting Pharaoh and assisting in the delivery of Moses. "*Mitzrayim*," which is translated into English as "Egypt," actually means "narrow straits." The soon-to-be child crosses through narrow straits and is born.[13] Exodus grows to be a story of Moses, in the service of God, resisting Pharaoh and assisting in the deliverance of a nation. And always, the women of Exodus are there, saving, guiding, and supporting Moses throughout his lifetime, using their understanding of a relational community, their wisdom, courage, and moral certitude to help us move toward becoming a sacred nation. And every day, in our own lives, we are asked to continue that journey by accepting the mutual responsibility and feeling the mutual caring necessary to develop our own sacred communities.

NOTES

1. This contribution also appears as a chapter in *She is a Tree of Life: Learning About Ourselves and Our Relationships from our Biblical Foremothers* by Marsha Mirkin. I would like to

acknowledge how much the teaching of Rabbi Alan Ullman influenced my thinking in this chapter. I would also like to thank my husband, Mitch Mirkin, for his support and editing. This chapter would not have been possible without them.

2. This chapter is dedicated to all the Jills I've been privileged to know through my years as a therapist. There is no single "Jill." The interaction between Jill and me in this chapter is a synthesis of many conversations with many young women with whom I have worked during the past twenty-five years.

3. Exodus *Rabbah* 1:12, *Sotah* 11b.

4. Michael Lerner used this term in *Tikkun* magazine.

5. Their names are not Egyptian, but as Everett Fox tells us, the word "Hebrew" is usually used when foreigners talk about Israelites. See Everett Fox, *Five Books of Moses*, Schocken Press.

6. It is said (*Shemot Rabbah* 1:15) that Shifra and Puah kept the children alive by collecting food from rich women to give to the poor Hebrew children.

7. *Jacob's Rescue* was written by Malka Drucker and published by Yearling Books in 1994.

8. I was taught this interpretation by Rabbi Alan Ullman. He also suggests that Pharaoh's daughter made the conscious decision to go to the Nile, and once she saw with her own eyes, she could not simply turn away and return to the palace.

9. Personal Communication, 1998.

10. Exodus *Rabbah*, 1:2, 1:30.

11. The female manifestation of God's presence; the presence that joined us in exile.

12. Harriet Lerner, personal communication, 1999.

13. I would like to thank Gail Reimer, personal communication, 1997, for the parallels between the birth process and the Exodus.

RENEWAL AND INSIGHT FROM MIRIAM'S WELL
Rosie Rosenzweig

*The classical reference to Miriam's Well can be found in the Talmud
Tractate Shabbat 35a. Below is a summary found in Ein Yaakov, a
collection of agaddic material of the Talmud, compiled by Rabbi Yaakov
ibn Chaviv, the fifteenth century Talmudist.*

*R. Chiya said: If you want to see the well of Miriam, (footnote: "The
well that miraculously followed the children of Israel on their
wandering through the desert and supplied them with water thanks to
the merit of Miriam.") climb to the peak of Mount Carmel.
When you look down toward the sea you will notice a round rock,
shaped like a sieve.
That is Miriam's well.
Rav said: A movable well is* tahor *[ritually pure, and, like a mikveh,
may be used to cleanse people and utensils of* tumah *(contamination)
by immersing them in it.] The only movable well in existence is the
well of Miriam.*

◈

A story about the famed mystic Isaac Luria
exemplifies how Miriam's well was used for purification.
In his book *Safed: The Mystical City,*[1] David Rosoff refers to
the story of Chayyim Vital, who in 1570 became singled
out to study and write about the mystical philosophy of
Rabbi Yitzchak (Isaac) Luria, the Arizal. Rabbi Vital once
confessed his inability to absorb the Arizal's wisdom of his
teacher. Rabbi Luria's remedy involved rowing to the
southern end of the Kinereth (Sea of Galilee). At that spot,
a flask was filled with seawater, and Vital was ordered to
drink from it. Upon obeying, Vital was promised by his
teacher that he would never again forget anything that the
Arizal taught. And so it came to pass that Chayyim Vital

became the main authority and disseminator of the great Ari's Kabbalistic system.

It seems that the Miriam's well remedy cleared away all of Vital's *klepot* (obstacles), so that nothing interfered with the transmission of learning. He became a clear channel for wisdom. Perhaps we can learn from this how to help ourselves.

How much more then can we make of Talmudic references to our aggadic heritage? We can take these stories and retell them to ourselves to bring down insights by which we can live our lives. So it is with Miriam's well. I first heard such an attempt through a guided visualization entailing Miriam, told by Matia Rania Angelou, founder of the Boston women's spiritual network called *Nishmat haNashim*, and past *darshan* of Boston's *P'nai Or*. Since then I have adapted it to numerous situations such as *S'lichot*, Passover, and the writing of one's ethical will. Here is a brief outline of how to use this technique in a group or for one's individual insight.

Meditation and Visualization (to be done slowly):

One should sit, either in a chair or on a pillow or bench with a straight back. Listen to your breath, not breathing too deeply or too quickly, just normally. Try to hear the heart beat. With each breath relax slowly each part of the body, from the toes to the calves, thighs, torso, solar plexus, chest, shoulders, arms, hands, neck, jaw, face, eyes, and the head. Pretend there is a golden string from the top of the head to the heavens above. This string is attached to the spine, and as one breathes, the light is pouring down into the body. With every breath more light enters the body. Slowly and evenly. There is a direct connection to the light above, a direct channel.

Each breath fills the body with light until the whole body is full of light rising to the skin.

Go to your favorite place and observe your favorite things. Touch them in your mind's eye and at each touch give them light. Go through everything there in this manner until the place and its objects are emanating light. Clear light.

Now you must leave this place and walk through a grassy knoll to a path that goes through some woods to a clearing. Perhaps you are a little warm or even hot. As the horizon becomes visible you will see a body of water. You are walking to its closest shore. A boat approaches you and comes to the shore. It is a boat of light. You enter this boat and it is being steered by light, God's Light. In the middle of the water you see a fountain spouting up and the water around it is circling mildly. The boat slows and stops at this oasis. It is pleasantly cool here.

Drink from this in any way that is comfortable— drink from your hands, or find a cup in the boat.

Enjoy the cool, sweet taste of this heavenly water. Enjoy yourself being refreshed as you sit in the boat and enjoy the well.

Now you notice that your boat indeed has an oarsman, and it is a woman. It is Miriam the prophet who foresaw Moses' mission before he was born. She offers you more water. A comfortable silence falls. You can ask her a question if you like. Or not. Now she is speaking to you. Her voice is music. She is telling you something very important about something you need to know.

Listen to what she says. She may even have something she is showing you.

Let the silence fill with the sounds of Miriam.

(Silence)

Wait for her to tell you the last words.

She is taking the boat back to the shore. The lighting is becoming more normal as you disembark. The boat fades back into the sea. It is the Sea of Galilee, Kinereth.

Don't forget what she told you.

Come slowly back to this room. Feel your feet on the ground. Be aware of your legs, your torso, your arms, your heart, your neck, and your head. Breathe a few more breaths before you open your eyes. Open them when you are ready, but don't speak.

≈

Keeping the silence and the memory of the message is important. At this point the participants can write down that message and perhaps later discuss it. Or not. The idea here is that we carry our own prophecies within us about our own lives and missions.

This is an excellent meditation to use during Nisan and perhaps the Passover Seders.

I have adapted this guided meditation before workshops in the writing of feminist ethical wills, entitled "The Ethics of Our Mothers." The person who appears and delivers the message could be any important woman in one's life who has something to impart. This woman could be on Miriam's arm, with Miriam introducing her. She can be any woman, living or dead—an acquaintance or a woman never met, an ancestor, a historical or inspirational figure alive at any point in the past, present, or future, who has influenced the participant/writer of the ethical will at any time in the writer's life. This important woman will, in the guided meditation, elicit the important issues of one's life.

Miriam or this important woman could also deliver a written or spoken message, which then gets transmitted to the participant's ethical will.

I have used variations of this guided meditation before *S'lichot*, and the message could be about unfinished business with other women in one's life or with oneself. The female figure that appears could be a woman asking forgiveness for something. A dialogue could ensue that Miriam facilitates, all contained in the private visualization. Another variation could have Miriam prophetizing the results of a certain forgiving act. This could also be incorporated into the bedtime *Sh'ma* during the part that includes forgiving all those who have bestowed hurt. This is especially useful to get through rocky times in a mother-daughter dialogue.

Another variation of the Miriam visualization could be used at *Shavuot* to impart some feminist figure of Torah, including our foremothers, who is significant to the participant that year.

Other variations, used during the appropriate Rosh Hodesh ceremony in a women's group, could also be used for any number of occasions involving a birthday, an anniversary, or a *yartzeit*. Miriam could bring a message or bring the actual figure of the woman involved in these life cycle events. The birth of a baby girl could elicit a visualization with the girl brought out at any future age on Miriam's arm with a dialogue ensuing. The father might enjoy this as well.

Any reference to Miriam in Torah and/or Talmud can be converted into a dialogue for self-discovery and growth.

One is limited only by one's imagination.

NOTES

1. Sha'ar Books, Feldenheim Distribution, 1991.

CAN PRAYER HEAL? A VIEW FROM TRADITION
Erica Brown

Today's new age spirituality places great emphasis on healing. But our own more ancient traditions also emphasize this healing process; from visiting the sick, to praying as a community for the sick to the strong commitment to the healing professions, Judaism has consistently demonstrated the centrality of healing in our heritage. In this process, there is always a tension between divine agency and human responsibility. We must do our utmost to preserve our health, and yet prayer, particularly, has consistently reflected urgency, dependence, and the submission of human control to divine destiny.

In traditional prayer, three times daily we supplicate in the plural for "complete healing to all our wounds," to a God who "is a faithful and merciful healer." Yet, this does not stop us from reading between the lines and wondering about the efficacy of such prayer. Is it optimistic but wasted breath? Perhaps in the era when much of our prayer was composed, medical treatment was still in such a primitive state that prayer stood just as much a chance of healing as any other method. But today, in light of medical advances, are we so confident in the power of the word to heal?

There have been medical trials that have attempted to demonstrate that intercessory prayer even without the patient's knowledge that he or she was the subject of prayer has beneficial effects on medical outcomes.[1] Individual doctors have written persuasively as witnesses of prayer's psychological value and even documented how their own prayers for patients have helped assist in the healing process.[2] But in an age of antibiotics, inoculations and ultrasounds it is hard not to be skeptical. Is prayer supposed to come with any medical guarantees or are its benefits measured differently?

In the Hebrew Bible, Numbers 12, we have one of the most beautiful and poignant prayers for recovery. Miriam was stricken with what has been classically called leprosy for slandering her brother Moses. The text reads:

> The cloud had departed from atop the Tent and behold! Miriam was afflicted with leprosy like snow. Aaron turned to Miriam and behold! She was afflicted with leprosy. Aaron said to Moses, "I beg you, my lord, do not cast a sin upon us, for we have been foolish and have sinned. Let her not be like a corpse, like one who leaves his mother's womb with half his flesh having been consumed." Moses cried out to God, saying, Please, God, heal her now." God said to Moses, "Were her father to spit in her face, would she not be humiliated for seven days? Let her be put outside the camp for seven days and then she may be brought in." So Miriam was put outside the camp for seven days and the people did not journey until Miriam was brought in.   (Numbers 12:10-15)

This passage is riddled with curiosities. Miriam's challenge to her brother resulted in a heavy punishment, and if biblical punishments are generally commensurate with and colored by the crime committed then the reader must struggle with the mystery of Miriam's illness. The repetition of the term "behold" almost forces us to look at Miriam's bodily derangement the way that Aaron himself did. Not all sickness had as crippling an effect on the appearance as did leprosy. Aaron, who participated, even passively, in this crime was left unblemished. As powerful as Moses' prayer was—and it is still evoked every Yom

Kippur—God maintained that Miriam had to be punished. The children of Israel waited for Miriam's return, and strangely, a narrative that focuses on the intimate details of sibling tension ends with the entire camp involved.

Miriam challenged her brother's authority in the beginning of the chapter. She suggested that she and Aaron were just as capable of communicating with God as Moses was. Yet she did so by unfairly evoking an image of a tarnished husband. Moses desisted from normal domestic relations, according to the midrash and several exegetes.[3] His service to God was so demanding that he was freed from the bounds of family life. Miriam was troubled by this and found it indefensible. She and Aaron were also prophets but indulged in their human needs. Did Moses think he was a higher-grade prophet than they? But here she questioned not Moses but God's choice of him, and the unusual demands God made of him. In addition, she did not focus on the nature of revelation but on Moses's intimate personal life, one that she had no right to question.

Slander by its nature is a public activity, even if that public is limited to one. By slandering her brother, she tried to promote some defect in his character to someone else. In turn, the commensurate punishment would be to experience some form of public deformity. Leprosy is described in detail in Leviticus. It was an illness with very visible signs. The passage itself is very visual, and the repetition of the term "behold" in verse ten alerts us to the shock of looking at the leper. The slow movement of Aaron turning and witnessing his sister in this state is recorded twice. The text narrates it and then the reader experiences it with Aaron as he sees his beloved sister in physical anguish. Based on this visceral reaction, Aaron pleads with Moses not to let this dignified leader look like a stillborn child in front of the entire encampment.

R. Moses Feinstein, a leading Orthodox rabbi, was asked if one could fulfill the commandment to visit the sick with a phone call.[4] He demurred to the convenience of the telephone and admitted that it may provide some comfort. However, he advised that not only is there more commiseration with a visit but that unless an individual actually *sees* his friend in pain, he will not adequately pray for him. The visual enhancement of seeing a sick person will inspire more powerful prayer. This is clearly demonstrated in our narrative.

Did Aaron also suffer this affliction? The Talmud is, as expected, divided on the matter.[5] One camp claims that the text does not confess Aaron's punishment so it must have been withheld or undeserved. In the text, it is Miriam who speaks. The other camp claims that for his participation in the discussion, even as passive listener, he received the same punishment. Why not mention it? Aaron could very well have had leprosy but that is not what the text wants to emphasize. It is his shock and mercy that are paramount here. If Aaron were ill that would only highlight the beauty of his concern: despite his own illness, he beseeched Moses to cure his sister.

Why did Aaron not turn to God himself? Here, it is important to see the text as a composite, and go beyond a line-by-line reading. God had just stridently informed Aaron and Miriam that Moses' prophecy was superior to theirs. Thus, when it came to communicating with God, Aaron humbled himself before his younger brother. Notice the appellation Aaron attached to his speech, "I beg you, *my lord* . . ." instead of "I beg you, my brother." Aaron had learned his lesson.

But Miriam evidently had not. One medieval commentator remarked that the whiteness brought on by the illness was the price she paid for accusing Moses of taking a dark-skinned woman as wife. Her whiteness now was not something to be proud of but the extreme coloring or absence of color that was a badge of shame. It was as branding as any mark Hawthorne could assign. Had she insulted her father she would have been publicly humiliated, all the more so, when she called into question the divine mechanics of the universe. God chose Moses; who was she to question? She tried to slander her brother, to put him metaphorically outside the camp, so she had to be put outside the camp herself.

Being put outside the camp was essentially a heightened form of the illness itself. Sickness is isolating. Being exiled is merely an exacerbated form of the same anguish -- isolation. Pain isolates because it makes you acutely aware of yourself, often blinded to the pain of others because of the intensity of personal anguish. This self-focus is itself a punishment. Wittgenstein, the famous twentieth century philosopher wrote convincingly about the deficiency of language to convey pain because even when we confess similar illness to a friend, relative or colleague, we know that the way we experience toothaches, sprains, and splinters is unique to ourselves. Pain is very individualized. "Both of us cry, contort our faces, give the same description of the pain, etc. Now are we to say we have the same pain or different ones?"[6]

When we gossip, we are not thinking about ourselves. We focus on the blemishes of others. When we are sick, especially with an illness which has physically unpleasant manifestations, we think only about ourselves.

Miriam was alienated by a very public sickness. What cured her? It was not the prayer of her brother. God refused his request. It was knowing that her brothers prayed for her. But it was still more. The narrative ends with the resumption of Israel's sojourns in the wilderness. The camp waited for her. The same camp from which she has been excluded inconvenienced itself for an entire week to wait for her healing. The very brother she insulted petitioned God for her recovery. What cured her was not prayer, since God told Moses that she must not be spared punishment, but the almost unconditional love that inspired prayer. If sickness is isolating on one level it is also embracing on another. We stop thinking about ourselves when others think about us.

We do not get better because we have responsibilities to others that only we can fulfill, but because we want to better enjoy the love that others have displayed while we were ill. In a room filled with flowers and cards, when several people a day visit and ask for our Hebrew names so that they may gently suggest divine assistance, we heal through love. Moses taught his sister that although she may not have been thinking kindly of him, he still prayed for her. Aaron healed his sister by expressing such personal anguish at her suffering. The children of Israel healed Miriam because they waited for her.

We do not know what the answers to our prayers are. Maybe they will be 'no.' We cannot pray audaciously expecting a change in divine will. It is the prayer itself which must ultimately concern us, the way it molds our character, the way it forms our concern for others, the way we demonstrate to the sick that our love may help carry them to good health. In that capacity it is healing. In a touching personal essay on being the recipient of such prayer, a woman struggling with cancer wrote of hearing that someone prayed on her behalf, ". . . I was overwhelmed. This woman whom I barely knew, had said my name and prayed for me everyday for months. It was a great gift . . .And it is good for the person who is ill to know that we are praying on their behalf, so that through the act of praying, they will feel the love of the community embracing them in their hour of need. And in the process, please God, it helps all of us feel God's care more deeply as well."[7]

We should not be seduced by medical statistics on prayer's efficacy. Prayer is not medicine, nor is it meant to be. Unlike medicine, it cannot be taken; it can only be given. It cannot be mechanical; it must be personal. Prayer is neither a prevention to pain nor its cure; it is a response to pain. It is the emotional, intimate recordings and reflections of Miriam outside the camp, the vociferous pleadings of her brothers inside the camp, and the patient wait of the entire camp that inspired prayer and ultimately began the healing process. Love that inspires prayer inspires healing.

NOTES

1. See, for example, the 1988 study done by Dr. Randolph C. Byrd entitled, 'Positive Therapeutic Effects of Intercessory Prayer in a Coronary Care Unit Population" (*Southern Medical Journal*: July, 1988, vol. 8, no.7). He concludes there that the "data suggest that intercessory prayer to the Judeo-Christian God has a beneficial therapeutic effect in patients admitted to a CCU." Other interesting studies include "The Efficacy of Prayer: A Double Blind Clinical Trial" in the *Journal of Chronic Disease* 18:367-377, 1965 and P.J. Collipp, "The Efficacy of Prayer: A Triple Blind Study" in *Medical Times* 97:201-204, 1969. These studies have aroused some controversy as to the clinical methods used to derive the positive conclusions.

2. In one such publication, *Healing Words* by Dr. Larry Dossey, the writer describes the difficulty in praying for the outcome of his patient given that a simple prayer for recovery did not necessarily match the complexity of the diagnosis or the needs of the patient or his or her family. His prayer was reduced to a simple formula "May the best possible outcome prevail." in the hope that this would make him more attuned to the patients individual needs.

3. *Midrash Tanhuma* 96:13 as cited by Rashi, *Sifrei Ba'alotekha* 99. See also BT *Bava Batra* 109b. This midrashim are not an indictment of Moses as much as they demonstrate sympathy with Tzipporah's difficult position.

4. R. Moses Feinstein, *Iggerot Moshe*, Y.D.I, #223.

5. Babylonian Talmud, *Shabbat* 97a.

6. Ludwig Wittgenstein, *The Blue and Brown Books: Preliminary Studies for the 'Philosophical Investigations'* (New York: 1958), p.54.

7. Elana Kanter, "The Healing Power of Prayer," *Sh'ma*, 28:554, 1998.

MIRIAM: *PARASHAT BEHA'ALOTECHA*
Marion Weinberg*

A wise and inspirational teacher once said that in order to fully appreciate Torah—to experience it not as a text, but as a living breathing life force—we must bring to study not only our minds but our hearts and souls. I have learned that Torah has the mystical properties of mirroring just who and where we are in our lives at that particular moment in time. So perhaps it is not so surprising that I'm approaching the conclusion of this *parashah* from the eyes and experiences of Miriam. Miriam, whose name means "bitter water," is often cited in text and midrash near water. Time and again she brilliantly navigates through the rising currents of her time. Miriam has been not only an archetype, but my constant companion during this past year—and for probably much longer than that. I have seen Miriam in dream and mirrored reflection. She has been my friend, my voice, my comfort, and at times my deep unrest.

The conclusion of this *parashah* is a troubling one, in which Miriam is a central figure together with Aaron, Moses, and God. Set against a backdrop of constant complaining and questioning of leadership, it ends with what is usually described as "divine punishment." Here Miriam and Aaron confide in each other, many say criticizing their brother Moses for marrying a Cushite woman. Miriam and Aaron then ask, "Does not God speak through us as well as through Moses?"

Their questioning provokes the wrath of God, and God's admonishment that only Moses has a unique and

---

* Marion Weinberg died on March 13, 1997, nine months after she delivered this essay as a *d'var torah* at her adult Bat Mitzvah.

unparalleled relationship with God. In a cloud, God departs and Miriam has *tzara'at*, which may be translated as "scales white as snow," which some call leprosy. Following Moses' and Aaron's pleas for her healing, Miriam is banished from the camp for seven days. The people wait for her return. In order to derive some meaning from this episode I'd like to briefly go back to the earlier occasions in the text and midrashic commentary where Miriam is mentioned and her character unfolds.

Initially, we see Miriam among the reeds of the Nile watching over the baby Moses, when Pharaoh's daughter finds him in a basket on the water. Instinctively protecting and caring for Moses, Miriam asks, "Shall I find you a Hebrew nursemaid for the baby?" In this critical moment Miriam's voice and actions altered the course of history. Speaking out as she did, a brave and bold act, could have cost Miriam her life. But her priorities were clear. Miriam helped save Moses' life and kept her family together.

Midrashic commentary adds more about Miriam's early life. As a child Miriam witnessed Pharaoh's decree to kill all newborn Hebrew boys. The commentary states that Miriam encouraged her parents to resume conjugal relations arguing that their decision to have no children was worse than Pharaoh's decree for it prohibited *all* births, while Pharaoh's edict was against the birth of boys alone. Based on Miriam's argument, the Talmud says that her parents resumed relations and Moses was born. Additional commentary notes that Miriam actually prophesied that her parents would one day give birth to the future leader of the Jewish nation. So in text as well as commentary we see that Miriam is determined to speak and act for what she believes to be important. Her powerful delivery, supported by clear priorities, affects the course of events in a profound way.

The next textual account of Miriam prior to today's *parashah* occurs just after the Israelites safely cross the parted Sea of Reeds. The pursuing Egyptians drown in the converged waters. I imagine that this moment was filled with an array of powerful confronting emotions. Amidst the chaos, fear, elation, distress, relief, and the stress of the impending journey, Miriam emerges as a leader: She feels the awe of the moment; she knows what to do. Miriam lifts a timbrel in her hand and celebrates. She leads the women with joy and fervor. In this moment, amidst all possible responses, Miriam has an inner voice which says: Yes! Celebrate life! Celebrate the source of all life. Miriam inspired the women to celebrate with her in song, in dance, in thanksgiving to God, the *Shechinah*. At this celebrating moment the text first identifies Miriam by name and title. Miriam the prophetess. Miriam meaning "bitter water." We see that Miriam has had both difficult and challenging moments by the water. Midrashically she is associated with a well that follows her and provides life-sustaining water for her people in the desert. Miriam the prophetess. We never read that Miriam communicates directly with God. Paradoxically, the only moment of direct communication occurs in today's *parashah*, when God angrily tells her and Aaron that only Moses receives the word of God directly. Yet, Miriam has powerfully impacted the course of human history. Does she perceive the future or is she merely forward-thinking? Is she divinely inspired or simply listening to the still, small voice inside? Is there a difference?

The *Kabbalah*, Judaism's mystical tradition, teaches us to know our true nature through self-realization. The mystics say that through self-knowledge we can actually participate in and align ourselves with the divine plan. By fulfilling our own destiny we are able to ultimately serve the holy *Shechinah*.

Miriam impresses me as a woman who is true to herself. Her embrace of life takes form as conviction and courage. Speaking and acting, celebrating and questioning. Significant moments in history unfold beneath her wings. Even moments of suffering. Miriam is covered with scales—perhaps leprosy. I want to scream, "It's not fair!" Miriam is ill. Why? Is it wrong to question? To share concerns between siblings? True to Miriam's character, she was concerned about family matters. Should she back down when it comes to a sister-in-law? We don't know what is so troubling about Moses marrying a Cushite woman. The interpretations are many, and rather inadequate. Rashi suggests that Miriam was concerned that Moses never had time for his wife Tzipporah due to his leadership responsibilities and divine communication with God.

Now that has a familiar ring!

Is it wrong for Miriam and Aaron to question their authority to communicate with God relative to Moses' authority? Why is Miriam the only one punished? The questions are numerous, and the midrashic explanations insufficient. What we know is that when God departed, Miriam was left with scales, and here the heart of the passage unfolds. For what happened next represents a profound and dramatic moment between Miriam, her brothers, and the entire Israelite community.

Everything stopped. The silence was deadening. People stopped kvetching and priorities of the moment, day, and week shifted. Miriam was ill. Even the thinking stopped. Suddenly what was important shone like a moonbeam in the clear desert sky. And all that remained were the heartfelt inner voices of brothers, family and friends. Aaron pleaded with Moses to save Miriam. This was an unusual reversal of communication between these brothers. Moses listened to Aaron, and with heartfelt simplicity, spoke to God. *"El na, refa na lah."* Please God, pray heal her. It was a moment of faith and submission.

Miriam was sent out to the wilderness for seven days and the people waited. Miriam was sent to the wilderness—a wilderness not unlike the nothingness described in Kabbalah upon which all existence would be based. Not unlike the nothingness of Genesis into which God spoke existence: "Let there be light."

Miriam, what was it like for you, there in the wilderness? What were you thinking, feeling, there in the nothingness? What was your inner knowing? My questions may not be the usual ones that come to mind in studying this *parashah*. I am not concerned about punishment. I don't believe in a vindictive, punishing God. I'm not concerned with why Miriam fell ill and not Aaron. Some things we cannot know or make sense of. Rather, central to this *parashah*, and central to my life and I think all of our lives, one way or another, is healing. Now as I grapple with illness, and plant myself firmly on my own healing journey, Miriam has been my guide, like the cloud and the fire in the wilderness. Miriam, share with me your inner wisdom. If only I could know more. There's so little I know about your experience in the wilderness. What did you do there? Was it a scary place? Were you frightened? Were you sick? Was the water bitter? What were you creating in the nothingness? Did you know that everyone was waiting for you?

Some of these questions came up two weeks ago when I took myself to the beach. There, sitting on a rock, I started thinking about life and death. I started thinking about my dear family and friends waiting for me. I thought about how lucky I am in so many ways, and what a trying time this is for me just as it must have been for Miriam. But then something happened. I stopped thinking. I stopped wondering what Miriam was thinking alone in the wilderness, the nothingness. Seeing the grains of sand, the earth and sea in front of me, I felt the rhythm of the waves. I heard their song. I saluted the sun and felt the sand, the grains of sand, beneath my feet. And at that moment, I knew what Miriam did in the wilderness. She danced.

And so did I.

THE CULT OF MIRIAM
Rabbi Susan Schnur

Who *was* the biblical Miriam? A minor character, backstage sister to the palace-reared Moses, occasional Rosencrantz-and-Guildenstern-type helpmeet? Or was she a real historical leader in her own right—with her own substantial cult following that was entirely separate from her brother's? New biblical scholarship strongly suggests the latter.[1]

It seems that at some point in biblical history the centrality of Miriam's role in the text was excised, leaving only telltale fragments. For example, there are two versions of the crossing of the Red Sea in the book of Exodus—one having Moses as the protagonist, the other celebrating Miriam. The question is, why does the Bible bother to tell the story twice? "Biblical scholars agree that the [Miriamic] passage is the older, original narrative. Editors of the Torah tried to change the story, focusing attention on Moses," writes lay-researcher Lorrie Greenhouse Gardella, "but the tradition honoring Miriam was strong, and editors dared not eliminate it completely. They retained bits and pieces of Miriam's story."

If you squint while rereading the books of Exodus or Numbers, you'll pick up the existence of a cult of devotees who demonstrate extraordinary allegiance to Miriam. Generally the Bible is a text of haiku-like economy, so it's worth wondering why the Bible has taken such careful pains to note both Miriam's death and funeral, as well as documenting that the Hebrew community stays devotedly at her side when she's leprous, and that it discovers when she dies that their only source of water is, indeed, coterminous with her life. "Miriam died and was buried," records the book of Numbers.

"Now there was no water for the congregation" (Num 20:1).

This is potentially strong stuff (without water, a wilderness community is slated for death)—*was* Miriam, in fact, the sole person upon whom the community's sheer biological survival depended? Why should Miriam and water be coterminous—is there the residue here of excised stories about a Miriam who once nurtured not only a community's body, but its desiccate soul? In general, it's always wonderful to be stopped short in our readings of the Bible, to realize how we dance lightly, again and again, over key narratives, without stopping fully to really grasp them.

Interestingly, Dorothy Zeligs, in a psychoanalytic study, takes a look at the biblical incident that directly follows Miriam's death and the concurrent disappearance of the Hebrews' gentle, reliable source of water. Moses strikes the rock, and, against God's wishes, begets water violently. Scholar Mhairi MacMillan, citing Zeligs, points out that "Moses' aggressive, sinful act follows directly on the death of Miriam, his older sister, who had been like a mother to him from infancy. Moreover, Miriam had been 'the group mother and source of nurturance' to the wilderness community, and her loss to them was likely to have been followed by deep distress and anger. Zeligs suggests these feelings were unacknowledged and uncontained, and may have led to Moses' aggressive acting-out in anger against the Lord."

Miriam is also of note as the *only* female mentioned in Hebrew scriptural genealogies who is not someone's wife or mother. This exception to the (very depressing) rule can be read in several ways, but one possibility is that Miriam was real, beloved and formidable—too vital a figure to suffer reduction solely to a fictive marriage. On the other hand, as a populist cult figure she threatened biblical editorial policy—she couldn't look *too* large.

Maybe appending her to Moses and his family was a kind of compromise.[2]

Archetypally, Miriam derives from the Goddess who is "the infinite depths of the waters, the Great Mother, the Queen of the Sea," writes Mhairi MacMillan. She's the Goddess "whose tears, representing purity, have special powers of healing," and who symbolizes "the profound mystery of the Deep; the reservoir and source of life"— those waters which, said Mircea Eliade, "precede every form and sustain every creation."

Clearly the Miriamic story and related ancient Miriamic legends abound with associations with both water and birth: She is a central, religiously ecstatic figure at the crossing of the Red Sea (metaphorically birthing/midwifing a new free nation); she hides her baby brother Moses in a river (and has involvement in his conception); and she's associated with her miraculous well, a magical spring of water that travels with her wherever she goes, and which is famous for its ability to heal, both psychologically and physically. Jewish legend claims that Miriam's well was brought into existence at *the* most spiritually liminal moment of Creation—during twilight of the sixth day of the world.[3] It was miracle worker Miriam (her very name translates in part as "water") who re-found the magic well after it had been lost for millennia.

Indeed, Jewish legend recounts that the rivers that flowed from Miriam's well were so big that the Hebrews needed boats to cross over from one part of their camp to the other. Many legends tap into Miriamic metaphors; the mystical book of the Zohar, for example, speaks of rivers which come from the Emanation of Understanding called "Marah the Great Sea, the Mother of all living."

The biblical scholar Rita Burns points out that when God punishes Miriam with leprosy, her skin turns "white as snow," a term used in other contexts to designate purity, not ritual uncleanliness. Maybe, she posits, beneath the overt narrative of Miriam's punishment there lurks an earlier, suppressed story of a spiritual initiation rite. [For more on this topic, see "*If There Be A Prophet* in this volume.] When Miriam challenges Moses' unique position as sole spokesperson/prophet of Yahweh, she is perhaps not claiming to be his equal (although she's called a prophetess, the Bible never, oddly, offers evidence of her prophetic activities). Rather she's "asserting that there were other, equally valid ways of conveying the divine message," writes MacMillan. "That is, that Miriam had *her* way, which we may assume to be somehow the women's or feminine way," of calling the sacred into existence. Miriam offers herself also as a beautiful model of ecstatic faith—as dancer/drummer/singer she enjoins us not to neglect in spiritual Judaism the crucial role of disinhibition.

From these musings, let us turn to the Passover seder. Can we take what we know about Miriam and integrate her into the Haggadic proceedings? Toward the ceremony's conclusion, we open the door for the prophet Elijah, inviting him to drink from his brimming goblet of wine, beseeching him to lead us towards a future of peace and love. Since Elijah's ceremony comes near the end of the seder, how about bracketing it with a goblet for Miriam—a cup of *mayim chayyim* (living waters) marking the seder's beginning?

Perhaps, holding Miriam's cup aloft, you feel that it stands for healing in its broadest sense. Maybe it symbolizes for you the need to infuse women's perceptions into Judaism and into our own private valued lives. Maybe Miriam's cup stands for process—the trek *through* the wilderness. Or, it might represent women's special abilities to celebrate struggle, change, or growth. What's most absent at your seder, demanding to be present? My personal angle on *Kos Miryam* (Miriam's

Cup) has to do with magic—the magic of touch: that one can sometimes touch and heal, be touched and healed.

Jung once said that ancient archetypes are like riverbeds which dry up when the water deserts them, but which can be refilled again at any time. The longer water has flowed in a channel, he writes, the more likely it is that sooner or later the water will return to its own bed. Miriam's cup, once glistening with water that energized the soul, calls to us in confident invitation. Let all who are ready come and fill it. Let all who are thirsty come and drink.

NOTES

1. See for example, Rita J. Burns' *Has the Lord Indeed Spoken Only Through Moses?* (Atlanta: Scholars Press, 1987); Mhairi MacMillan's "Miriam: Wilderness Leader, Priestess, Ancestor of Mary," in Alix Pirani's *The Absent Mother: Restoring the Goddess to Judaism and Christianity* (HarperCollins, 1991); Phyllis Trible's "Bringing Miriam Out of the Shadows," *Bible Review*, 1989; or read Exodus and Numbers again, bur with a refreshed eye.

2. The Talmud, in contrast with biblical scripture, does name Miriam both wife and mother, and the rabbis generally agreed that she was married to Caleb.

3. See Louis Ginzberg, *Legends of the Jews* (Philadelphia: Jewish Publication Society, 1911).

THE CUP OF MIRIAM
Susan Schnur

We place Miriam's goblet on the Seder table as a counterweight to the cup of Elijah. The latter is a symbol of messianic redemption at the end of time; the former, of redemption in our present lives. Elijah lived in the desert as a lone, howling visionary, focused on the millennium. Miriam sojourned in the same wilderness, but she accompanied the Hebrew people. Tireless tribal parent, she offered hope and renewal at any stage of the journey.

We place Miriam's goblet on the Seder table to remind us of Jewish women, whose stories have been too sparingly told. On Passover in particular, a holiday celebrating many kinds of birth, we recall women, whose domain, of course, is birth.

We raise her goblet and recite this prayer:

You abound in blessings,
God, creator of the universe,
Who sustains us with
living water. May we, like
the children of Israel leaving
Egypt, be guarded and
nurtured and kept alive in the
wilderness, and may You give
us wisdom to understand that
the journey itself holds the
promise of redemption.
AMEN.

KOS MIRYAM
Matia Rania Angelou

Many years ago, Joyce Rosen led our Rosh Chodesh group in a meditation on Miriam's Well. She invited us to take a goblet, fill it with the healing waters of Miriam's Well, and drink. Another member of our group, Stephanie Loo, was so taken with the image of the Well and the water, that she began using a crystal goblet filled with spring water to remind her of the *mayim khayyim* (living waters) from Miriam's Well. She called this goblet *Kos Miryam*.

I am delighted by the growing interest in *Kos Miryam*, the Cup of Miriam. Since our Rosh Chodesh group began using *Kos Miryam* in the late 1980's, the custom has become more widespread and is now being used in a variety of settings. Stephanie Loo was the first in our group to use a crystal goblet filled with spring water to represent the living waters of Miriam's Well. It was Stephanie who gave the cup its name and who wrote the first ceremony using *Kos Miryam*.

It seems to me that Stephanie "discovered" this custom more than she "created" it. It's as though *Kos Miryam* were lost in history, and that it is just now being rediscovered and reused. As Penina Adelman said in *Moment* Magazine, "The ritual is 'new' in the sense that such a cup had never been used on the seder table . . . or for a bat mitzvah celebration . . . or during any of the other myriad uses this particular group found for the Cup of Miriam. However, the ritual is 'ancient' and even 'traditional' in the sense that . . . it felt so natural to start blessing this cup full of pure spring water from Miriam's well, using it at the appropriate times" (August, 1997, pages 26 and 27). Indeed, we read in *The Book of Our Heritage* by Eliahu KiTov that, "There is said to be a custom to draw water from a well at the end of Shabat [sic], for at that time, the water of the well of Miriam fills every other well and whoever comes in contact with it, or drinks it, is cured of all his ailments" (volume 2, page 162).

It is fitting that *Kos Miryam* is being used at this time in Jewish history because we are now rediscovering the women of the Torah and beginning to relate to them differently. We are ready spiritually to uncover these women's lessons and to understand their teachings in a new way. Now is the time for women's voices to be heard along with the men's voices. It is no surprise to me that *Kos Miryam* was revealed to Stephanie at this time through her study and spiritual journey.

Miriam died on the 10th day of the month of Nisan. Midrash tells us that when Miriam died, the miraculous well that had been given by God in her honor disappeared, leaving the Israelites without a source of water in the desert. In our generation, Miriam's Well has become a symbol of our thirst for spiritual nourishment. As we search for Miriam's Well with its healing waters, let us remember the lessons of Miriam and all of our women ancestors. May their voices be heard loudly to guide us on our journey from slavery to freedom.

KOS MIRYAM RITUAL
Matia Rania Angelou

God gave us many gifts when we left Egypt. We were fed with Manna every morning to satiate our hunger. Clouds of Glory protected us and led our way through the desert. With awe and fear at Mt. Sinai we accepted God's gift of Torah which continues to influence our lives today. Manna is associated with Moses, and Clouds of Glory with Aaron.

One other special gift was given for the sake of the Prophetess Miriam. Because of Miriam's righteousness, God gave us a wandering well filled with *mayim khayyim*, living waters. This sparkling well traveled with us on our journey through the desert as a constant source of pure water, as a source of spiritual nourishment, healing, and redemption. The well became known as "Miriam's Well", and it is said that when Miriam died, the well dried up.

Today we are trying to rediscover Miriam's Well and its pure sparkling waters. We fill this goblet with spring water as a symbol of God's *mayim khayyim*. Let us drink deeply from Miriam's Well and feel God's ever-present spiritual sustenance, God's continual strength and healing, moving through our lives. May we be blessed to find Miriam's Well whenever we need it. May its living waters sustain each of us in our search.

Lift Cup

Reader: *Zot Kos Miryam, Kos Mayim Khayyim.*
  Khazak Khazak V'nit-khazeik.

All: *Khazak Khazak V'nit-khazeik.*

ALL THE WOMEN FOLLOWED HER

This is the Cup of Miriam, the Cup of Living Waters.
Strength, Strength, and may we be Strengthened.

N'varekh et Eyn ha-Khayyim she-natnah lanu Mayim Khayyim.
Let us bless the Source of Life Who has given us living
waters.

(blessing for drinking water)
*Barukh Atta Adonai, El-heinu Melekh ha-Olam, she-ha-kol
nih'ye bi-d'varo.*
Blessed are You Adonai our God, Majestic Spirit of
the Universe, by Whose word everything is created.

Drink

∾

KOS MIRYAM FOR PASSOVER
Matia Rania Angelou & Janet Berkenfeld

We begin our seder with *Kos Miryam*, Miriam's Cup, symbolically filled with *mayim khayyim*, living waters from Miriam's Well. Elijah's Cup, of which we speak at the end of the seder, represents our future redemption in the Messianic Age, when peace will fill the world. Miriam's Cup represents our past redemption, when our people were brought out of Egypt and delivered from slavery.

Miriam's Well was said to hold Divine power to heal, sustain, and renew. It became a special source of transformation for a people leaving slavery to form a new identity. Throughout our journey as a people, we have sought to rediscover these living waters for ourselves. With this cup of clear spring water, we remember God's gift of living waters from Miriam's Well.

Tonight at our seder, we continue this journey. Just as the Holy One delivered Miriam and her people, just as they were sustained in the desert and transformed into a new people, so may we be delivered, sustained and transformed on our own journey to a stronger sense of ourselves as individuals and as one community. May the living waters of Miriam's Well nourish us and give us inspiration as we embark on our journey through the Haggadah.

Lift Cup

Reader: *Zot Kos Miryam, Kos Mayim Khayyim.*
             Zakheir l'tzi-at Mitzrayim.

This is the Cup of Miriam, the Cup of Living Waters.
Let us remember the Exodus from Egypt.

All: These are the living waters, God's gift to Miriam, which gave new life to Israel as we struggled with ourselves in the wilderness.

Blessed are You God, Who brings us from the narrows into the wilderness, sustains us with endless possibilities, and enables us to reach a new place.

N'varekh et Eyn ha-Khayyim she-natnah lanu mayim khayyim.
Let us bless the Source of Life Who has given us living waters.

(blessing for drinking water)
Barukh Atta Adonai, Eloheinu Melekh ha-Olam, she-ha-kol nih'ye bi-d'varo.
Blessed are You Adonai our God, Majestic Spirit of the Universe, by Whose word everything is created.

Drink

⋘

TRANSLATION OF BIBLICAL TEXT

All translations from *"The Five Books of Moses"* translated by Everett Fox (Schocken Books 1995), unless otherwise noted.

Exodus 1:15   Now the king of Egypt said to the midwives of the Hebrews – the name of the first one was Shifra, the name of the second was Pu'ah – he said:
When you help the Hebrew women give birth, see the supporting-stones:
if he be a son, put him to death,
but if she be a daughter, she may live.
But the midwives held God in awe, and they did not do as the king of Egypt had spoken to them, they let the (male) children live.
The king of Egypt called for the midwives and said to them:
Why have you done this thing, you have let the children live!
The midwives said to Pharaoh: Indeed, not like the Egyptian (women) are the Hebrew (women), indeed, they are lively; before the midwife comes to them, they have given birth!
God dealt well with the midwives. And the people became many and grew exceedingly mighty (in number).
It was, since the midwives held God in awe, that he made them households.
Now Pharaoh commanded all his people, saying:
Every son that is born, throw him into the Nile, but let every daughter live.

Exodus 2   Now a man from the house of Levi went and took to wife a daughter of Levi. The woman became pregnant and bore a son. When she saw him – that he was goodly, she hid him, for three months.

And when she was no longer able to hide him, she took for him a little-ark of papyrus, she loamed it with loam and with pitch, placed the child in it, and placed it in the reeds by the shore of the Nile.

Now his sister stationed herself far off, to know what would be done to him.

Now Pharaoh's daughter went down to bathe at the Nile, and her girls were walking along the Nile.

She saw the little-ark among the reeds and sent her maid, and she fetched it. She opened it and saw him, the child – here, a boy weeping!

She pitied him, and she said: One of the Hebrews' children is this!

Now his sister said to Pharaoh's daughter: Shall I go and call a nursing woman from the Hebrews for you, that she may nurse the child for you?

Pharaoh's daughter said to her: Go!

The maiden went and called the child's mother.

Pharaoh's daughter said to her: Have this child go with you and nurse him for me, and I myself will give you your wages.

So the woman took the child and she nursed him. The child grew, she brought him to Pharaoh's daughter, and he became her son.

Exodus 15:20   Now Miriam the prophetess, Aaron's sister, took a timbrel in her hand,

And all the women went out after her, with timbrels and with dancing.

Miriam chanted to them:

Sing to YHWH, for he has triumphed, yes triumphed!

The horse and its charioteer he flung into the sea!

Numbers 12 Now Miriam spoke, and Aaron, against Moshe
on account of the Cushite wife that he had
taken-in-marriage, for a Cushite wife had he
taken.
They said: Is it only, solely through Moshe that
YHWH speaks? Is it not also through us that he
speaks? And YHWH heard.
Now the man Moshe is exceedingly humble,
more than any (other) human who is on the face
of the earth.
And YHWH said suddenly to Moshe, to Aaron
and to Miriam:
Go out, the three of you, to the Tent of
Appointment! The three of them went out.
And YHWH descended in a column of cloud
and stood at the entrance to the Tent; he called
out: Aaron and Miriam! And the two of them
went out.
He said: Pray hear my words:
If there should be among-you-a-prophet of
YHWH, in a vision to him I make-myself-
known, in a dream I speak with him.
Not so my servant Moshe: in all my house,
trusted is he; mouth to mouth I speak with him,
in plain-sight, not in riddles, and the form of
YHWH (is what) he beholds. So why were you
not too awestruck to speak against my servant,
against Moshe?
The anger of YHWH flared up against them,
and he went off.
When the cloud turned away from above the
Tent, here: Miriam has *tzaraat* like snow!
When Aaron faced Miriam, here: she has *tzaraat*!
Aaron said to Moshe:
Please, my lord, do not, pray, impose on us
guilt-for-a-sin by which we were foolish, by
which we sinned!
Do not, pray, let her be like a dead-child who,
when it comes out of its mother's womb is eaten
up in half its flesh!

ALL THE WOMEN FOLLOWED HER   313

Moshe cried out to YHWH, saying:
O God, pray, heal her, pray!
YHWH said to Moshe: If her father spat, yes,
spat in her face, would she not be put-to-shame
for seven days (at least)? Let her be shut up for
seven days outside the camp, afterward she may
be gathered-back.
So Miriam was shut up outside the camp for
seven days, and the people did not march on
until Miriam had been gathered-back.

Numbers 20   Now they came, the Children of Israel, the entire
community, to the Wilderness of Zin,
in the first New-Moon.
The people stayed in Kadesh.
Miriam died there, and she was buried there.
Now there was no water for the community.

Numbers 26:59 Now Kehat begot Amram;
The name of Amram's wife was Yocheved
daughter of Levi; who bore her to Levi in Egypt;
She bore to Amram: Aaron and Moses, and
Miriam their sister.

Deut 24:8 – 9   Be careful regarding the affliction of *tzara'at*,
take exceeding care to observe (the rules);
According to all that the Levitical priests
instruct you
as I have commanded them, you are to carefully
observe.
Bear-in-mind what YHWH your God did to
Miriam
On the way at your going-out of Egypt.

Micah 6:4   For I brought you up out of the Land of Egypt
and from the house of slavery redeemed you;
and I sent before you Moses, Aaron and Miriam.
(*translation Rebecca Schwartz*)

ABOUT THE AUTHORS

SARA O'DONNELL ADLER is a poet, writer and rabbi. She was ordained by the Jewish Theological Seminary, and lives with her husband and cat in Riverdale, NY.

MARJORIE AGOSIN is a Chilean Jewish American poet, author of twelve collections of poetry and Professor of Spanish at Wellesley. She has won numerous awards for her poetry such as the *Letras de Oro* prize, the Latino Literature prize, and most recently the Gabriela Mistral Medal of Honor. Her collections include: *An Absence of Shadows* and *Lluvia en el Desierto* (Rain in the Desert).

MATIA RANIA ANGELOU, *Eshet Hazon*, is a poet, singer, and spiritual teacher. She is a member of the musical trio, Ashira, who released their first CD of original songs, "The Indwelling Presence" in September, 2000. She currently performs with The Tribe of Dinah, a collective of women dancers and musicians, and the drumming group, Olamot. Her poem "New Moon of the Daughters" is published in *Celebrating the New Moon: A Rosh Chodesh Anthology*, edited by Susan Berrin. In 1990, Matia founded *Nishmat HaNashim*/WomenSoul. Matia enjoys teaching about the various forms of Jewish spiritual expression, including Kos Miryam, The Cup of Miriam, which originated with a member of her Rosh Chodesh Group. At the end of her term as Spiritual Leader for P'nai Or of Boston, the community bestowed upon her the title *Eshet Hazon*/A Woman of Vision.

CAROL ANSHIEN is a Telephone Reference Librarian at the New York Public Library, after working more than twenty years in neighborhood branches. She has been a community videomaker, labor and social justice activist and is an active member of Congregation Ansche Chesed and P'nai Or NY. As one of the founders of *Bridges* magazine, she still serves on its Advisory Editorial Committee. Her spiritual studies include chanting, meditation, midrash and bibliodrama. Other interests are theater, traveling, birdwatching, and sketching. This is her first published poem.

ANNE K. BLAU has a PhD in sociology; she is an independent scholar who has dedicated almost all of her scholarly life to an exploration of the Dead Sea Scrolls and the works of Josephus.

RANDI S. BRENOWITZ is a Palo Alto, California based organization development consultant dedicated to improving productivity through teamwork and collaboration. She is a National Vice President of Women's American ORT and a member of the World ORT Board of Directors. She also serves on the board and ritual committee of her Reconstructionist synagogue, and helps to coordinate a monthly Rosh Chodesh group. At the age of 40, after very little Jewish education, Randi joined a monthly Torah study group and thus began a continuous journey of Jewish education and exploration.

ERICA BROWN has served as the scholar-in-residence for the Combined Jewish Philanthropies (Federation) of Boston and taught in several Jewish adult education programs in the Boston area, in addition to lecturing throughout the United States. She received her BA from Yeshiva University in philosophy and Jewish studies; an MA in religious education and an MA in Jewish Studies from University of London; and an AM from the Department of Near Eastern Language and Civilization from Harvard University. Erica has published several articles on education, women's role in Judaism and the Hebrew Bible in *The Jewish Educator*, *Le'aylah*, *Ten Da'at*, *Amit Magazine*, *The Journal of Jewish Communal Service*, and *Bible Review*, and has a chapter in *Jewish Legal Writings by Women*. She lives with her husband and three children in Efrat, Israel, and is currently a Jerusalem Fellow.

ABBE DON, president of Abbe Don Interactive, Inc. is an interface designer and interactive multimedia artist best known for her innovative interactive family album "We Make Memories," which documents the stories of four generations of women in her family. Her ongoing collection of family stories can be viewed and contributed to on the World Wide Web at "Bubbe's Back Porch" (http://www.bubbe.com). She is currently working on "Digital Drash" an interactive multimedia collection of midrash, focused on women's stories in the Torah. Ms. Don holds a master's degree from the Interactive Telecommunications Program at New York University

JANET RUTH FALON is a writer and writing teacher in Elkins Park, PA. This poem is from her as-yet unpublished book, *In the Spirit of the Holidays*, which has readings for all the Jewish holidays.

DEBBIE FINDLING holds a doctorate in philosophy of education from the University of San Francisco, graduate degrees in education and Rabbinic literature from the University of Judaism, and a bachelor's degree in women's studies from the University of Colorado at Boulder.

NAOMI GRAETZ has been living in Israel since 1967. She is the author of *S/He Created Them: Feminist Retellings of Biblical Stories* (Professional Press, 1993) and *Silence is Deadly: Judaism Confronts Wifebeating* (Jason Aronson, 1998). Her many articles on women and metaphor in the Bible and Midrash have appeared in such journals as *Conservative Judaism, Shofar, A Feminist Companion to the Bible* (ed. Athalyah Brenner, Sheffield Academic Press) and *Gender and Judaism* (ed. Tamar Rudavsky, NYU Press, 1995). She was the founder of the Negev branch of the Israel Women's Network and on its National Board (1989-91).

SUSAN GROSS is a freelance writer specializing in feminist midrash and Jewish American history. She volunteers at her local animal shelter and as her synagogue's archivist. She lives in Shreveport, Louisiana with her husband and two daughters.

JILL HAMMER is a poet and writer whose specialty is midrash. Her work has been published in anthologies such as Naomi Hyman's *Biblical Women in the Midrash* and Miriyam Glazer's *Dancing on the Edge of the World*, as well as in journals such as *Lilith, Bridges, Kerem, The Jewish Spectator, Frontiers,* and *The Jewish Women's Literary Annual.* Her upcoming book, a collection of midrashic short stories entitled *In the Shadow of Wings: Tales of Biblical Women,* will be published by the Jewish Publication Society in November 2001. Jill Hammer is currently a rabbinical student at the Jewish Theological Seminary, and will be ordained in 2001. She received her PhD in social psychology from the University of Connecticut in 1995. She currently lives in Manhattan.

BARBARA D. HOLENDER, of Buffalo, NY, is the author of three volumes of poetry: *Shivah Poems: Poems of Mourning* (Andrew Mt. Press, 1989), *Ladies of Genesis* (Jewish Women's Resource Center, 1991), *Is This The Way To Athens?* (Quarterly Review of Literature, 1996), and a children's book in Hebrew, *Ani Cli-zemer* (1996). Her poems have appeared in numerous journals and anthologies, and her prose in *Lifecycles Vol. I* (ed. Orenstein, Jewish Lights, 1994) and in *Jewish Mothers Tell Their Stories* (ed. R. Siegel, E. Cole, S. Steinberg-Oren, The Haworth Press, 2000).

LAURIE HORN wrote dance criticism for *The Miami Herald* from 1978 to 1996. She is a 20-year member of Havurah of South Florida and author of *The Song of Miriam*, a novel based on the life of the prophetess. She lives in Miami, Florida.

YAEL LEVINE KATZ has a Ph.D. from the Talmud department of Bar-Ilan University, Ramat Gan. She has published numerous articles, focusing mainly on women and Judaism. The midrash she composed, "The Women's Supplication for the Rebuilding of the Temple," is read in various communities as an extra-liturgical text on Tisha Be-Av. She is also owner and webmaster of an educational website devoted to the song "*Yerushalayim Shel Zahav*" ("Jerusalem of Gold"). She resides in Jerusalem.

MARSHA MIRKIN, Ph.D., is a clinical psychologist and a Visiting Scholar at Brandeis University's Women's Studies Program where she is writing *She is a Tree of Life: Learning about Ourselves and our Relationships from our Biblical Foremothers*. She teaches Torah from a psychological perspective at various community agencies, synagogues, and schools. Dr. Mirkin is also on the faculty of the Jean Baker Miller Institute, Stone Center, Wellesley College, and is the editor of three texts.

ELAINE MOISE has been involved in Jewish women's rituals since the late 1970's, when she wrote her first Rosh Chodesh service She is the author of several *haftarah* translations, which were written to be chanted to the trope of the original Hebrew. A music student from the age of six, she has Master's degrees in Voice and in Music History from SUNY at Buffalo. Elaine helped to found Keddem Congregation, a Reconstructionist congregation in Palo Alto, California. She served as editor for Keddem's *machzor, Chadesh Yamenu,* and of its *siddur,* and is currently president of the congregation. She is, with Rebecca Schwartz, co-author of *The Dancing with Miriam Haggadah,* an expression of her desire that women's voices may always be heard in Judaism.

ALICIA OSTRIKER'S most recent volume of poetry, *The Little Space,* was nominated for a National Book Award in 1998. She is also the author of *The Nakedness of the Fathers: Biblical Visions and Revisions,* a combination of midrash and autobiography. Ostriker teaches midrash workshops for the Institute for Contemporary Midrash, and around the country. She is a Professor of English at Rutgers University.

SUSAN PHILLIPS is a writer, photographer and graphic designer. Her work has been published in many newspapers and magazines. She has presented many midrashic stories as *divrei Torah* and has been invited to other events to read her stories. An eager Jewish learner, she has studied with many teachers at Hebrew College in Brookline, MA, at Congregation Beth El in Sudbury, MA, and at *kallot* sponsored by the Union of American Hebrew Congregations and Hebrew Union College. She began to write midrash as part of a homework assignment in an adult education class. Susan continued to read classical midrash and to write stories long after the course ended.

GEELA RAYZEL RAPHAEL was ordained at the Reconstructionist Rabbinical College. She has also studied at Indiana University, Brandeis, Pardes and the Hebrew University of Jerusalem. She has served Leyv Ha-Ir Reconstructionist Congregation of Center City, Philadelphia as rabbi for eight years. As well, she is the Rabbinic Director of the Jericho Project, an Interfaith Family Support Network of the Jewish Family and Children's Service of Greater Philadelphia. Rabbi Rayzel Raphael is a songwriter/liturgist and sings with MIRAJ, an *a cappella* trio and Shabbat Unplugged. She teaches in numerous locations in the

Philadelphia area. "Bible Babes A-beltin'" is Rayzel's recent recording.

ROSIE ROSENZWEIG is a resident scholar in Women's Studies at Brandeis University and the author of *A Jewish Mother in Shangri-la* (Shambhala).

CIA SAUTTER is a dancer, writer, and instructor, with a Ph.D. in Religion from the Graduate Theological Union in Berkeley. She teaches classes in world religions, with emphasis on the connection between the arts, culture, and ritual. Her current work is in Jewish and Hindu comparative studies, and she is interested in modern American uses of both traditions. Her dissertation on Sephardic women's history is entitled *The Dance of Jewish Women as Torah*.

SUSAN SCHNUR is a rabbi and has been an Editor at LILITH magazine for thirteen years. She lives in Princeton, NJ.

REBECCA SCHWARTZ holds a Master of Arts in Jewish Studies from Baltimore Hebrew University. She teaches workshops on Jewish women's spirituality and creative ritual, and on women in the Bible. She has been fascinated by the character of Miriam since attending her first women's seder in Jerusalem in 1989. In 1996 she co-authored *The Dancing with Miriam Haggadah: A Jewish Women's Celebration of Passover* with Elaine Moise. She lives in the San Francisco Bay Area with her husband and daughter, and serves as Director of a community academy for adult Jewish education. She is also active in *Shalom Bayit*: Bay Area Jewish Women Working to End Domestic Violence.

ALIZA SHAPIRO, CMA, DTR is a faculty member at the Laban / Bartenieff Institute of Movement Studies in NYC. She gives movement and movement theory workshops in the USA and in Israel. And she enjoys collaborating on projects with artists and scientists.

ITA SHERES is Professor of English, Comparative Literature & Judaic Studies at San Diego State University. Her main area of teaching and expertise is Biblical Literature; she offers a graduate seminar every year on the topic of "Women of the Bible." Her publications include: *Dinah's Rebellion: A Biblical Parable for Our Time*, and *The Truth About the Virgin: Sex and Ritual in the Dead Sea Scrolls* (also co-authored with Dr. Blau). She has also published numerous essays in the field of Biblical Literature (e.g. "Biblical Monotheism," "Women Anonymous: The Dead Sea Scrolls Gender Legacy") and essays in the field of Jewish American Literature.

RUTH H. SOHN teaches Jewish texts at Milken Community High School and in various other settings in Los Angeles, where she lives with her husband and three children. She was ordained at Hebrew Union College-Jewish Institute of Religion in 1982. Ruth's articles, biblical commentary, midrash and poetry have appeared in various periodicals, prayerbooks and books including *Reading Ruth* (New York: Ballantine Books, 1994) and *Kol Haneshama*, the Reconstructionist Prayerbook.

VIRGINIA (BERURIAH AVNIEL) SPATZ writes, directs the Jewish Study Center, and learns with two homeschooling children and her husband in Washington, DC. This midrash was created for, and nurtured by, the Fabrangen havurah, with crucial support from Alicia Ostriker and fellow writers of the Institute for Contemporary Midrash. Her writing has recently appeared in *Living Text* and in Shma.com's *Living Words: the Best High Holiday Sermons of 5760*.

ALANA SUSKIN is a rabbinical student at the Ziegler School of Rabbinic Studies, the Conservative seminary of Los Angeles. Her work has been published in a number of places, including *Bridges*, *Lilith*, *Sophie's Wind*, and several anthologies. She is neither a dog person, nor a cat person, but a ferret person.

DAVI WALDERS is a poet, writer and educational consultant whose poetry and prose have appeared in *Ms. The American Scholar, Cross Currents, Seneca Review, Kalliope, Washington Woman*, and many other literary journals and Jewish publications such as *Midstream, Judaism, Lilith* and *Jewish Spectator*. Her poems are included in such anthologies as *Worlds in Their Words: Contemporary American Women Writers* (Prentice Hall); *Grow Old Along With Me – the Best is Yet to Be* (Papier

Mache Press); and *Beyond Lament: Poets of the World Bearing Witness to the Holocaust* (Northwestern University Press). Her poetry on Jewish themes has won Virginia Poetry Society's Franklin Dew Award. She developed and directs the Vital Signs Poetry Project which serves parents and guardians of children who are in treatment for life-threatening illness at the National Institutes of Health and its Children's Inn in Bethesda, MD.

MARION WEINBERG was a speech and language pathologist whose primary focus was with special needs children. She saw her true calling as mothering, and she took a long leave from work to spend time raising her two daughters, Jessica and Gabrielle. Marion was a student of Torah and believed she had a deep spiritual connection to the Prophetess Miriam that sustained her through her long struggle with breast cancer. She died on March 13, 1997.

CHAVA WEISSLER is Professor of Religion Studies at Lehigh University, where she holds the Philip and Muriel Berman Chair of Jewish Civilization. Among the courses she teaches are Women in Jewish History, Jewish Folklore, Hasidic Tales, and the Mystical Tradition in Judaism. Her most recent book, *Voices of the Matriarchs: Listening to the Prayers of Early Modern Jewish Women* (Boston: Beacon Press, 1998) was a finalist for a 1998 National Jewish Book Award, and won the Koret Prize for Outstanding Work in Jewish History for 1999.

About the Artist

LYDIA ANNE BROSE, MFA, was born and raised in Detroit, MI. As a second-generation artist, she grew up steeped in art and craftsmanship. She studied art at Michigan State University, Wayne State University and Center for Creative Studies. She has taught art on the pre-K through college levels. She has authored and illustrated two books for children. Ms. Brose has exhibited widely in Michigan, Boston and the Bay Area, where she currently resides. For further information about Ms. Brose's art work, please contact the publisher. The cover art for this book originally appeared in the film *Timbrels and Torahs*.

PERMISSION ACKNOWLEDGMENTS

"The Songs of Miriam" by Alicia Ostriker was previously published in *The Nakedness of the Fathers* (New Brunswick, NJ: Rutgers University Press), 1994. Reprinted by permission of the author.

"Immanence" and "Tzipporah: Exodus 4:22" by Alana Suskin appear by permission of the author.

"Births" by Laurie Jane Horn appears by permission of the author.

"Journeys" and "I Shall Sing to the Lord" by Ruth Sohn appear by permission of the author.

"The Silencing of Miriam" by Ruth Sohn previously appeared in *The Women's Torah Commentary*, ed. Elyse Goldstein (Jewish Lights Publishing, 2000), p. 270. Contact Jewish Lights Publishing, Sunset Farm Offices Rte 4, Box 237, Woodstock, VT; or www.jewishlights.com. Reprinted by permission.

"Miriam's Well" by Barbara Holender appears by permission of author.

"Miriam at the Red Sea" by Barbara Holender previously appeared in *Ladies of Genesis* by Barbara Holender (New York: Jewish Women's Resource Center, 1991). Reprinted by permission of the author.

"The Mirrors" and "The Names of Miriam" by Jill Hammer appear by permission of the author.

"The Well Dried Up: Miriam's Death in Bible and Midrash" by Erica Brown appears by permission of the author.

"The Dance of Miriam" by Cia Sautter appears by permission of the author.

"Can Prayer Heal? A View From Tradition" by Erica Brown first appeared in *AMIT* magazine, Summer, 1999. Reprinted with permission.

"*Parashat Beha'alotecha*" by Marion Weinberg appears by permission of Thomas Redner.

"The Cult of Miriam" by Susan Schnur previously appeared in LILITH, the award-winning independent Jewish women's magazine. For a sample copy or subscriptions contact 1-888-2LILITH or www.lilithmag.com. Reprinted by permission of the author.

"The Cup of Miriam" by Susan Schnur previously appeared in *The New Schocken Haggadah*. Reprinted by permission of the author.

"Kos Miryam" by Matia Rania Angelou first appeared in *Neshama*, Spring 1992, vol 2, #2, p 8. (*Neshama*, Box 545, Brookline, MA 02446). Reprinted by permission of the author.